D0445273

Better Capitalism

BETTER
CAPITALISM

Renewing the
Entrepreneurial
Strength of the
American Economy

Robert E. Litan and
Carl J. Schramm

Yale UNIVERSITY PRESS
New Haven & London

Published with assistance from the Mary Cady Tew Memorial Fund.

Yale University Press books may be purchased in quantity for educational, business, or promotional use. For information, please e-mail sales.press@yale.edu (U.S. office) or sales@yaleup.co.uk (U.K. office).

Set in Postscript Galliard Old Style with Copperplate 33 bc display type by Westchester Book Group.
Printed in the United States of America.

Library of Congress Cataloging-in-Publication Data

Litan, Robert E., 1950–
    Better capitalism : renewing the entrepreneurial strength of the American economy / Robert E. Litan and Carl J. Schramm.
        p. cm.
    Includes bibliographical references and index.
    ISBN 978-0-300-14678-3 (cloth : alk. paper)
  1. Entrepreneurship—United States.   2. Capitalism—United States.
  3. United States—Economic policy.   I. Schramm, Carl J.   II. Title.
    HB615.L496 2012
    338'.040973—dc23
                                                              2012006665

A catalogue record for this book is available from the British Library.

This paper meets the requirements of ANSI/NISO Z39.48–1992 (Permanence of Paper).

10 9 8 7 6 5 4 3 2 1

CONTENTS

PREFACE

Hollywood has a tendency to produce sequels because they seem "safe." Movie producers who have success with the first movie of its kind are often sorely tempted to repeat the formula of the initial venture, with an updated story line and perhaps a few new characters. Simply put, sequels seem to be less risky than trying something entirely new.

This book is a sequel to a book that the two of us published with New York University economist William Baumol, *Good Capitalism, Bad Capitalism,* through this same press in 2007. But we have two very different non-Hollywood motives for writing it (beyond the obvious one; namely, that this book will never be a movie!). And we like to think and hope readers agree that this book is very different from the earlier one.

First, the economic world suddenly changed less than a year after the prior book's publication, with the emergence of the subprime mortgage crisis in the fall of 2008 (actually there were signs this was coming months before), followed by the Great Recession of 2008–9, which engulfed primarily the developed economies of the world. We did not predict this crisis in the earlier book, though we concluded with a number of warnings and concerns about the long-run sustainability of the United States' model of entrepreneurial capitalism that was the main character, as it were, of the book.

Then, just as we had almost finished this manuscript and were ready to submit it to the publisher for editing, the world was convulsed again by another crisis, in August 2011. This one was largely triggered by the near default by the United States on its debt and the revision in U.S. GDP statistics that showed the economy to have been barely growing during the first half of that year when, up to then, the data had been showing at least some growth. The ensuing global sell-off in stocks, coupled with the realization that U.S. economic policymakers were out of the conventional macroeconomic ammunition—fiscal and monetary stimulus—that ordinarily works during downturns, added fuel to the economic anxieties. So, we updated parts of the following book to reflect these new realities but left its central message unchanged, because that message, as we are about to explain, has an eternal quality to it.

That message turns on the fact that despite the new gloom over the apparently "new normal" in the U.S. economy, one feature—our entrepreneurial culture and activity—remains widely admired here and throughout the rest of the world, and for good reason. As we lay out more fully in the following chapters, entrepreneurship, especially the formation and growth of scale firms, for at least the past several decades has been the driving force behind U.S. job growth. Over an ever longer period, entrepreneurs have been disproportionately responsible for many of the innovations that define what it is to be a modern economy.

And so, in the wake of these back-to-back crises, it seems appropriate—indeed necessary—not only to revisit some of the themes of the earlier book, but to discuss them solely in the U.S. context, where soul-searching about the nature and future of capitalism rightly continues. Thus, the first purpose of this new book is to contribute to this reconsideration and debate about the future of capitalism in the country where both crises started and whose economy is still critical to the health of the global economy.

Second, we have written this book to spell out in considerably greater detail the specific policy recommendations we believe the United States must now implement if it wishes both to mount a solid recovery from the recent crises, and even more important, to permanently lift the growth rate of its economy considerably above where many economists otherwise believe it to be. The key to achieving both objectives, it may not surprise many readers who are familiar with our earlier work, is an entrepreneurial resurgence—not just as a one-time event, but as a process of constant and continued entrepreneurial revolutions. This marks a somewhat different path than one of the main theses of *Good Capitalism, Bad Capitalism,* namely, that the recipe for sustained rapid growth in any economy lies in a mix of entrepreneurial and managerial (or "Big Firm") capitalism. We still believe in the importance of incremental innovation of large, established firms. But we now also believe that to accelerate growth in both the short and long runs, we need an even stronger dose of entrepreneurial capitalism than has existed recently and than we implied in our earlier work.

Readers may note that we have written this book without the third author of our earlier venture, William Baumol. But readers will also find that we have been heavily influenced by Baumol's writings, especially his most recent tour de force, *The Microtheory of Innovative Entrepreneurship,* and our continuing conversations with him. We have nonetheless proceeded here on our own because many of the specific ideas expressed here grow out of our experiences and programs funded by the Ewing Marion Kauffman Foundation, where both of us have had the privilege to work for nearly a decade, and interactions during this period with our colleagues at the Kauffman Foundation. In this regard, we owe special thanks to the following Kauffman colleagues—Brink Lindsey, Lesa Mitchell, Munro Richardson, Dane Stangler, Nick Seguin, Wendy Guillies, and Ted Zoller—whose views have greatly influenced our thinking about economic policy broadly, and entrepreneurship more specifically, and whose comments on earlier drafts we valued greatly. As a result, this book, much more than our earlier work, is a product of the Kauffman Foundation, and for this reason we decided it would be most appropriate not to hold Will to the views we express here. But we will be forever grateful to him for teaching us much of what we know about entrepreneurship and its importance to all economies.

We also owe much to others who made important contributions to this book. For outstanding research assistance, we are grateful to Michael Anton, Alyse Freilich, Jared Konczal, Jacob Madel, and Kate Maxwell. For reading and providing excellent comments on earlier versions of portions or all of this manuscript, we thank also Ramana Nanda and two anonymous referees. For editorial assistance and all-around help throughout this project, we thank Glory Olson. And for her continuing inspirational artwork on all Kauffman projects, including the cover design of this book, we thank Melody Dellinger.

Of course, we alone remain responsible for the content, which we hope readers will enjoy, and any errors, which we hope will be few.

1

TOWARD BETTER CAPITALISM

It was not an American who coined the word "capitalism," which has long been used to describe the U.S. economy. That honor falls, ironically, to capitalism's most famous critic, Karl Marx, who inveighed against an economic system he believed was dominated by a few "capitalists"—owners of buildings, equipment, and the dreaded corporations—whom he believed exploited the masses.

But Marx the wordsmith was cleverer than Marx the economist. The emerging economic system that he decried for enslaving the poor turned out instead to be the greatest anti-poverty force the world has ever known, lifting living standards for ever-growing numbers of people beyond what they could have imagined. Economic output per capita has multiplied manyfold in most places around the world since the beginning of the nineteenth century, overwhelmingly because "capitalists" built companies with technologies that have vastly increased the productivity and wages of the workers they employed. *The Economist* was able to report in early 2009 that, by one measure, more than two billion people—close to half the people on the planet—were then living what could be called middle-class lives, a triumph that could not have happened unless "capitalists" had motives to profit from their risk-taking endeavors and investments.

Yet 2009 and the year before it, as all readers of this book surely know, were years that many would rather forget. During these years, the Great Recession in the United States began and then spread to the rest of the developed world, following the bursting of an unsustainable bubble in residential real estate prices heavily fueled in the United States by large volumes of unsound "subprime" mortgage loans that in the decade before had been packaged into securities and sold to banks, financial institutions, and other investors around the world. When the losses came, they ate into thin cushions of capital at many of these institutions, bringing some of them down and, by September 2008, threatening a systemwide financial panic in much of the developed world.

Governments of these economies responded with massive measures, "bailouts" of the creditors of large firms (not all of them financial), injections of government funds into many large financial firms themselves, unprecedented expansions of money and credit by central banks, and extraordinary fiscal stimulus packages. The emergency efforts stopped the bleeding, for the most part, but never really jump-started the economic "patients." Consumers remained hesitant to return to their prerecession free spending ways, and so businesses stashed away cash rather than ramp up investment spending. As a result, the postrecession recovery has been weak by historical standards. GDP advanced for the first two years after the recession at roughly just a 3 percent pace—barely fast enough to absorb new workers coming into the labor force and the continued rising productivity of U.S. firms. As a consequence, the unemployment rate that peaked at 10 percent (only the second time this has happened in the post–World War II era) only dropped to 8.3 percent through the spring of 2012.

Something clearly was seriously amiss. The 2009–10 fiscal stimulus in the United States in particular had bumped up federal spending to a historic high of 25 percent of GDP, roughly five percentage points above its forty-year average, and thus exacerbated what was already an upward trend toward higher spending to honor obligations made by many previous Congresses and administrations to support the incomes and medical costs of Americans when they retired and pay for the medical costs of the indigent. Just several years earlier, a Republican president and a Democratic Congress had agreed to add reimbursement of prescription drugs to the list of "entitlements," while in 2010, in a strictly partisan vote, the Congress and president added yet another health care program, subsidizing the costs of extending health care to all citizens, regardless of age.

By 2011, it dawned on politicians in Washington and many voters living outside the capital that the country could not afford all these obligations as baby boomers aged and began retiring en masse. By the summer of that year, the stage was set for an epic, and unprecedented, showdown between the two political parties (and a subset of the Republican party, the Tea Party, that had revolted against all this spending) over the magnitude of a long-term deficit reduction deal that would be tied to the otherwise routine matter of annually raising the ceiling on the amount of U.S. debt that could be issued for the coming year and beyond. In the end, the United States did the almost unthinkable: as July ended and August of that year began, the country had to choose either to default on its debt or massively cut into federal spending, perhaps not sending out Social Security checks to tens of millions of senior citizens who needed them to pay their monthly bills.

Yet even when a final deal came, the markets shrugged it off, focusing instead on recently revised statistics showing that the U.S. economy *barely grew at all during the first half of 2011,* despite record amounts of stimulus that was supposed to have kick-started the private economy. And then to pour salt into the economic wound, one of the three leading ratings agencies downgraded the quality of U.S. Treasury debt for the first time, citing the political dysfunction that was on full display during the deficit reduction negotiations and the failure of the August 2011 deal to really tackle the underlying source of the government's long-term fiscal imbalance: the huge and growing gap between tax revenues collected and the rising costs of the big three "entitlement programs": Medicare, Medicaid, and Social Security. Ever since, at least as of this writing, the U.S. economy has been weak, while a pall has continued to hang over much of Europe (except Germany and some of the Eastern European countries), whose governments have faced the same, or even worse, fiscal challenges.

Understandably, fingers point in all directions, looking for people and ideas to blame for these events. The United States and other developed economies that have suffered along with it had experienced and now confronted something they never thought would happen again after the Depression: an extended period, perhaps a decade or more, of anemic growth and high unemployment. The conventional macroeconomic tools—temporary fiscal stimulus (higher spending and tax cuts) and the printing of money—did not seem to work as the textbooks had said they would. And though deficit reduction over the long run is clearly necessary, the efforts to do it immediately in a fragile economic climate make it difficult, if not impossible, for the affected economies to mount a recovery sufficiently rapid to return most of the unemployed promptly to work.

Some of the fingers looking for blame have pointed to a fundamental failure in "capitalism." If by this term one means the unbridled *financial capitalism* that reigned in the United States in the run-up to the financial crisis, then the blame clearly is well deserved. With the benefit of hindsight, it was crazy to have allowed people with less-than-stellar credit histories to buy homes with little or no money down, outcomes made possible through the sale of securities backed by subprime debt that should never have been sold. Likewise, years of many different policy mistakes led financial institutions and individuals to become excessively leveraged, so that when the U.S. housing and subprime mortgage markets began melting down, the losses suffered by banks and households quickly depleted their limited amounts of net worth and thus amplified the economic damage well beyond the losses suffered by those holding mortgage securities.

Fortunately, this particular mutated form of opaque and reckless financial capitalism is now dead. But here's the surprising and not fully appreciated thing: the "entrepreneurial capitalism" that drove the U.S. economy positively for several decades until the financial crisis—the one that accounted for the proliferation of new "gee-whiz" products, technologies, and services introduced by a seemingly never-ending supply of new firms—has continued to be admired and envied not just in the United States, but throughout the world. It was entrepreneurs, after all, who commercialized the telegraph, telephone, and automobiles of the nineteenth and early twentieth centuries, the airplane, radio and television, computer, and transistors that followed, and most recently, personal computers, software, and an amazing array of medical therapies and technologies. No wonder that other countries, notably Brazil, India, Indonesia, and China, among others, even as they struggle with their own current economic difficulties (excessively rapid growth that has led to too much inflation) want to copy and improve on our entrepreneurial model even as—and indeed especially as—the global economy continues to struggle to recover from the financial crisis.

That is not the way things would have looked fifty years ago, had we been writing this book then. The 1950s and 1960s were the halcyon days of "managerial capitalism," when large firms such as General Motors, Ford Motor Company, U.S. Steel, IBM, and AT&T (in its previous monopoly incarnation), among others, were the driving forces of the U.S. economy. Taking advantage of the pent-up demand for consumer goods during World War II, large firms expanded their reach into new markets at home and abroad. They used their economies of scale, access to internal capital, and in-house research labs to generate new products, drawing on technologies that had been developed during or before World War II. This managerial capitalism delivered rapid growth and thus rising living standards for almost three decades after the end of the war. Indeed, our particular brand of this capitalism was not only envied, but feared. In the late 1960s, European intellectual Jean-Jacques Servan-Schreiber warned European governments and citizens that without aggressive counter-measures, the multinational companies birthed and headquartered in America—the quintessential managerial capitalists—would dominate the world economy.[1]

But then the U.S. economy hit the proverbial wall in the early 1970s. Inflation had been edging up throughout the Vietnam War, eventually leading to a run on the dollar that forced the United States to quit exchanging gold at the price fixed after World War II. Soon thereafter, the fixed exchange rate system that had governed world currency markets and international trade that had been in place since World War II came undone. The coup de grace was the quadrupling of oil prices in 1973, which pushed both inflation and the unemployment rate nearly into double digits—then post-Depression highs. Even though growth later resumed and the unemployment rate fell back to near 6 percent, inflation stayed uncomfortably high until the economy was hit by yet another oil shock, this one in 1979 during the Iranian hostage affair. From 1973 to 1980, stock prices dropped in real terms (adjusted for inflation) by roughly 40 percent, reflecting a loss of faith in the managerial capitalism that at least until the first oil shock had produced such rapid growth and widely shared prosperity.

There was ample reason for the loss of faith. Big Auto and Big Steel—along with steadily Bigger Government—that helped define managerial capitalism proved too bureaucratic and uninventive to withstand the seeming onslaught of cheaper (and often better) imports from Japan and

elsewhere. While many Americans feared the United States was thus losing out to the Japanese on the economic front, they had also been steadily
losing faith in government. The U.S. military not only suffered its first-
ever defeat in Vietnam, but the Watergate scandal that ultimately forced
President Nixon to resign shocked Americans of both political parties. The
decade ended with the seizure of the American Embassy in Iran and the
humiliation of U.S. government employees being held hostage for over a
year, unable to be rescued by the one failed military attempt to do so.

In one narrative, what saved America and rejuvenated its economy was
the election of the optimistic, anticommunist, free market enthusiast
Ronald Reagan to the presidency in 1980. Rather than wade into contentious political waters about the correctness of this explanation, we suggest
here that an uncontroversial but important contributing reason for at least
the economic turnaround was the transformation of the U.S. economy
from managerial to entrepreneurial capitalism. This apparently new form
of capitalism was not new at all, but is in fact what powered the American
economy from Revolutionary times until the early 1900s: the cleverness
and hard work of waves of entrepreneurs of all types whose efforts gradually lifted the living standards of American citizens. Entrepreneurs began
to take center stage in the U.S. economy again in the 1970s (before Reagan
was elected) with the formation of such companies as Intel, Microsoft,
Apple, Federal Express, and Southwest Airlines, among others. But entrepreneurial capitalism really took off in the 1980s and 1990s and flowered
under presidents of both major parties.

Five years ago, in *Good Capitalism, Bad Capitalism,* we described this
remarkable transformation with our coauthor and distinguished colleague, New York University economist William Baumol.[2] In that book,
we argued nonetheless that economies perform best when they have a
blend of dynamic entrepreneurial companies and larger, established enterprises. (Baumol has also made this argument in other papers and books
authored by him.) A continuous supply of new firms, especially those that
eventually scale, is required to develop and commercialize the disruptive
technologies that are the key to sustained productivity growth and, hence,
to rapid advances in living standards. A large base of large, established
firms, meanwhile, is required to refine, incrementally improve, and mass
produce the new disruptive technologies brought to market by entrepre-

neurs. The precise mix of new and established firms that best maximizes growth varies from economy to economy, but the notion that both are required was a central thesis of the prior book.

This book appears at a very different time—radically so—after a financial crisis that, frankly, we (and most others) did not foresee, followed by a budget-related loss of confidence in the United States, by Americans and citizens from elsewhere around the world, that we did warn about earlier (along with plenty of others). The challenge, clearly, is what to do now: not just to get economies back on track to recover from these recent traumas, but even more important, to sustain rapid growth once again for the indefinite future after some measure of recovery has been accomplished.

We modestly believe we have at least part of the answer and it is one reason we have written this book. Readers are unlikely to find this explanation in the expansive postcrisis literature on how to get out of our economic troubles, which tends to focus on the traditional macroeconomic fixes (tax cuts, spending increases, and expansionary monetary policy) that have worked in past recoveries. Instead, we offer a different, and we hope more compelling, narrative that focuses on the central role of the *continued formation and growth of scale firms* in driving economic growth, both in the short and long runs. To use terminology familiar to economists, we argue that to better the macro trends in overall jobs and output growth, citizens and policymakers must strengthen the micro underpinnings of our economy; specifically, the formation and growth of scale firms.

In particular, we argue that the "better capitalism" the United States needs now more than ever is one that fosters continuous *entrepreneurial revolution*—the economic equivalent of what Thomas Jefferson called for when he famously uttered, "Every generation needs a new [political] revolution." Whether or not that statement is appropriate for governing, it could not be more relevant today as an economic proposition. For countries at the technological frontier like the United States, sustained rapid growth is only possible through the continued commercialization of new, disruptive—and, yes, revolutionary—technologies, products, and services.

We are not sufficiently clairvoyant to predict what those technologies will be. Futurists in the past have missed the mark, and no doubt their heirs today will be equally unsuccessful. Nonetheless, it is does not take much imagination to believe that eventually some form of computer chip will be in almost everything we buy, enabling many household and business chores to be carried out by robots rather than humans. Cars at some point may not need drivers, but instead will be carried along expressways with computer guidance. New therapies, devices, and medicines will extend average life spans, with good quality of life, by decades. And so on. Just as entrepreneurs have shaped the lives most readers enjoy today, they will shape the tomorrows of the billions of people living now and born into the future.

Of more immediate interest, sustained and continuous entrepreneurial revolutions of the kinds just listed also are what America needs to meet five large challenges that confront it in the wake of the financial crisis and subsequent recession:

- Generating a faster recovery in jobs and incomes that is now needed more than ever;
- Eliminating a deficit of imagination about what our country and its economy could look like if our entrepreneurial spirit could be more effectively harnessed, consistently;
- Restoring faith in our political system;
- Averting a potential fiscal crisis that could produce an even deeper and more lasting financial crisis than the one that began in 2008 (and has continued to show aftershocks in subsequent years);
- Maintaining U.S. economic power in an age where it may matter more than military force (but where force is required, stronger growth will make it easier to finance); and

In outlining our views on these topics in the balance of this chapter and throughout the rest of this book, we are cautiously optimistic. Time and again, Americans have faced enormous challenges and overcome them, so those who bet against the United States coming back strong after the Great Recession do so at their peril. At the same time, we also recognize the huge nature of these challenges. Those who say America is "in decline"—as a *Time* cover story by the journalist Fareed Zakaria argued in March 2011—or who fear the inexorable rise of the Chinese or Indian economies, or both, have plenty of arguments on their side.[3] It will take successive entrepreneurial revolutions *in the United States* in many spheres of life to prove the pessimists wrong. Our main purpose in writing this book is to outline how those revolutions can be spawned, maintained, and put to use in lifting living standards for all Americans at a faster rate over a sustained period than conventional wisdom now thinks possible.

Faster Job Growth

The economic metric that matters most to elected officials and probably the people they represent turns in one way or another on one word—jobs—and how many any particular program or set of policies will create (or destroy). This should not be surprising. People by nature want to be busy and to be valued for the work they do. When individuals do not have work they care about and that gives them meaning, they doubt themselves and their worth. As unemployment drags on, its ill effects show up in people's physical and mental health and in their interactions with friends and family.

Because of the human toll that unemployment exacts, economists and political leaders have long been occupied with trying to understand, and reduce, both the incidence and length of spells of unemployment, which of course get worse during recessions. In the typical post–World War II recession, the U.S. economy has bounced back in a V-shaped pattern; the deeper the downturn, the steeper and more rapid the recovery. For example, in the sharpest recession before the most recent one—actually the twin recessions (coupled with double-digit inflation) of 1980–82—after the unemployment rate topped out at 10.8 percent at year-end 1982, a snapback rebound pushed it down to just 6 percent two years later.

The 2008–9 recession, it already is evident, is much different. For one thing, the financial crisis that preceded it was much deeper than in the 1980–82 recession and so the financial system—banking in particular—is much less able and willing to finance a rapid recovery. Moreover, going into the post-financial-crisis recession, consumers (like many financial institutions) were excessively leveraged—the personal savings rate was essentially zero—and thus have not been eager to buy, even as output began slowly recovering. The precarious employment situation, with officially measured unemployment topping or staying near 9 percent and the unofficial number (counting all those involuntarily working part-time plus discouraged workers who have dropped out of the labor force) much higher, has made consumers even more nervous. Anxious consumers make for anxious businesses, which likewise have been slow to add new plants and equipment.

In short, by historical standards, the recovery from the Great Recession so far has been listless and indeed fell back in 2011, as already noted. Absent some fundamental change in the national psyche, the U.S. economy is unlikely to gather much momentum any time soon. Indeed, many are already worried that this current decade will turn out to be a "lost" one, much like the 1990s in Japan after the stock market and real estate bubble in that country popped in 1989. In early 2010, the President's Council of Economic Advisers in its annual *Economic Report of the President*—a document not typically known for its pessimism in any administration—essentially validated this judgment by projecting the unemployment rate not to return to its precrisis level of 5 percent until *2020,* more than a decade after the Great Recession began. In August 2010, economists Carmen and Vincent Reinhart presented a paper at that year's "Jackson Hole" meeting sponsored annually by the Federal Reserve Bank of Kansas City demonstrating that GDP growth rates after financial crises typically fall 1 percent below precrisis growth rates, and continue in that fashion for roughly one decade after the crisis. If this pessimistic pattern holds, and so far it has the ring of truth, the U.S. economy will not return to anything close to "full employment"—the highest level of employment consistent with a low, stable rate of inflation—until well *beyond* 2020.[4]

We will have much more to say in the next chapter about how and why the formation and growth of new firms is the key to a more robust recovery in both jobs and income, in the short and long runs. But a preview of that straightforward argument is worth stating here. If you want to see where the jobs of the future will come from, look at the historical record, at least since entrepreneurial capitalism has come to the fore. Between 1980 (the earliest date for which we have this data) and the years immediately preceding the Great Recession, the best estimates suggest that new young firms (those five years old or less) accounted for virtually all of the 40 million *net new jobs* created in the U.S. economy. This is a remarkable statistic, for it implies that a much stronger entrepreneurial economy is essential for a more rapid return to pre-crisis economic conditions.

If the United States can make real progress on the jobs front by accelerating the rate of formation and growth of scale firms, it will find it easier to address other problems or challenges that confront the nation: the disturbing fiscal deficit (which we address below) and perhaps its main underlying cause, the continued rapid escalation of health care costs (which we discuss in more detail in Chapter 8). It is also likely that in a more rapidly growing economy, growth will be more widely shared since there are greater opportunities for upward mobility when the economy is growing quickly than when it is limping along.

The Imagination Deficit and the Need for Growth

Once the U.S. economy recovers, what will happen then? Economists often speak of the long-run or "potential" rate of economic growth, that being the pace at which the economy is most likely to expand once all resources, workers in particular, are fully employed. This potential rate of growth, or the expansion of the "supply side" of the economy, is of critical importance because it determines the rate at which general living standards advance. In turn, whether we are consciously aware of it or not, what we have come to consider the "American dream"—realizing a better life in the future for ourselves and our children if we work hard and play by the rules—is largely determined by the potential rate of growth. If potential growth is rapid *and there is collective optimism about that fact,* people have bold and ambitious dreams for themselves and their children. Conversely, if there is a popular belief that future growth will be slow (as seems to have been the case since the financial crisis), that could put a damper on ambition and imagination. These beliefs are important, because they all too easily can become self-fulfilling prophecies.

Unfortunately, up to now, it has been virtually impossible to know with any precision what the potential growth of an economy is likely to be *in the future.* Economists nonetheless make educated guesses, usually starting with extrapolations from the recent past and then making adjustments for factors that may cause a deviation from the historical trends, such as projected changes in the labor force composition (a higher fraction of older workers usually boosts productivity because they are more experienced), educational attainment (a more educated workforce is likely to be more productive), and so on. We will argue in the next chapter that an even more important and generally overlooked factor driving long-run growth is the formation and growth of "scale firms."

Looking back, for the first quarter century after the end of World War II, the potential growth of the U.S. economy was rapid, largely because of the significant pent-up supply of good ideas generated during World War II that could be readily transformed into valuable goods and services by many of the same large companies that were critical to the successful war effort. Per capita incomes—perhaps the best measure of average economic welfare—grew rapidly as a result. Even taking the ups and downs of the economic cycle into account, average income per person advanced at an annual rate of 2.5 percent. This may not sound like a lot, but due to the magic of compound interest, a growth rate of this magnitude meant that by 1973, the typical American household was about twice as well off as it was coming out of World War II.

But then, as we noted earlier, the U.S. economy hit a wall in the early 1970s, and for roughly the next two decades, productivity growth and thus the growth in per capita income slowed markedly, to a little more than 1 percent. No wonder Americans turned pessimistic. To be sure, the seeds of resurgence were planted in the transition to a more entrepreneurial form of capitalism that began during this period, but the full benefits of this transition did not become evident until the mid-1990s. By that time, the accumulated advances in information technology and communications—ushered in by a wave of new companies—had pushed the annual growth rate in productivity and per capita income up to around 3 percent. This rate was even faster than growth in the golden quarter century after World War II, and it continued through the mini-boom years that followed the 2001–2 recession. For a brief period, some (perhaps many) economists thought we had entered a new age of rapid productivity growth that would last for decades.

Ironically, it was during this period—which we now know was artificially inflated by a housing boom fueled by a wave of *destructive* financial entrepreneurship—that the concept of economic growth itself was being challenged from many different quarters. Some argued that growth was (and is) bad for the environment. Others asserted that there is more to life than what the markets value, and that "happiness surveys" confirmed this.

We responded to these and other critiques in *Good Capitalism, Bad Capitalism*.[5] Simply put, economic growth can be "clean" and does not have to be dirty. Indeed, the richer societies are, the more likely it is that their citizens will demand a cleaner environment and the more resources will be available to deliver on that demand. Furthermore, recent evidence confirms the common-sense notion that, holding other factors constant, people tend to be happier the higher their income. Of course, money does not guarantee happiness, but it sure helps. Contrary to the once widely believed "Easterlin paradox" (named after demographer Richard Easterlin who touted it to be true)—that the subjective feeling of well-being apparently did not increase with income—the latest evidence is that higher incomes do indeed make people feel better.[6] But higher incomes need not translate into just having more *things*. Increasingly, developed economies are *service* economies, and as the United States and other developed economies grow, their residents are likely to spend more at the margin on highly valued services—noninvasive life-saving medical procedures and therapies, education and training, entertainment, and the like—that not only will extend life but make it more enjoyable.

But these are academic quibbles. Since the financial crisis, there has not been much criticism of economic growth. To the contrary, citizens around the world if anything are impatient, wanting faster growth and the job formation that comes with it. People have seen what a world without growth looks like and almost universally, we suspect, they do not like it.

The Great Recession has not only tempered the optimism of consumers and businesses, but of economists who estimate potential growth. To the extent that there is a consensus now on this topic, it seems to be that per capita income in the United States can at best grow at only about 2 percent, or perhaps at an even lower annual pace into the indefinite future. One of the most pessimistic forecasts, issued in the fall of 2010 by distinguished productivity expert Robert Gordon of Northwestern University, would mean that per capita growth—and thus advances in living standards—over the next twenty years would advance at its slowest pace *in U.S. history* over a comparable period.[7] Although he did not express it in quantifiable terms,

George Mason University Professor Tyler Cowen has a written an entire book in which he argues that America's best economic days are behind it now that we have allegedly reached a technological plateau.[8]

These discouraging projections—driven by the exit of the labor force of high productivity baby boomers and their replacement by a less educated and less productive generation, as well as concerns that the information technology revolution is slowing down—could turn out to be accurate, but they represent a failure of imagination. We can do better, and indeed we have done much better during the entrepreneurial boom that preceded this downturn. We just need continued booms like it to put us back on that trajectory of 3 percent per capita GDP growth. That extra 1 percent (relative to the somewhat more optimistic baseline growth estimate of 2 percent) may not look very big, but again, compounding makes all the difference. An economy whose per capita income grows at 3 percent per year will in seventy years *be twice as large—and thus average living standards will be twice as high*—as an economy that grows annually at the currently projected 2 percent. Many of us now may not appreciate this difference, but our children and their children surely will, if a higher growth rate comes to pass.

In emphasizing the importance of economic growth as it is traditionally measured—by the total output of goods and services—divided by an economy's population or calculated for the median household, we do not mean to neglect other aspects of what determines the standard of living: the range of available products and services, the quality and comfort of workplaces, the length and quality of life, the amount and quality of "public goods," and so on. It is likely, however, that those aspects of the standard of living not traded on the market are highly correlated with the output of goods and services that are. And so when we speak of "economic growth" throughout the rest of the book, we implicitly include these broader measures of human welfare.

In our next chapter, we illustrate one way to generate significantly faster growth: fostering the formation and growth of what we call "billion dollar" firms, or more precisely, those firms whose revenues eventually scale to an average of $1 billion. We focus on these "scale firms" because they are most likely to commercialize technologies with wide social benefits, much larger than can be captured by any one or even many entrepreneurs.

In subsequent chapters we outline policies that could spawn more such firms and in the process generate the added growth and its social benefits we believe would be broadly welcomed.

Fixing the Trust Deficit

Historians, economists, and journalists no doubt will debate for years the wisdom of the many unprecedented steps taken by two administrations, the Federal Reserve, and other financial agencies during the 2008 financial crisis and its aftermath in an effort to head off a much more damaging crisis.

At the request of the Bush administration and the Federal Reserve, Congress created a $700 billion fund to rescue weak banks, which was expanded to rescue two auto companies (General Motors and Chrysler), a few finance companies, and certain life insurers. Part of this fund was also used, in conjunction with other funds, in the Federal Reserve's unprecedented $182 billion rescue and takeover of the nation's largest insurer, AIG. In addition, Congress essentially gave the U.S. Treasury Department a blank check to take over Fannie Mae and Freddie Mac, the two quasi-governmental corporations that collectively held or guaranteed over half of all mortgages outstanding in the United States (and since have bought or guaranteed a much higher percentage than that).

Beyond these company-specific interventions, Congress adopted at President Obama's behest in early 2009 a two-year "fiscal stimulus" package of almost $800 billion; the Treasury Department found a way to deploy its rarely used "emergency stabilization fund" to guarantee roughly $4 trillion in money market fund deposits after Lehman Brothers failed; and the Federal Deposit Insurance Corporation (FDIC) guaranteed the uninsured long-term debt of the nation's banks. Perhaps most significant, the Federal Reserve implemented a host of innovative steps to keep the financial system afloat by purchasing roughly $2 trillion in U.S. Treasury bonds and mortgage-backed securities to keep interest rates at all maturities low (a program extended in 2010 under the name "Quantitative Easing 2" and modified in 2011 by "Operation Twist"), opening its "discount window" to investment banks and primary dealers of government securities, and creating a temporary lending facility to assist purchasers of securities backed by non-mortgage loans (small business and credit card loans in particular).

Readers can turn elsewhere for more thorough assessments of the effects thus far of this dizzying array of initiatives and interventions, where the arguments have become somewhat predictable. Defenders of some or all of these measures have argued that the imaginative improvisation was necessary given the suddenness and severity of the financial crisis, especially as it played out in the fall of 2008, and that, in combination, the steps taken did, in fact, avert a much deeper downturn. They also point out, quite rightly, that the ultimate cost to the federal government of some of the bailouts turned out to be far less than the initial layouts of funds (the large banks paid back all of their borrowed monies, with interest, as did many of the smaller ones, and the U.S. government even got some of its money back from the GM bailout when that company offered shares to the public in late 2010). Whether the United States and global economies would have experienced another Depression had certain of these rescue efforts not been mounted, we will never know. Critics have responded by not only discounting that possibility, but expressing fear that the monetary stimulus in particular has laid the foundation for an explosive increase in inflation down the road, while the company-specific bailouts have prompted cries of unfairness that Wall Street was protected but "Main Street" was not.

Perhaps it was the bonuses that AIG and the large banks that had been rescued wanted to pay their top executives (until they were stopped by the public outcry and more formally by the Treasury's "pay czar") that turned the tide. Or perhaps the company-specific bailouts of the larger institutions alone would have done the trick. But in combination, all of the government's financial rescue measures alarmed many Americans that something was fundamentally unfair about the way the financial crisis was handled—even if, by most expert accounts, these steps did "save" the economy from something worse, thereby helping many of the same people (without their being aware of this fact) who have voiced such strong opposition to those measures.

In sum, the one unintended but highly significant consequence of the various government financial rescue efforts during the financial crisis of 2008—and one that we believe few, if any, saw in advance or even shortly after these initiatives were undertaken—has been a significant erosion in the public's confidence and trust in government generally. This dissatisfaction and indeed anger showed up in public opinion polls in early 2010, and later in the election of so many Tea Party candidates to federal office. Much (we suspect most) of the public has become even more disaffected in the wake of the budget brinksmanship during the summer of 2011, when the U.S. government nearly had to default on its debt or massively cut back federal expenditures.

Putting aside one's views about all of these events, the loss of the public's trust in government is not a healthy outcome, especially for a country that faces the kinds of challenges we have already mentioned. And looming on the horizon is yet another challenge that could turn into a future crisis—perhaps more severe than anything experienced so far—if it is not soon addressed.

Dramatically Cutting Long-Term Fiscal Deficits

By this we mean, of course, America's long-term fiscal deficits at all levels of government, but first and foremost the long-term projected federal government deficits. Even before the recession, the warnings had been clear. Whether from official government forecasts—such as those from the nation's two Congressional budget watchdogs (the General Accountability Office and the Congressional Budget Office)—or from leading think tanks and economists across the political spectrum, the federal budget projections had been showing for at least a decade that in the absence of firm policy decisions to reverse course, the federal deficit will soar, both in absolute terms and relative to GDP, over the course of the twenty-first century. The main driving factor behind the projections is the mounting costs of the nation's big three "entitlement" programs—Social Security, Medicare, and Medicaid—due in part to the aging of the baby boom generation, but even more so to projected continued growth in health care costs.[9]

The various economic stimulus measures enacted in 2008 and 2009, coupled with the deep fiscal wound associated with the Great Recession, have only made the deficit projections worse. In addition, although the health care reform plan adopted by Congress and signed into law by

President Obama in March 2010 was projected to cut the federal deficit modestly over a ten-year "scoring window," many economists, elected officials, and members of the public remain skeptical, fearing that the projected savings in Medicare, among other factors, designed to offset the costs of expanded health care coverage will never materialize. Accordingly, health care reform (assuming the Supreme Court upholds it) may worsen the deficit even within the narrow ten-year period mandated by law, and very likely will worsen the deficit in the long-term, well beyond that window.

And so what had been a major concern of a relative handful of budget analysts and perhaps a few federal legislators in years past is now very much in the national consciousness. This was clearly reflected in the huge budget battle during the debate over whether to lift the government's debt ceiling in August 2011. Although the final outcome of that battle made some dent in the medium-term budget trends, it did precious little to change the long-term deterioration in the nation's fiscal finances.

The deficit problem is just as real and more immediate for state and local governments that cannot simply print money to cover expenses, and instead by law must balance their operating budgets. State and local governments can borrow money, but precisely because they cannot print it, these governments must demonstrate to the ratings agencies, however discredited they may be in the wake of the financial crisis, that they have the resources to service their debts. The financial crisis only aggravated an already dire long-term budget outlook for many states and localities, which have their own "entitlement" commitments: principally "defined benefit" pension and health care obligations to growing numbers of retired state and local government workers. This combination of short- and long-run budget problems may eventually force some, if not many, local governments to declare bankruptcy.

We will discuss in more detail in Chapter 8 the danger that the projected deficits pose to the nation's finances, economy, and even national security.

We hope it will not take a full-blown crisis—a run from the dollar and U.S. government bonds and other investments—to trigger the major corrective actions that ultimately will be required to put America's fiscal house truly in order. For if such a crisis occurs, the United States no longer has the fiscal cushion to try another set of stimulus measures, nor may the financial markets be so accepting of the kind of monetary easing that helped get the United States through the post-2008 financial crisis. Accordingly, a future economic crisis could easily be far worse—deeper and longer-lasting than the most recent one, whose negative impacts will take years to reverse.

As for the fiscal challenges confronting states and localities, as daunting as they are, they also may contain a silver lining. Just as bankruptcy has forced some of our largest companies to restructure their debts and their operations, the same fate for municipalities—states cannot legally declare bankruptcy though they can default on their debts—may be the necessary trigger for some long-overdue restructuring of government. Among other things, bankruptcy may permit local governments to fundamentally rework their contracts with municipal employees, especially teachers, in ways that give supervisors and school superintendents and principals greater ability to incentivize good teachers while removing poor performers. Such reforms have at least a chance of making government work more like the private sector and encouraging government workers to be more entrepreneurial. For schools especially, bankruptcy or the threat of it may be the crisis that is needed to finally give economically disadvantaged students in particular a better chance to receive the quality education and opportunities to succeed later in life that they deserve.

And while tight state and local budgets should make it increasingly difficult for governments to finance the new infrastructure—roads, sewers, communications networks, and the like—that will be necessary to support faster growth, the fiscal challenges should open the way for a new era of *private sector–led infrastructure projects,* and indeed a new class of *infrastructure entrepreneurs.* We will argue in Chapter 8 that a privatized system of infrastructure is likely to be more efficient and more responsive to citizen demands than the traditional government financed and operated infrastructure that we have come to believe is the natural order of things. But it need not be, and in the future, it probably will not.

Maintaining and Projecting Economic Power

Ever since the rise of the nation-state, and even well before, the power of any given jurisdiction was largely if not exclusively measured by its military might. Indeed, the history of the world is very much marked by the movements of armies, the taking and yielding of land, and of course the deaths of hundreds of millions.

Yet as pervasive as military conflicts have been, they and the deaths they have caused have been on the decline since the end of World War II. If power is to be measured as influence, then, as Les Gelb, the former president of the Council of Foreign Relations has argued, *economic power* today may be as important as military power. The limits of U.S. military power—and the United States after all has by far the strongest military on the face of the planet, perhaps stronger relative to its competitors than any other nation or power in history—have been grossly apparent in just the past decade. After taking Iraq by storm (or perhaps by "shock and awe") in 2003, American forces became enmeshed in a multiyear counterinsurgency campaign that still has not fully wound down at this writing, and whose results are still up in the air. The verdict on the U.S. military involvement in Afghanistan, which was ramped up early in the Obama administration, likewise is still very much out. In each case, the military edge of U.S. forces over their opponents has been overwhelming, but still no clear-cut "victory" is in sight.

Meanwhile, the principal scenes of engagement in the rest of the world are almost entirely economic, especially in the wake of the financial crisis and ensuing recession. A battle is on for the hearts and minds, and even more for the pocketbooks, of people around the world regarding which economic systems work best: the formerly freewheeling U.S. style of financial and entrepreneurial capitalism, or the more state-directed variation seemingly practiced so successfully in China (despite a huge dose of entrepreneurship there too) and to a lesser extent in countries like South Korea and Singapore. The spoils for the "winner"—which will be heavily determined by growth outcomes—include influence in both policy circles and on the streets of countries throughout the world. An America that could find a way to engineer consistently more rapid growth than now seems to be the case will enjoy a much stronger position in this battle than the one mired in slow and uneven growth, and perhaps subject to future crises. Likewise, just in case military force is needed to address threats that cannot be addressed in any other matter, a more rapidly growing economy would equip the U.S. military with more resources—especially more innovative technologies that can reduce both American military and innocent civilian casualties.

Outline of This Book

Although government will not create the new scale firms the U.S. economy needs to grow more rapidly—that job must fall to the private sector—the rules government sets and enforces have a huge influence on how successful private firms will be. We devote ourselves in this book to exploring which rules need to be changed—mostly without spending more money or necessarily giving more tax breaks—to foster faster entrepreneurial growth, which in turn would help address (though we admit not entirely solve) all five of the foregoing challenges we have outlined.

In the process, we cover many and diverse subjects, not all of them likely to be covered in a book of this sort. Accordingly, readers who want details on some but not all of our ideas are welcome to read only those chapters in which they have a deep interest, and then get summaries of the other proposals here in this initial chapter. Other readers, we hope most of them, will find the details in *all* the chapters sufficiently compelling to read the book straight through.

The central proposition on which all of our arguments rest is that *faster economy-wide growth over the long run rests on the formation and growth of high-growth companies.* In Chapter 2, we lay out this thesis and outline some "arithmetic of growth" to show how large new companies, those with at least a billion dollars in revenues, are likely to contribute most to growth because they are likely to generate the largest positive spillovers to other firms and to consumers relative to the gains they produce for their founders. In the most extreme case, if all additional growth above some baseline, say 2 percent growth in annual per capita income, were derived from these "home run" companies, it would take roughly sixty of them to be created *each year* to lift the economy-wide growth rate *permanently* by one percentage point. The formation and growth of highly, but somewhat less, successful new companies—triples and doubles, to continue the baseball analogy—would reduce the required number of home runs to generate that extra percentage point of growth.

How can the U.S. economy produce such additional numbers of new scale companies? The conventional policy levers one would pull would include more federal spending on scientific research and lower taxes on income. In Chapter 3, we discuss the limits of both these answers (although we make a plea for a comprehensive federal budget accord as rapidly as possible since, among other reasons, this should bring greater permanence to the federal income tax code, which in recent years has been a disturbing source of business uncertainty). Instead, we put our emphasis on the formation and growth of "entrepreneurial ecosystems" (some would say "clusters") as the real key to generation of more high-growth firms. While government policies can play some role in nurturing these ecosystems, we are heartened by the efforts of universities and new forms of privately owned accelerators in generating more scale companies. With the right policies in place, additional scale companies should be able to form and grow independently as well.

Who will be the entrepreneurs who create these new high-growth firms? As in earlier generations, they will come from all walks of life and backgrounds. But in a world where new advances emerge out of new scientific discoveries, often based in universities, faculty entrepreneurs are— or should be—high on the list of the creators of new scale enterprises. In Chapter 4, we describe how this has been true in the recent past, and why it is likely to be even more so in the twenty-first century. There is one major problem, however: the bureaucracies that universities themselves have created, ostensibly to facilitate the rapid commercialization of faculty-developed innovations, instead are impeding this process or at the very least behaving suboptimally. We outline in the chapter several ways of surmounting this roadblock, which must be overcome if society is to gain maximum benefit from the continued advances in knowledge generated by our world-class institutions of higher learning.

Speaking of the world, it is now widely recognized that all economies, with a few exceptions, function in a highly global setting where goods, services, capital, and people constantly move across national borders. The global economy provides a much larger stage for giving firms everywhere better and more rapid opportunities to grow to scale.

Nonetheless, in part because of the terrorist attacks of 9/11 and in part because difficult economic times create much anxiety, many people understandably worry that immigrants will "take their jobs" or at the very least push down their wages. As a result, the United States is not as open to immigration—or the cross-border movement of people for the purpose of work and firm creation—as would be in its own best interest. In Chapter 5, we focus on one class of immigrants, those already with advanced skills or seeking to come to the United States to gain them, who have been and could in the future be especially helpful to the country in achieving rapid growth. Ideally, we would like immigration policy changed to automatically give permanent work permits ("green cards") to all the foreign students who come here to get degrees in science, technology, engineering, and math ("STEM"). Ideally, as a supplement but at the very least as a political fallback, we favor a graduated but expansive system that would permit entry by skilled immigrants who launch businesses here and employ U.S. citizens. Visas for "job creators" who threaten no one and indeed promise new jobs for many Americans should be an easy political "sell." As soon as our elected officials recognize this and lead, we are confident that their American constituents will follow.

Beyond the identity of future entrepreneurs, there is the issue of money. How will these new high-growth firms be financed? Fortunately, advances in technology have reduced the entry costs for many new firms—especially those doing business on the Internet—so that many business launches today are more feasible than people think. Still, all new and growing firms need capital at some point. During the roughly two years we worked on this book and in the intervening period that it took to be published, the unavailability of finance—especially bank loans, but also outside equity—has been one of the hottest and most difficult to resolve of the economic issues plaguing the U.S. economy since the recession ended.

In Chapter 6, we take a close look at what portion of this capital shortage is due to unusually deep, but still mostly cyclical, problems confronting the financial system during and since the recession, and what portion can and should be remedied by specific policy measures. The data do not yet permit us to provide a definitive split, but we do identify some changes in government policy—specifically, in the rules governing equity finance—that would reduce the cost and enhance the availability of capital for new and potential high-growth companies at different stages in their life cycle: at the beginning, during their early growth phase, and during their later growth spurts.

Thus, one important financial market failure in the early growth stage of technology-oriented growth companies concerns the so-called "Valley of Death": the inability of private markets to provide sufficient risk capital to finance the "proof of concept" that demonstrates the commercial viability of promising technological breakthroughs. The private sector can help overcome this problem by developing so-called "white swan" venture funds, those that reward investors only if the companies they finance pass some significant revenue or profit milestone. For its part, the federal government should expand funding, on a matched basis with other funds, of proof of concept centers, which can finance and thus accelerate the commercial development of promising new technologies.

An even more general way to induce equity capital to support early growth stage companies is to eliminate or substantially reduce capital gains taxes for investments in startups held for at least five years. In offering this suggestion, we recognize that all capital gains preferences could be eliminated as part of a future comprehensive federal budget deficit reduction plan. In that event, the case for *any* capital gains preference is harder to make, even though we believe there are positive social benefits to providing one for start-up financing. In that event, we would accept as a reasonable compromise a temporary capital gains preference for startups, perhaps lasting five or so years, or just enough time to get the country through the slow recovery period and help re-ignite the appetite for risk taking that the recession has so damaged.

Policy changes also are necessary to facilitate the growth of high-potential companies at what we call the "growth spurt" stage—and specifically make it more attractive for companies that reach this stage to go public and gain the necessary funds from public investors. For various reasons, however, growing companies (except for a few hot new Internet plays in 2011) have found it more difficult over the past decade to offer shares to the public and instead, if they have been financed by outside investors, have been forced to sell out instead to larger, more bureaucratic and thus less entrepreneurial companies or private equity firms looking for quick returns. Imagine, for example, if Apple, Microsoft, or Intel had been forced in their early stages to sell to IBM or its equivalent. The world would have been far different, and we submit, less well-off.

In Chapter 6, we outline several ways to improve the market for IPOs. One fix would give the shareholders of all companies with market capitalizations of less than $1 billion, or of all new public companies within the first three years of their public listings, the choice of whether their companies should comply with the costliest provisions of the Sarbanes-Oxley Act—those that relate to internal auditing. This act (often called by its abbreviated initials, SOX) was enacted to protect shareholders, so why not let them decide whether the benefits of compliance with these provisions outweigh the costs? Fortunately, just as we were completing this book, Congress passed the JOBS Act in March 2012, which essentially exempts young public companies from SOX while relaxing other legal impediments to early-stage equity financing.

Our most controversial way of enhancing public offerings by growing companies would be to slow the proliferation of "exchange traded funds" or ETFs that consist in part or whole of indexes of small cap or early growth stage public companies. Drawing on earlier Kauffman Foundation research, we note that the shares of new growth companies are increasingly held and traded by ETFs rather than by individual or other institutional investors—to the point where movements in ETF prices largely determine price movements in these smaller cap stocks. In such an environment, growth companies considering going public are less inclined to do so, knowing their financial performance will probably not be the major factor driving the price of their shares, but rather investor interest in the larger baskets of ETFs to which they unwillingly may belong once their company's shares are publicly traded. We offer several regulatory solutions to this problem that would reduce, if not entirely eliminate, the negative impact of ETFs on the "going public" decision.

Until the 2008 financial crisis plunged the economy into its deep recession, one of the arguments against growth that appeared to resonate best with at least a healthy number of Americans was that further growth was not "good for the environment." More cars, machines, and the like, it was feared, would lead to more pollution, greenhouse gas emissions, and thus climate change, while aggravating our dependence on unreliable sources of oil from abroad.

In Chapter 7, we lay out how faster growth can indeed be made "sustainable." Two energy-related challenges confront us. Because virtually all of our cars and trucks operate only on oil-based gasoline, we are heavily dependent on the whims of a foreign oil cartel for its supply. This puts our national security at risk while exposing the U.S. economy to the continued fluctuations in oil's price. Constant oil price fluctuations and the continued threat that the cartel could, if it wanted, pump enough oil to cause oil prices to plummet, make it difficult for entrepreneurs who want to develop and market alternative transport fuels to attract the capital they need to become viable suppliers.

The second challenge, climate change due to rising human-generated carbon emissions, is more controversial and only growing more so. We see no need to resolve that scientific debate here, however, for two reasons. For one thing, many states already have mandated that some minimum portion of electricity generated within their borders be derived from renewable or close to carbon-free fuels (solar, wind, and the like). In addition, there is strong public demand for "green" products and energy that is driving electricity generators and users of energy to turn to renewable energy sources.

The conventional answer to both challenges offered by most economists is deceptively simple: put a permanent tax on carbon, either directly or through a government imposed cap coupled with tradable rights to emit carbon below the cap. With a tax in place, consumers and firms would cut back their use of such carbon-intensive fuels, while firms developing alternatives would have greater incentives to do so.

Yet as congressional votes and public opinion polls have consistently shown over time, the American people are highly resistant to government mandated taxes on energy, even as they accept the energy "taxes" imposed by the foreign powers that control the market and thereby set the price for oil and other energy products that at least compete with oil somewhat. But even without this resistance, the oil cartel can always offset increased efficiency, induced either by higher taxes or mandates, simply by cutting oil production. It can and will do the same as more oil is being found outside the cartel countries. As long as cars and trucks in the United States (and in most other countries) operate only on oil, consuming nations always will be at the mercy of the cartel with excess production capacity, no more how much more efficient any economy becomes and regardless of how much oil (and natural gas) is discovered outside the cartel.

Is there a way out of this seemingly intractable dilemma? Fortunately, the answer is yes, and it is one we outline, drawing on the pioneering insights of energy engineers Gal Luft and Anne Korin.[10] The central reason that any monopoly—or a cartel, which is a monopoly by a group, albeit frequently with some cheating on the side—is able to dominate a particular market is that, by definition, there are no effective substitutes for monopoly products. Such is the case with cars that operate only on oil. The solution to this dilemma, however, is equally simple, though it will take some time to be fully effective: phase in a mandate that all new cars operating on liquid fuels be "flex vehicles," capable of running on *multiple fuels* such as alcohol, ethanol, and methanol. To encourage a rapid buildup of production capacity in these alternative liquids, it may be appropriate to use temporary flexible taxes to keep oil prices to consumers above some floor. Unlike a permanent carbon or gasoline tax, however, the tax we have in mind not only would be temporary but would apply only when oil prices fall below some threshold at which at least one of the alternative fuels is not competitive with oil-based gasoline.

Policymakers also may want to consider adding variations of electric power to the platform—hybrid motors, longer-lived batteries and plug-in vehicles—as certain cost thresholds are met. The additional electric mandates would act like prizes and provide strong market incentives for companies to meet the targets to trigger the mandates, which in turn would open up huge markets for the technologies.

With an open fuels platform, America over time would no longer be hostage to the cartel-based suppliers of gasoline, but would have alternatives, one of which would continue to be oil. OPEC's market power would be further reduced to the extent that other countries also adopt flex-fuel transportation platforms, which in fact some already have done (Brazil being the world's leading example). The powerful insight of Luft and Korin is that simply by converting the transportation fuel market to a competitive market, *one with choices or alternatives,* U.S. foreign policy and consumers would be free of the kinds of threats, implicit or explicit, of future supply interruptions, embargoes, and cartel-induced price hikes that have roiled our foreign and economic policies for nearly four decades.

Oil is no longer relevant as a source for electricity, powering less than 1 percent of all electricity generated in the United States, down substantially from the days before the 1973 OPEC oil embargo. The main source of electricity in the United States (and in much of the rest of the world) instead is coal, which is also a principal source of carbon emissions. Even with "cleaner coal" or coal sequestration, the United States will continue for some time to burn coal and thus contribute to any climate change fueled by carbon emissions.

Sensing this future, some states have required electric utilities in their jurisdictions to generate some portion of their power with less carbon-intensive fuels. Yet as economist Frank Wolak has pointed out, these mandates are inefficient. It makes no sense to require utilities in every state to use solar and/or wind to generate electricity when in many states the sun does not often shine or the wind does not blow. The sensible course is for states to allow utilities to gain credits for meeting their renewable mandates by purchasing credits from utilities that can more cheaply generate electricity in this manner. Much the same trading process has been under way for some time, with widely acknowledged success, for emissions of sulfur dioxide and other pollutants. Such a trading system could and should be established by a compact among the states without the need for federal intervention (although a federal statute could accelerate the creation of such a system).

In addition, incentives for using cost-effectively renewable sources of electricity generation must be buttressed by a more rational system of building additional electricity transmission capacity. Since it is unlikely that Congress will give to a single federal regulatory body (such as the Federal Energy Regulatory Commission) authority to approve all new transmission lines, preempting states and localities in the process (except perhaps for small generation facilities), states could (and should) nonetheless agree among themselves to change their standards for approving new transmission facilities so that they take account of the potential benefits not only to a narrow metropolitan area or even state, but to the nation, of expanded transmission facilities.

Taken together, these reforms can not only move the United States toward real energy independence (not autarky, but rather effective choice in transportation fuel sources) and more cost-effective methods for reducing carbon emissions, but also open new opportunities for entrepreneurs. Historically, entrepreneurs developed the automobile and the energy source (oil) that powered it, and also assembled the electricity generation network that defines a modern economy today. With the right rules in place and with little need for expanded federal research in clean energy, a new generation of entrepreneurs can power our economy of the future without the downsides of our current energy system.

If growth will not be stopped or significantly slowed through a shortage of energy, then—as we noted earlier in this chapter and argue in more detail in Chapter 8—it could be significantly interrupted during one or more financial crises of the sort that nearly triggered another depression just a few years ago. Although such crises could be generated by yet another set of destructive financial innovations or practices (as they have been many times in the past), we and others fear a more old-fashioned source of crisis: one triggered by a loss of confidence in U.S. Treasury instruments and our currency due to continued and excessive borrowing to cover the cost of public expenditures, especially the mounting costs of Medicare, Medicaid, and Social Security. The United States got a taste of what a variation on such a crisis could look like after U.S. Treasury debt was downgraded by one major ratings agency in August 2011.

But a future crisis could be much worse. Even the $2.5 trillion-plus, ten-year deficit reduction package negotiated as part of the debt ceiling talks at that time will make only a modest dent in the long-term federal deficit projections, *assuming that all parts of that plan are fully implemented*. To really tackle the longer-term problem will require much more significant compromises by the two parties—a willingness by Democrats to accept significant modifications to entitlement program benefits and openness by Republicans to additional tax revenue. The entitlements pain will be easier to absorb if it is imposed on *future* beneficiaries, while it may be easier politically and certainly more defensible economically if additional tax revenue comes about by closing loopholes and capping deductions on current income taxes rather than lifting marginal income tax rates for any class of taxpayer.

Unfortunately, the long-term federal deficit problem is one that faster growth will not solve, though it would help mitigate it somewhat. Ultimately some combination of benefit cuts (almost certainly those of future beneficiaries) and tax increases will be required. When we published *Good Capitalism, Bad Capitalism,* we reflected the then-conventional wisdom that the solution, when it came, would reflect roughly a fifty-fifty split between benefit cuts and tax increases (and that the latter most likely would take the form of taxes on consumption rather than on income, which we preferred as a last resort and still do). But events since, most importantly the public animus directed toward government spending in the wake of the crisis-induced bailouts and the stimulus itself (whose impact will likely continue to be a subject of academic and public controversy for years), have changed our minds, and more importantly have deeply affected the politics of deficit reduction. The August 2011 package, for example, consisted *only of spending cuts* and had no tax increases. This formula is not politically sustainable as further required deficit reduction is undertaken. Bringing the long-term deficit under control entirely through spending cuts would eviscerate Medicare and Social Security as we have come to know it. Still, for reasons we have just outlined, any further package(s) almost surely will be heavily tilted toward spending cuts, probably on the order of 70/30 (spending cuts/additional tax revenues) or even 80/20.

The critical question, of course, is whether a future Congress and the next president will agree on a comprehensive deficit reduction plan before another financial crisis—triggered by a run on the dollar and by U.S. Treasuries—forces action to be taken. Until August 2011 we would have been far more pessimistic than we are now that this problem will be tackled before another crisis. Elected officials and the public at least now know the seriousness of the problem and the dangers of not acting. Nonetheless, the bitter partisanship that was on display during the summer of 2011 and has continued through this writing does not inspire too much confidence that elected officials will be able to slay the deficit monster before an economic crisis compels them to do so, at the worst possible time. We lay all this out in Chapter 8, along with some descriptions of a few silver linings in the otherwise dark deficit clouds.

Finally, faster sustainable growth is not and should not be the only objective of economic and social policy. It is important on moral, political, and economic grounds that the fruits of growth be widely shared. A society in which all or most of the gains in income and wealth accrue to a narrow few is the very definition of an oligarchy, a society where those at the top are likely to care only about themselves and not the general welfare of the vast majority of their fellow citizens. Such societies are potentially unstable, since those underneath will not accept their plight forever and will either agitate for populist measures that hurt growth, or in extreme cases, be tempted to violence.

At the same time, Americans have long had only a limited appetite for after-fact redistribution through the tax system or direct government transfers. Americans prize work and risk taking and do not resent the successes of entrepreneurs who build great companies and provide work opportunities for many others. The challenge that the United States has not always satisfactorily met is to ensure that all Americans from all socioeconomic backgrounds have at least a reasonable shot at being part of these entrepreneurial successes, either as cofounders or employees. In other words, there has always been stronger political support for broadening *opportunities to earn* the good life than to level the results of the economic game after the fact.

But that political dynamic will hold only as long as those opportunities realistically exist, and that tickets to the good life—handed out to those who get a good education—are broadly (and ideally equally) available. We know that is not the case now, especially for children raised in low-income families or neighborhoods with underperforming schools. Too few of the students in those schools ever graduate and go on to college, and for those who do not make it that far, future life prospects are difficult at best.

This is not a book about education policy, and even if it were, volumes have been written about how to better educate at-risk students. Much of this literature stresses the importance of introducing market-like measures to education, including expansion of parental choice through more charter schools, greater freedom for principals to run their schools (including hiring and firing of teachers), and performance-based pay for teachers, among others. We side with all these proposals, urge that more states, municipalities, and school districts adopt them, and believe, as we argue in Chapter 8, that budget pressures at all these levels of government will accelerate their implementation.

Yet these important and necessary reforms still will fix only what might be called the education "infrastructure." They do not necessarily influence what students in K–12 should be taught and how. In Chapter 9, we outline what we admit is a preliminary case for filling in this missing blank, and readers of this book who have made it this far—and certainly by the time they reach Chapter 9—will not be surprised by what we recommend.

Consider what it takes to achieve some modicum of economic success in the twenty-first century. In years past, once many individuals secured a job with a large firm, they could earn their way into the middle class and perhaps higher, and stay there. But those days are gone. Few Americans entering the workforce today or in the future will remain with a single employer. The far more common pattern will be that individuals will work for a succession of firms, often in different industries and in different occupations. A healthy minority, we hope, will not work for anyone else but themselves, and through starting and growing a business may employ many others.

To be successful in such an environment, people will have to manage themselves as if they were a business—acquiring and then reselling their skills. Does this activity sound familiar? It should. It's what an entrepreneur does, but with his or her business. Now and in the future, even individuals working for others will have to behave the same way. They must become entrepreneurs of their own careers, which means they not only need to learn skills suitable for the workforce they will enter upon graduation—one that will pay them more if they graduate college than if they simply finish high school—but they must both *know how to continue to learn and want to do so.*

We believe that the current K–12 curriculum and even too many colleges do an inadequate job of preparing their graduates for such a future, and, even more important to the quest for more equal economic opportunities, they fail to excite the far too many students who drop out of school before earning a diploma. At the K–12 level, the challenge is to infuse the entire curriculum in all grades with real-life materials, examples, and illustrations that prepare the students not only for specific occupations, but for entrepreneurship as a career. This means activities that provide opportunities to be creative, recognize opportunities, and perhaps most important, know how to launch actual businesses to implement ideas.

We provide some thoughts in Chapter 9 about how to impart these skills both inside and outside the classroom. Indeed, hands-on experiences in high school, and even more importantly in college, may be even more useful than what students are formally taught. We do not settle for classroom teaching of the fundamentals of baseball, basketball, or football. You actually have to play the game. The same is true with entrepreneurial skills.

Entrepreneurship is also likely to be one element, not yet really tried, of giving adults already in the labor force (with or without diplomas) who are unemployed or have little or no income a better ticket to the good life than they might have if they continue trying to hop from job to job throughout their lives. At the very least, entrepreneurial training—recognizing opportunities, knowing the basics of how to launch a business and what a growing business requires—will provide students and adults with useful skills whether or not they ever actually start their own business.

Policymakers can help too. At the local level, they need to remove counterproductive licensing requirements for many occupations and services. Entrepreneurship training should be widely offered, especially for low-income individuals and the unemployed, and if necessary funded either out of general revenues or with a tiny increase (for that is all it would take) in the current unemployment insurance tax.

We want to be clear: we are not arguing that lifelong education, infused with an entrepreneurial outlook, is the silver bullet that will cure poverty and completely level the playing field of economic opportunity. Rather, we simply suggest that it should be part of the solution to achieving these goals, one that has not yet been given sufficient recognition or support.

Regardless of the measures that government policymakers may or may not take to ensure more equal opportunities at living the American dream, a faster rate of growth driven by continuous entrepreneurial innovation, however disruptive it may be, need not lead to greater inequalities in either income or opportunities. Recent American economic history supports this optimistic view. Incomes in each of the five income distribution quintiles advanced at roughly the same pace during the twenty-five-year period between 1948 and 1973, regarded by many as a golden age because of annual productivity growth that neared 3 percent. A similar pattern occurred during the 1990s after the recession at the beginning of the decade. In short, a rising tide can lift most boats, even if unequally, and this is not an outcome that should be resisted.

We conclude the book in Chapter 10 with some thoughts about the political economy of the policy changes we recommend in earlier chapters. We do not understate the difficulties of getting these changes implemented or the magnitude of the challenges that lie ahead. In particular, our calling for continued entrepreneurial revolutions during one of the most difficult economic periods in U.S. history is ambitious. Yet in our concluding chapter we provide some reasons that history gives reason for hope.

We nonetheless do not expect all the ideas for accelerating growth to be implemented at once, or even a few of them in response to future crises. The best we can hope for is that citizens and policymakers (current and future) who read this book will be inspired about how a few changes here and there, not all of them within the province of government, can significantly enhance the chances that more rapid, sustained growth can be and will become an engrained part of our economy—so engrained that it will not even be noticeable, except one day to future historians who will look back and marvel over how the Americans yet again reinvented themselves, their society, and their economy to produce steady improvements in standards of living for all citizens. That story is our history. It is a story that can and should be our future.

2

TOWARD A NEW UNDERSTANDING OF THE
ECONOMY: AN ENTREPRENEURIAL SYNTHESIS

There are silver linings to economic crises. They tend to cause a major rethinking of economics itself. Fortunately, there is already evidence that the Great Recession and its aftermath are having this effect.

Given the relative stability of the U.S. economy in the twenty-five years preceding this traumatic event, macroeconomics—that part of economics which deals with the performance of the overall economy and had once attracted some of the profession's brightest stars—had become much more theoretical (and esoteric) and of less interest to most economists and even less to the wider public. The best evidence for this perhaps is the surprising commercial success of *Freakonomics,* which was published and topped the nonfiction best seller lists just before the crisis got under way. To be sure, the book offers a fascinating look at how some of the fundamental insights of economics can be applied to some unusual problems (cheating by teachers on student tests or drug dealing), and its economist coauthor, Steven Levitt, has been awarded one of the profession's most coveted prizes, the John Bates Clark award, given only every two years to an economist under age forty for outstanding original work in the field. But there is not one word in that book about the economic cycle or the potential for a financial or economic crisis, two of the topics that have since dominated the public's attention and seem to be refocusing what many economists now consider to be important and worth understanding. We do not mean to pick on Levitt, who is clearly a brilliant economist. The fact is that few of the winners of the Clark Medal, which is usually a precursor to a later Nobel Prize, have won primarily for their work in macroeconomics.

It is safe to predict that this will change in the years ahead. The Great Recession has prompted a major resurgence of interest within the profession, not surprisingly, in both macroeconomics and in understanding financial markets and institutions. Indeed, there seems to be a growing consensus within the profession that the next great challenge for economists is to integrate "macro" with "finance" so that future models of the economy (for that is how economists think, by building models) take account of the impact of financial sector developments on the wider economy, and vice versa.

We do not dispute the need for such a synthesis. Economists obviously need to be better able to explain how economies behave in the short run, over the so-called cycle. Specifically, given the failure of most macroeconomists to "call" either the 2008 recession or of many experts to predict the weakness of the recovery, there clearly is a need to identify factors that will better explain the "turning points"—when economies reach their tops and output and employment begin to slow or actually fall and, just as important, when economies bottom out and output and employment begin to turn up—in the future.

Of equal import, however, is the need for improvements in "growth theory," that branch of economics which seeks to explain *over the long run* how rapidly economies generate more output, and thus the rate of improvement in living standards for their members. In effect, growth theory looks at the "supply side" of the economy, or how fast economies grow in their ability to produce goods and services *assuming all current inputs, namely capital and labor, are fully employed*. In contrast, traditional macroeconomics looks at the "demand side" of the economy, or what factors determine how close actual output is to *potential* output at any given point in time.

In this chapter we advance a bold thesis: that there is way of looking at the economy, and specifically the U.S. economy, that can help economists, policymakers, and interested readers better understand *both* its short- and long-run dynamics. The way to do that, we submit, is through the lens of *firm formation and growth*.

Ironically, this may seem more obvious to noneconomists than economists. To those without formal economic training, it may come as no surprise to learn that the overall economy, or at least the private sector, is nothing more than the summed activity of all of its firms (including part- or full-time self-employed individuals with no employees). But that is not the traditional way economists measure the economy. Rather, the national income accounts, which add up all private sector economic output, are apportioned into the part that is consumed (recently nearly 70 percent of GDP in the United States), the part that is "invested" (used for the purchase of long-lived assets, such as new homes for individuals and buildings and equipment for businesses), and the portion that is exported abroad, minus the goods and services that are imported from other countries. In short, GDP is measured as the sum of aggregate *demand*. Nothing about firms here, except narrowly, in their investment activities.

We do not challenge the accounting conventions for adding up GDP. They are uncontestable and of course useful. But growth policy, and specifically growth theory, is about more than accounting. The objective should be to focus on the key drivers of economic activity, and in this narrative it is hard to escape the central role of firms. Firms not only produce, they also purchase—supplies and services—including the labor of those who work for them. Firm activity is thus an engine of demand as well as supply.

Moreover, it is not just any entrepreneurial firms that are important; we will argue that there is special place in the U.S. economy for *new firms*. In the roughly three decades preceding the Great Recession, firms less than five years old (and perhaps as young as only one year old) accounted for virtually *all* of the net new jobs created each year in the private sector. Over time, this means that newly formed firms have accounted for a growing fraction of total output in the economy. By one accounting, roughly *one third* of total employment and therefore private sector output today is being generated by firms that did not exist before 1980.[1] We do not have the data to know whether new firms are as important in other countries as they are in the United States, but we suspect that at least in the most dynamic economies of the world—India, China, Brazil, and Israel—a very similar story can be told.

It may surprise some readers, but we believe our focus on new firm activity is very much consistent with the Keynesian focus on aggregate demand, which in Keynes' view was driven very heavily by what he called "animal spirits," a term he meant to loosely refer to the degree of private sector optimism. Although Keynes never mentions the word "entrepreneur" (unlike his contemporary rival, Joseph Schumpeter, for whom entrepreneurs are the main drivers of growth) in any of his books, we will argue that the level of entrepreneurial activity, especially of potentially scalable firms, is an ideal measure of Keynes' animal spirits and thus an excellent guide to the health of both aggregate demand and growth of potential output at any point in time. Put differently, the surest way to provide a *lasting* Keynesian stimulus is to foster the creation and growth of new firms, for this is likely to be the surest way of giving confidence to consumers and other firms at home and abroad that the future is bright. Having confidence in the future, in turn, encourages people and firms to spend, which lifts aggregate demand without necessarily requiring as much (or, depending on the circumstances, conceivably *any*) traditional fiscal and/or monetary stimulus. At the same time, an economy with a vibrant entrepreneurial sector is likely to be developing and commercializing new technologies, products, and services, which expand an economy's productive capacity. In sum, entrepreneurs are the glue that binds together both the demand and supply sides of the economy.

Of course, we do not claim this "entrepreneurial synthesis" to be a silver bullet to understanding everything about the short- and long-run performance of economies. Economies are complex phenomena with multiple actors, each with different motivations and intentions. But the very best science can often be reduced to the quest to identify the *simplest* plausible, and ideally verifiable, explanations of the forces or behavior at issue—what scientists and economists frequently refer to as "Occam's razor" (named after the English logician and theologian, William of Ockham). Entrepreneurs are the razor in our narrative, and while they may not be the only "blade"—the adoption of best practices by existing firms has been and always will be a source of much potential productivity growth—we believe and will argue here that the new firm phenomenon is much more important than has heretofore been recognized by many economists and policymakers interested in both short -and long-run economic performance.

Firms and Growth in the Short Run

One frequently heard adage is that in the U.S. economy, "small business" is central to job creation and, by inference, economic growth. In a series of studies sponsored by or conducted by the Kauffman Foundation, we have learned that this is not strictly true. It's not small business that is central to job growth, it is *new business,* especially firms that grow. Indeed, more broadly, it is a mistake to equate small business with entrepreneurship when thinking about public policy. Many small business owners have no intention of growing beyond their present size, preferring the lifestyle of self-employment. True entrepreneurs bring new products, services, or methods of production or service to the market, and are interested in building growing enterprises. Growing economies are built on such endeavors. And, as it turns out, the greatest job growth is associated with *new firms.* For example, Professor John Haltiwanger of the University of Maryland and two colleagues from the U.S. Census Bureau, Ron Jarmin and Javier Miranda, found that between 1992 and 2005, all net increases in jobs were located in start-up firms, or those less than five years old.[2] Time in business, not size, mattered for job growth. One of us (Litan) and our Kauffman Foundation colleague Dane Stangler extended this analysis over a longer period and found it to be true for the years 1980 through 2007.[3]

Some may be tempted to dismiss or downplay these results by observing (correctly) that, by definition, startups can't lose jobs because they don't have any employees to begin with. So any success they have must generate an increase in jobs. All true, but this fact says nothing about the net job generation of all other existing firms. Some generate more jobs, others lose jobs. What is surprising in the data is that *on balance* the jobs added by existing businesses are almost precisely offset by the jobs shed by other existing businesses. The net result (no pun intended) is that taking whichever study one wants, the inescapable conclusion is that when it comes to new job creation, it's new firms that count most (although we don't want to entirely dismiss existing firms because for many startups, existing firms are customers or suppliers—or both).

But do we know that the jobs created by new firms last? Actually we do. Another study conducted by one of us (Litan) and former Kauffman

Foundation researcher Mike Horell found that fully 80 percent of the jobs generated by startups, in aggregate number, were still there five years later.[4] This is not to say that the *same firms* were there, because we know that isn't the case. Indeed, one of the other surprising things from Kauffman Foundation firm research is the stability of firm failure rates: in good years and bad, just about half of all firms launched are still in business five years later, and the other half are gone.[5] Of course, when looking over a longer period, failure rates go up considerably, as one would expect in any dynamic economy. Dane Stangler and Paul Kedrosky find that a company formed today has an 80 percent chance of disappearing over the next twenty-five years.[6] But the data also are telling us that the jobs generated by the successful startups over their first five years offset almost all the job losses from the firms that fail, indicating that the jobs created by startups are not "flashes in the pan" that then quickly vanish.[7]

This isn't to say that the pace of new firm formation explains short-run fluctuations in output and employment. Another surprising fact, illustrated in the top line in Figure 2.1, is that the number of new firms formed each month as a percentage of the overall workforce on an annualized basis was remarkably stable between the mid-1990s (when we first had good data to track this important trend) and the onset of the Great Recession, showing no cyclical trend to that point. Since then, the business formation rate has increased, but only due to an increase in firms without employees. We know this because the formation rate of firms with employees dropped after 2007. This suggests that the uptick since then in the overall rate of business formation is probably due to "necessity entrepreneurs," most likely previously unemployed individuals who couldn't find a suitable job and opened a business out of necessity (or those with a job who needed to supplement their income after the recession began).

The statistics in Figure 2.1 tell us nothing, however, about the "quality" of the firms being formed at any time, specifically the rate of formation of potentially scalable firms. It is highly plausible that the pace at which truly scale firms are being formed and growing strongly reflects and influences consumers' and firms' degrees of optimism or pessimism about the economy in general. In particular, if we had a measure, which we don't, of new firms linked to the introduction and commercialization of new products and services, or what we call "scale entrepreneurship" (since those firms

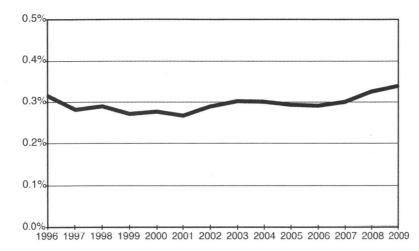

Figure 2.1 Trends in Start-up Activity 1996–2009
Source: Kauffman Index of Entrepreneurial Activity

most likely to scale are those that are truly "entrepreneurial," doing something that no one has done before), that would be as good an indicator
as there is of the Keynesian "animal spirits" in the economy at any point in
time. After all, "the new" is what excites people to buy, and if consumers
are spending, firms are more likely to invest. It is not an accident, for example, that the U.S. economy grew relatively rapidly in the 1980s and
1990s, decades marked by high-tech entrepreneurship.

This reasoning is highly relevant to figuring out how to accelerate the
pace of the recovery from the Great Recession, a topic that was of great
interest through much of the time we were working on this book, and one
that we suspect will be timely for a number of years after its publication. It
has become apparent that the recovery from this recession will be much
slower than the typical "V"-shaped recovery from other post–World War
II recessions because, going into this recession, the American consumer
was considerably overleveraged and not saving sufficiently for retirement.[8]
The crashes of the stock and housing markets that marked the financial
crisis have added strong headwinds to the recovery by inducing not only
Americans, but also consumers in other developed nations rocked by the
recession, to save more—a good thing in the long run, but not in the short
run. These events also dampened the animal spirits of firms, reflected in

the relatively anemic pace of investment spending (outside of information technology) since the Great Recession began and technically ended, in late 2009.

Much of this downbeat psychology would change with another entrepreneurial revolution—not just another new iPad or iPhone equivalent, but *many* "gee whiz" devices and services that would excite not only American consumers but also those in other countries. We're not claiming or even urging that Americans go on yet another leveraged consumption binge. Not only must the de-leveraging process continue, but banks won't let Americans use their houses as ATMs again, especially when roughly a quarter of them are "underwater" (valued at less than the combination of any first and second mortgages). But a bit faster consumption growth, combined with faster export growth (without the need for further dollar depreciation), would accelerate the pace of the recovery. Unemployment would come down faster, budgets at all levels of government would improve (though not avoid the severe structural problems most governments must deal with, as we discuss later in this book), and perhaps most important, Americans would get back that optimism about the future they once had.

There is much urgency to rejuvenating America's start-up performance. Despite the importance of startups in generating new jobs in the United States, there were signs even before the recession that the start-up engine was sputtering. The numbers of new *employer startups*—those that hire at least one employee in the first year after launch—were beginning to fall in 2005–6 and fell even faster through the recession and into 2010. Just as important, the average number of employees working at new "establishments" (a mushier statistic that includes both startups and new facilities of existing firms) has fallen steadily since 2000, from 7.5 to just 4.9 in 2010. In part, this latter trend can be traced to the dramatic reduction and ease of use of information technology, coupled with the ease of outsourcing work even at the beginning stages of launching a company.[9] But the two trends combined—fewer employer startups and fewer employees per startup—can only spell trouble unless and until America's start-up engine is retuned, if not overhauled.

We don't have the data to know how important the continued flow of new firms is to other economies, especially the most rapidly growing

economies of the past decade—China, India, and Brazil. We strongly suspect, however, that growth in each of these economies also is being
strongly driven by high-growth firms.

The same may or may not be true of other smaller but rapidly growing
economies such as Israel and, until the Great Recession, Ireland, or some
of the emerging success stories in Africa. Up to now, smaller economies,
due to their geographic or population limits, have been limited by the relatively small size of their domestic market in supporting truly scale growth
companies. But in an increasingly global economy linked by the Internet,
it is not inconceivable in the future that some truly large global brand-name
firms could get their start in smaller economics.

Firms and Growth in the Long Run

Entrepreneurs, especially those founding scale companies that
commercialize innovative products and services, are important not only
for short-run cyclical recovery, but also for raising the long-run growth
rate and thereby the rate of living standards improvement. The reason is
straightforward. As we observed in the first chapter, entrepreneurs throughout modern economic history, in this country and others, have been disproportionately responsible for truly radical innovations—the airplane,
the railroad, the automobile, electric service, the telegraph and telephone,
the computer, air conditioning, and so on—that not only fundamentally
transformed consumers' lives, but also became platforms for many other
industries that, in combination, have fundamentally changed entire economies.

The successful radical or disruptive innovations of the nineteenth century were brought to us by entrepreneurs, because the modern, large corporation with its huge resources, thousands of employees, and yes, bureaucracy
(with a few exceptions), did not become a presence in *any* economy until the
twentieth century. Large companies, with their large fixed costs of plant,
equipment, and to some extent personnel, have perfected the economic arts
of economies of scale production and incremental innovation. But, as William Baumol has explained, most large companies are less eager to pursue
radical innovations—those that disrupt current business models in which
the firms are heavily invested. There are exceptions to this pattern, most

notably Apple, which in two eras when Steve Jobs was running the company came up with a series of game-changing innovations. But Apple is one exception to the rule that larger companies tend not to invest in and develop disruptive innovations precisely because its founder, Steve Jobs, was brought back from exile to direct the firm's growth. Whether Jobs's creative entrepreneurial spirit can and will live past his death is one of the great unanswered questions in the business world.

In any event, because entrepreneurs are willing to work for "nonpecuniary rewards"—fame, control over one's life, and the feeling of "changing the world"—that do not show up in their "wages," it makes economic sense for large companies to effectively outsource the riskiest innovative activity, and then either copy and improve the most successful outcomes or purchase proven entrepreneurial ventures.[10] Of course, this research and development (R&D) outsourcing story does not always end well for large, established companies, which can miss the boat on truly revolutionary new businesses. Just ask IBM, which had a chance to own the operating systems for personal computers but ceded control of this technology to Bill Gates and hence to Microsoft. The rest, as they say, is history.

The contributions of entrepreneurs to our modern way of life are easily taken for granted. Today's children and students, for example, do not know of a life without the Internet or mobile phones that act like computers, just as our generation couldn't have imagined life without the television or air conditioning. Similar statements can be made for earlier generations.

But for today's readers, it is useful to briefly go back in time to the nineteenth century to review how what is now considered to be a mundane industry—the railroad business, which was launched in the United States by a series of unsavory entrepreneurs—had a truly revolutionary impact on the U.S. economy and society. The railroad story is a microcosm of how other entrepreneur-created industries have had similar impacts, by spawning other inventions and industries and by changing the lives of people who bought the new products and services.[11]

Railroads, of course, made it possible for people to move much more rapidly and generally more safely than on the main alternative mode of transportation at the time, the horse. But these new steam-powered vehicles had even more far-reaching economic and social impacts because of the *things* they carried. With the invention of the refrigerated railroad car by Gustavus Swift, for example, railroads enabled people to eat a much wider of variety of foods—vegetables, fruits, meat, and milk—than the limited choices that were available from local sources.

Railroads also enabled the emergence and subsequent rise of large-scale national companies, and thus were critical to birthing managerial capitalism, which later became the dominant form of capitalism in the United States, Europe, and Japan in the twentieth century. Consider the first two large retailers—before Walmart—namely, Sears Roebuck and Montgomery Ward, which began by accepting orders by mail. With the mail-order catalog, anyone could have access to the same wide menu of items that Sears and Montgomery Ward provided, only because the goods could then by shipped by rail. Later, each of these companies along with others developed the modern "department store" that physically offered the same items that were available by catalog, but again, only because the inventory they stocked was delivered by rail.

The railroad not only greatly increased choice and led to lower prices for a vast array of items due to the enhanced competition among retailers and economies of scale in retail that rail shipping helped make possible, but, by improving access to quality food and clothing, it also made Americans healthier and enabled them to live longer. Both stature and life expectancy have risen steadily since the late nineteenth century in particular, due in no small part to the multiple commercial opportunities opened by rail (and later automobile and air) transportation.

Of course, public health and longevity also have increased because of the efforts of many other entrepreneurs and scientists who gave us new pharmaceuticals (especially antibiotics), new modes of trash collection and sanitation, and new and better methods for building houses and apartment buildings, all of which made America a far healthier place to live. It is important for Americans today to understand and recognize the unseen but hugely important contribution of the railroad pioneers, who also played a vital role in these trends. Similar stories can be told for many other breakthrough inventions and technologies that have been brought to the market and thus widely dispersed by entrepreneurs.

Spontaneous entrepreneurial, firm-centric growth explains the enormous surge of growth throughout the nineteenth and twentieth centuries in Europe as well. Italy, for example, developed a renowned technological base, driven largely driven by innovators and engineers whose training was often provided through military service where first-generation technology was developed to support innovations in munitions and warships. England's mercantile history is similarly characterized by innovations taking shape in new firms. The legendary Joshua Wedgewood and his china factory set the stage for the Industrial Revolution just as much as did Watt and his steam engine, arguably one of the most important innovations of the last two centuries.

The point is that firm-centric growth, although largely unrecognized by academic observers in both economics and business scholarship, has been perhaps the single most powerful force for economic expansion in every economy that ever experienced growth. While some studies argue the importance of banking, others of risk capital, the rule of law, or the criticality of physical infrastructure, none of these factors can produce economic activity outside the context of firms.

An economy that is centered on firms and their continuous creation, combination, and failure was anticipated and described with clarity by not only Adam Smith but also, in more modern times, the great Joseph Schumpeter, who emigrated to this country from Europe and had a sterling academic career at Harvard.[12] Both Smith and Schumpeter, though more than 200 years apart in their thinking and writing, each saw the firm as the instigation of one or more entrepreneurs who hoped to deliver an innovation in technology or processes that would prove economically valuable by either creating a new market or challenging existing firms through efficiency gains. Ironically, in the last great work of his life, *Capitalism, Socialism and Democracy,* Schumpeter was exceedingly pessimistic about the future of entrepreneurs, fearing that large corporations, with their sound finances and armies of scientists and engineers, would dominate innovation and, by inference, entrepreneurship in the future. The resurgence of entrepreneurial capitalism in the United States in the late 1970s through today fortunately has proved Schumpeter's pessimism misplaced.

Nonetheless, at least Schumpeter knew enough to credit entrepreneurs—whether inside large companies or operating outside of them—with advancing economies. Most other economists have failed to do even that, essentially ignoring entrepreneurs (the very word, let alone the concept entrepreneurship represents, is absent from nearly all beginning economics textbooks) in their increasingly mathematical models of the economy. Entrepreneurs, by definition, are unpredictable and the capitalism they create is inherently "messy," not the ordered capitalism of the economic textbooks. But there is a story that many economists also recite as a warning: that it is a mistake to look for lost coins only under lampposts because that is where the light is. Economists must look for the truth wherever it is, in the light or in the dark. In the case of economic growth, entrepreneurs operate far away from the lampposts, and the challenge for economists, policymakers, and citizens is both to recognize the huge contribution entrepreneurs make to economic growth and to establish and maintain an institutional, legal, and policy environment in which entrepreneurs can thrive, for we all benefit when they do.

The Billion Dollar Thought Experiment[13]

To illustrate concretely what we mean about the linkage between firm formation and growth on the one hand, and GDP growth on the other, we now lay out a thought experiment and ask: how could annual U.S. economic growth be permanently increased *in the future* by one additional percentage point (above the growth rate that would otherwise exist)? We offered one calculation of the significance of this question in Chapter 1. Here's another. If the economy were to grow at a 4 percent annual rate rather than 3 percent (the upper end of most economists' current estimates for the maximum rate at which the U.S. economy now can grow), GDP would double six years sooner (eighteen years versus twenty-four years). Given the magic of compounding, this extra 1 percent would cumulate over a century to produce a level GDP roughly *three times* higher than would otherwise exist.

Such a world would be a far more comfortable one than many of us may be able to imagine. It would mean a dramatically lower level of poverty, while the average American would have a living standard three times as comfortable as the one that he or she would otherwise enjoy (imagine today, for example, the average family income being roughly $135,000 rather than its current level of about $45,000). A richer society would also have more resources to address public challenges—upgrading infrastructure, doing more to clean the environment, and so on—to make life in America even more comfortable for all our citizens.

So what is the key to faster growth? Earlier in this chapter we reported recent research establishing that, at least in the U.S. economy, growth in output and employment is driven strongly by the creation and growth of new firms. It thus may be tempting to answer the "How do we get one percent faster growth?" question by figuring out how many more total firms need to be started each year.

But this is a shotgun approach, the proverbial equivalent of throwing a lot of "mud" (firms) against the wall and hoping that some of it sticks. A nuanced, and we believe more useful, inquiry is to try to estimate how many *very successful* new firms it would take each year to lift the economy-wide growth rate by 1 percent. After all, it is the most rapidly growing firms that, by definition, generate the most job growth.

Especially important are those truly *innovative* or *inventive* growing firms that bring to the market something *new*—a product, service, or process—that generates substantially more benefits for society as a whole than any single entrepreneur, inventor, or firm can capture for himself or itself. Think, for example, of the electric light, which literally opened up new horizons for all humanity to work and experience new forms of leisure when it is dark outside. Or, more recently, consider breakthrough computer programs such as the Microsoft or Linux operating systems that establish a platform on which tens of thousands of other productivity-enhancing applications can run. The same is true of other platforms, such as Apple's iPhone or Google's Android, or new technologies, such as genetic sequencers or cloud computing, which facilitate innovation of many other complementary technologies.

To be sure, not all innovations generating social gains in excess of private rewards find their way into measured GDP. Many health care innovations—new pharmaceuticals, medical devices, and treatments—both lengthen and improve the quality of lives for millions, if not billions of people. While the inventors of these marvels often (though not always) reap handsome rewards, the rewards also surely do not capture the health benefits enjoyed by all the beneficiaries of these innovations. Economists may attempt to put a price on these gains in health and thus quantify the overall improvement in social welfare, but these gains are not generally traded on the open market. Still, they are very real, and in some respect they do translate into additional GDP (since healthier individuals are more productive and can work longer). However they are considered, health benefits should be accounted for as if they added to GDP, and for our purpose here, they are.

If innovative firms are the drivers of growth in both output and jobs—largely because of the excess gains to society they generate over the private reward their founders, shareholders, and employees reap—then it stands to reason that the steady creation of more such firms will increase growth in the long run. Here we focus for illustrative purposes on one particular class of such firms—*those inventive firms whose revenues grow to an average of $1 billion or more*—and ask: how many such new firms would the U.S. economy have to create in order, in a steady state, to generate an additional one percentage point in annual economic growth?

The billion dollar revenue threshold is an admittedly arbitrary way of focusing on only the most inventive successful firms. It is based, however, on what we believe to be a plausible assumption: that the products, services, or processes whose social benefits *substantially* exceed their private benefits are most likely to be brought to market by "home run" firms whose revenues grow to some significant level, such as an average of $1 billion. This is not to say that *all* billion dollar firms generate social gains far in excess of their private gains, only that *on average*, firms of this size are likely to have been more inventive (as demonstrated by their revenue success) and to exhibit higher ratios of social to private gains than firms in smaller size cohorts. But we also don't want to be interpreted as denying the important contribution of smaller but successful new and existing firms, or the "singles," "doubles," and "triples," whose ratios of social to private gains are likely to be somewhat lower than the "home runs." Indeed, the home runs will need services and supplies from these successful "base hits," and the latter firms surely will purchase some of the output of the home runs.

Thus, to the extent that all successful firms generate additional productivity growth for the economy, this will reduce the number of billion dollar companies required to generate an additional 1 percent in economy-wide growth. Likewise, the more rapid adoption of best practices by existing firms would reduce the need for productivity acceleration generated by the formation of new home run firms. Thus, the order-of-magnitude estimates that follow—ranging from 30 to 150 new billion dollar companies each year, with a most likely estimate of 60—are likely to overstate the numbers actually required. This should make it a bit less daunting to achieve the 1 percent extra growth target than the estimates that follow may suggest.

Some Arithmetic of Growth

With U.S. GDP currently about $15 trillion, 1 percent extra growth would require an additional $150 billion in output annually.[14] Economists typically would say that the way to generate that additional GDP growth is for society to somehow increase its growth of "productivity"—the rate at which outputs increase for given inputs (labor in particular). This is a truism, of course. It doesn't translate at all into how many additional firms, and of what kinds, it would take to achieve such an outcome.

To dig deeper, we use the results of a pathbreaking analysis conducted several years ago, in which Yale economist William Nordhaus estimated that inventors, which we assume here to be proxies for innovative entrepreneurs, capture only 4 percent of the total social gains from their innovations.[15] The lion's share of inventors' gains "leak out" to benefit many other firms and industries that use the inventions in some manner.

The 4 percent figure implies that in order for *society* to benefit from an additional $150 billion in output, inventors (or entrepreneurs, for this purpose) must develop new products, services, and processes that collectively earn themselves only $6 billion a year ($150 billion times .04) after taxes. If, as seems reasonable, the average inventive firm returns 10 percent on its sales, it would take $60 billion in sales to generate $6 billion in profits.[16] If we spread this $60 billion evenly across all billion dollar firms, we have our answer! *The economy needs sixty inventive companies to be formed each year whose revenues eventually mature into an average of $1 billion* (because the figure is an "average," some new companies' sales can exceed $1 billion while other successful enterprises with large social benefits can fall short of this benchmark).

This is an order-of-magnitude estimate, and one that could easily be lower or higher than this level depending on the assumptions. For example, our impression is that the most successful high-tech companies—or those most likely to qualify for our required list of inventive billion dollar companies—have higher margins. Say, for example, that the net profit-to-sales ratio for these companies is 20 percent rather than 10 percent. In that event, generating $6 billion in annual profits would require a much lower $30 billion in collective revenue, implying the need for *just thirty billion-dollar companies to be created each year.*

Conversely, it is possible that Nordhaus's 4 percent estimate is too low for the purpose here, since it reflects only the most successful inventions. If the ratio of private gains was somewhat higher than 4 percent—say 10 percent—to reflect some mix of billion dollar companies whose external benefits are not as large as the Nordhaus average, then the "billion dollar club" may need to earn $15 billion collectively in profits. At a 10 percent earnings-to-revenue ratio, this implies the need for an additional $150 billion in annual revenue, or 150 companies whose average revenues grow to $1 billion.

Several fundamental points about this range of estimates—anywhere from 30 to 150 new billion dollar companies per year—are noteworthy. First, the estimated numbers of additional billion dollar companies required are *incremental.* That is, these are the *additional* highly successful companies that must be launched *each year*—over and above the number of such companies that are already being formed (a subject we address shortly)—to generate the sustained increase in growth of 1 percent. Actually, the required incremental figure is an *average* figure over time, since, as in the baseline now, the number of new companies that grow up to be home runs quite clearly does and will continue to vary from year to year.

Second, the required number of new successful companies will need to grow by roughly 15 percent a year to take account of the steadily larger economy. Recall that the calculations began with an estimated $150 billion increase in GDP being required in the first year. This additional amount will grow at the economy-wide growth rate and thus, so will the required number of billion dollar companies. Alternatively, one could adjust the billion dollar threshold upward by 15 percent a year (the growth in nominal GDP). If that were done, the required number of successful new inventive companies to be created each year would remain constant, but the level of their required success would grow over time, surpassing an average of $2 billion in roughly fourteen years, $4 billion in twenty-eight years, and so on.

Third, as noted already, the estimates here pertain to economy-wide growth in a *steady state*—or once the average successful company reaches a milestone of success (again, because we are referring to averages, that milestone will exceed a billion dollars for some of these companies, and for others the benchmark will be somewhat less). We have no hard data on how long this period of steadiness is likely to be, but it bears noting that the length of this period only influences the length of the initial transition required to get to the steady state of incremental 1 percent growth (say ten or twenty years, or whatever the right figure is). That is, the calculations refer to the number of companies that must be created each year that *eventually* will mature into the billion dollar average. It is possible, of course, that with continued advances in and diffusion of technology this transition period will grow shorter over time, and indeed may already have shortened compared to earlier periods in U.S. history.

Fourth, as noted in the introduction, the calculations here by design put all the weight of added GDP growth on new billion dollar companies, when in fact we know that new and existing companies of lesser size can certainly contribute to faster economy-wide growth. Furthermore, successful billion dollar companies surely rely on smaller companies to supply materials and services, and also, in many cases, smaller companies can make a significant mark on their own. Nonetheless, we have chosen to focus on the billion dollar enterprises since they are likely to have the largest ratio of social to private gains, and so the economy is likely to get its largest "growth bang for the buck" from the formation and growth of these home run firms.

Finally, the exercise here (also by construction) is a "supply side" one in that it implicitly assumes that any additional output generated by the incremental billion dollar firms is purchased, by domestic or foreign consumers, businesses, or governments. Put differently, the calculations assume that actual GDP grows at the rate at which *potential GDP* (increased by one percentage point) increases. This may not be a realistic assumption at all times since some of the new billion dollar companies will displace existing companies or reduce their sales and thus their employment, adding to the baseline amount of "job churn" already in the economy and perhaps temporarily aggravating mismatches between the requirements of the new jobs being generated by the new companies and the skills of the workers who are displaced. However, over the long run, with sufficient aggregate demand, workers do get reallocated to other firms or they start their own, which enables actual GDP to catch up to and eventually grow at the same rate as potential GDP.

The Billion Dollar Company Benchmark and Beyond

One natural question to ask is "How do the estimates of the required number of billion dollar companies per year compare to how many such companies are already launched?" That is, what is the baseline number of companies started each year that will eventually mature to sales that average $1 billion?

While we have no hard data to provide a good baseline estimate, there is one way to make an order-of-magnitude stab at one. Using a database of publicly held companies whose stocks are traded on U.S. exchanges, we have identified a total of 1,544 U.S.-founded companies whose current (2009) sales exceed $1 billion. This admittedly lowers the baseline since it does not account for firms with lower revenues that have the same ratio of social to private gains as those firms with revenues above $1 billion. But we had no other way to make the cutoff, and so this is the baseline we chose.

Assume that the 1,544 billion dollar companies today were formed over a roughly 150-year period (going back to 1860). In that event, the average number of such companies formed in any given year was, and is, roughly ten. It is plausible that because of advances in communication and transportation technologies—specifically the Internet—that permit companies to reach both internal and non-U.S. markets more quickly, companies formed in more recent cohorts take less time to reach the billion dollar benchmark, and thus the average number of such companies formed in recent decades—say, since 1980—may be somewhat higher than ten.

There are other reasons that the benchmark is likely to be a bit higher. For one thing, there is a substantial number of privately held companies— perhaps several thousand—with revenues over $1 billion. In addition, the current numbers of billion dollar companies reflect a survivorship bias; that is, by definition the current numbers do not include companies that in the past may have reached $1 billion in sales (in today's dollars), but then fell back from that figure, merged with other companies whose sales were below that threshold, or even went out of business altogether. In any event, however the benchmark is computed, it is unrealistically steady as presented here in that it assumes, as a baseline, that the number of new companies growing up to be billion dollar enterprises is constant year in and year out. In reality, this number changes from year to year: some years produce a bunch of winners, others a dearth.

Taking all these considerations into account, let's say the annual benchmark of billion dollar companies is roughly fifteen. Against this benchmark, it is clear that an additional sixty billion dollar companies per year would represent a huge increase over any baseline figure.

Looked at another way, however, the incremental figure is not as daunting. Every year, roughly five hundred thousand startups are born.[17] If sixty of them "grow up" to be billion dollar companies, that's only 0.12 percent of the annual number of business startups. Moreover, if the formation and growth of new billion dollar companies encourages the formation and growth of more somewhat smaller but highly successful companies, then we wouldn't need the sixty home runs to hit the 1 percent extra growth target.

Even in the midst of a sluggish recovery bordering on a relapse into another recession, there is cause for optimism. Each year, *Inc.* magazine puts out its list of the 500 fastest growing privately held companies. In introducing the list for 2011, which was released in September 2011, the editors referred to the essay from which we have drawn heavily in preparing this chapter and asked the founders or presidents of the 500 how many thought they could eventually hit the $1 billion sales target. The answer: 157, or more than 30 percent of the honorees.[18] These 157 aspiring "home runs" got their start in different years, and some of them are repeat honorees, so this number cannot be assigned to any single year's beginning cohort. But 157 aspiring home run companies with an impressive track record out of the gate—nineteen companies on the Inc. 500 list for 2011 had already surpassed $100 million in revenues—certainly indicates that the entrepreneurial spirit remains alive and well in America despite the difficult overall economic environment.

However many more home runs, triples, doubles, and singles are required to generate faster growth, the obvious question is "What can governments, in conjunction with the private sector, do to spawn the formation and growth of such enterprises?" We devote Chapters 3 through 6 to answering this question.

3

TOWARD A MORE ENTREPRENEURIAL ECONOMY

There are fundamentally two very different ways to generate more successful firms, and hence to spur economy-wide growth. Continuing the baseball analogy introduced in the last chapter, one can have more "at bats"—namely, encourage more people to launch their own firms—or increase the national batting average—namely, find ways to increase the percentage of new firms that successfully scale.

Of the two strategies, we believe the more likely route to success is to raise the entrepreneurial batting average. As shown in the last chapter, the number of new firms launched annually has been relatively stable over the past fifteen years, with some uptick in 2009 and 2010 due primarily to an increase in so-called "necessity" entrepreneurship. Though, as we will argue later in this chapter, it should be possible to do a better job inducing more individuals to voluntarily pursue entrepreneurial careers, if as a society we really want to move the needle on the formation of scale firms, we need to find ways of increasing the odds of success among those who decide to take the entrepreneurial path.

In the first half of this chapter, we discuss and examine the two conventional policy instruments for answering this challenge. We devote substantial time and space to these policies largely because they define the current limits of policy discourse. It is impossible, therefore, not to give them serious attention.

For example, one traditional answer to the challenge of launching more high-growth firms would be for the federal government to spend more money on basic scientific research, on the theory that more scientific breakthroughs should lead to more entrepreneurial opportunities for commercializing them, and thus more highly successful companies. The second (and not mutually exclusive) way to achieve the same outcome is to cut taxes or provide targeted incentives to let entrepreneurs keep more of their rewards and thereby encourage them to grow while motivating others to follow in their wake. We conclude that certain tweaks in our nation's R&D and tax policies almost certainly would help to promote the formation and growth of scale companies.

But we believe that neither of these somewhat conventional policy responses is likely to be a "game changer." Instead, in our view, the better answers for really moving the needle on economy-wide growth through scale firm formation and growth lie in improving the effectiveness of what we will call "entrepreneurial ecosystems." Accordingly, we devote the second half of this chapter to this important, and so far underappreciated, topic.

Some readers may equate our term "entrepreneurial ecosystem" with "clusters," or the web of successful firms and their support networks (venture capitalist and angel investors, lawyers, accountants, and skilled workers) in any given locality that generate a virtuous cycle of entrepreneurial activity. One immediately thinks of such places as Silicon Valley, Austin, Boulder, Raleigh-Durham-Chapel Hill, San Diego, and Seattle that exhibit these characteristics and are home to an increasing number of successful startups that became home runs. At first glance, therefore, our call for boosting entrepreneurial ecosystems would seem to be asking the federal and/or state and local governments to attempt to create more such clusters, or less ambitiously, to take measures to boost the batting average of the existing clusters.

Purposely creating more *geographically based* clusters, however, is very definitely *not* our aim, nor do we believe it is appropriate for the federal government even to try. There are too many examples of failed attempts at creating place-based clusters from scratch for this to be a good strategy for any level of government to follow.[1] The fact is that the clusters we have now are the products of serendipity—the locales where one or more entrepreneurs founded successful companies that launched the virtuous cycles we now identify as clusters. There is no example, perhaps apart from the

Research Triangle Park area in North Carolina, of a successful cluster being created as a product of a deliberate set of government policies, although clusters can develop as a by-product of federal funding (such as the emerging cybersecurity hub around San Antonio or the health services hub in Nashville, Tennessee, both encouraged by federal grants).[2] Local education, transportation, and safety policies, among others, are important in nurturing and sustaining a cluster once it has emerged, and therefore such policies may raise a particular cluster's batting average at some point; however, all of this is very different from trying to launch a cluster in the first place (or, in baseball terminology, trying to build a new team from scratch).

More fundamentally, in an age of instant communication and high-definition video conferencing that is rapidly replacing the need for business travel, it is becoming increasingly evident that successful clusters, or more precisely *ecosystems,* are no longer defined solely by a single *place,* but instead form more around particular subject areas or industries. This is self-evident to any academic, who typically has more colleagues at universities other than his or her home institution, not only nationally but around the world. The same is increasingly true for commercial activity. While workers with special industry-specific skills and money sources tend to be concentrated geographically, that is not true for potential managers, senior executives, mentors, suppliers, consultants, and other individuals or firms that can help boost small, growing companies into much larger, growing enterprises.

Indeed, from our experience at the Kauffman Foundation with entrepreneurs, investors, and academic scholars, it is our view that clusters increasingly are defined by industries or *"verticals,"* and that the right people who can help build companies are found throughout the country and indeed the world. This is not to say that geographically based clusters are dead, because they are not. Place still matters, because continuous human interactions generate innovative sparks which can turn into innovations offering significant commercial opportunities. Moreover, even successful vertical clusters need a physical home, even if much of the communication and work takes place electronically, in text, over the telephone, or through video technologies. But precisely because technology is now connecting people and firms without as much need for continuous physical presence, successful locally based ecosystems are likely to have their greatest impact *nationally* (and even globally) if they combine the virtual with the physical.

The challenge is how to build more vertical clusters that offer the best chance for substantially increasing the number of new scale companies formed each year. As we will describe below, fortunately there are already some highly successful models for these new ecosystems. We will conclude this chapter by describing some of these novel experiments, which if replicated and scaled, might be able to substantially enlarge the number of home run companies that the U.S. economy needs to significantly increase its growth rate.

Conventional Policy Instruments

Let's turn first, however, to a more detailed discussion of the two main conventional national policy tools that many believe would most likely affect scale entrepreneurship: more federal support of so-called "basic" research and making better use of tax incentives to encourage innovative entrepreneurship. We are a bit more optimistic about the effectiveness of the second tool (tax policy) than the first (more R&D support), and explain why below. However, each policy is not as likely to be as important, in our view, as both private- and public-sector efforts aimed at facilitating the development of entrepreneurial ecosystems that we discuss in the balance of this chapter.

More Federal Research Support

There is a textbook case for having the government spend money on "basic" research and it rests on two propositions. The first is that the most important driver of growth is something called "innovation," which is embodied in new and more valuable products or services, or methods of producing them. The second proposition is that new knowledge, especially advances in basic science that are not likely to be commercialized immediately but may be in the long run, are "public goods" in the sense that their benefits can and should be widely disseminated, and for that reason will not be undertaken to an optimal degree unless research activity is publicly funded. Private firms and investors will not be enthusiastic about underwriting the costs of R&D whose benefits leak out to too many others.

These textbook justifications for government support of R&D have been reflected in federal spending policy. Federally supported research in the United States in 2008, for example, totaled almost $85 billion, up from about $78 billion in 2003 (in constant 2000 dollars).[3] As a share of GDP, federally supported R&D has averaged about 0.7 percent since 1996. These data do not include the big one-time jump in federal research–related spending in 2009–10 included as part of the stimulus package, most of it concentrated in over $30 billion in grants and loans authorized for alternative energy projects to be spent by the Department of Energy (DOE).

Despite these trends, especially the record expansion in DOE research funding in 2009–10, the calls for even more federally supported R&D continue, no doubt premised on the view that additional federal R&D support will make U.S. firms more competitive with their counterparts abroad. We do not want to be skunks at the federal R&D party, but it is important to have a more clear-eyed perspective on claims that more federal R&D spending is necessary for and automatically will be translated into faster GDP growth broadly, or—more specifically—is necessary to spur the formation and growth of more "home run" firms that generate significant positive spillovers to the larger economy. We want to be clear: we are not contesting or asking for a rollback of *existing levels* of federal research support, but instead questioning whether *additional* federal research funding is *the most cost-effective way* to enhance growth.

Several reasons account for our skepticism. At the outset, a subject that cannot be avoided is whether, in light of the enormous current and projected future federal budget deficits (whose implications we explore in Chapter 8), it is even remotely politically possible to expect that Congress will approve any more permanent or sustained spending increases or tax cuts for *any* programs, even those as theoretically attractive as spending more money on scientific research. But even if this were not the case, calls for more research money should take account of what the late economist Arthur Okun called the "leaky bucket" principle. This is the notion that any federal program will entail some waste or ineffectiveness, and that the cost effectiveness of those programs should account for those leaks, but that the presence of the leaks themselves does not mean the programs should be abandoned.

In the research area, there are several leaks in the buckets that collectively are quite significant. One is the system of technology transfer at universities, through which most federal research spending is channeled. As discussed in considerable detail in the next chapter, the process by which universities translate innovations funded by federal research dollars into commercial opportunities is far from optimal. Pouring more money into the technology commercialization system and expecting more significant new commercial applications is less important, in our view, than fixing the system in the first place.

Another source of leaks is the federal system of awarding research monies through peer review. On the surface, this seems fair and certainly a way to prevent funds from being allocated according to political criteria (a problem visibly demonstrated by the controversy over federal guarantees for the failed solar company, Solyndra). The reality is very different.

One well-known by-product of the peer review system for awarding research monies is that it too easily tends toward creating and cementing a club of well-connected senior researchers, who collectively are, or become, resistant to novel thinking and research inquiries inconsistent with the reviewers' own findings. Moreover, competing scientists have incentive to scratch each others' back to ensure that each receives grants. These features of the current peer review system—however well-intentioned and sensible it may appear on the surface—have the effect of awarding federal monies to older researchers who are less likely than younger scholars to explore ideas that could upend the old order and usher in real breakthroughs. For example, the average age at which U.S. Nobel Prize winners made their Nobel-worthy discoveries is thirty-four. In contrast, the average age of the primary investigators who have been awarded research grants by the National Institutes of Health is over fifty, and has been steadily increasing.[4]

The importance of this age bias in peer review awards is gaining increasing recognition. The Bill & Melinda Gates Foundation, for example, has launched a special initiative, Grand Challenges in Global Health, that is aimed specifically at funding untested ideas with high innovative potential. The foundation wants to avoid the standard peer review process by reaching out to any researchers, regardless of age, who might have break-through ideas to fight global diseases.[5]

The federal government should follow suit in some form. Perhaps some fraction of federal research dollars should be set aside for younger scientists. Or there may be ways of fixing the current peer review system, such as putting younger scholars on the review panels. Until something is done to correct the age bias in grant awards, however, we should not expect that pouring more federal money into R&D will translate into the break-through innovations that really drive economic growth.

We are more sanguine about the positive impacts of tax incentives on R&D spending by the private sector. Economist Alan Viard has outlined a number of ways in which the current *temporary* tax credit for R&D might be improved to better promote innovation, without necessarily adding to the deficit.[6] These ideas include making the credit permanent, which would remove the uncertainty over its annual reauthorization that makes it incredibly difficult for companies to plan, thus reducing the credit's impact; replacing the incremental structure of the current 25 per-cent credit that rewards R&D spending over a particular baseline (which has been raised a number of times by Congress) to a flat credit, but with a lower statutory rate (say about 8 percent, to make the change revenue neu-tral); and narrowing the definition of research qualifying for the credit to only those activities aimed at exceeding, expanding, or refining com-monly held knowledge.

We have one other suggestion. Since the R&D credit is of little use to start-up firms that are not showing a profit, we propose allowing firms to carry the R&D credit backward or forward until their income can absorb the credit. This modest change should make the credit especially useful to the research-intensive new firms that probably have the greatest chances of becoming home runs once they begin making profits, thereby encourag-ing their formation and facilitating their growth.

Indeed, reforming the R&D tax credit to increase its effectiveness in promoting innovation would build on the fact that over time, the private sector—not the federal government—has been pushing up the "R&D intensity" of the U.S. economy, measured by the ratio of total R&D ex-penditure to GDP, over the past three decades. This is shown in Figure 3.1. United States R&D spending as of 2007 (the latest year for which

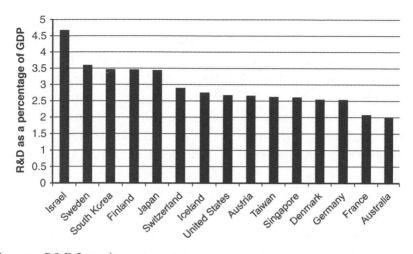

Figure 3.1 R&D Intensity
Source: Ewing Marion Kauffman Foundation

internationally comparable data were available at the time we wrote this book) accounted for fully one-third of the $1.1 trillion spent on R&D worldwide. Our closest competitor, Japan, accounted for just 13 percent, and Taiwan, the country whose national R&D spending policies seem to be of most concern to Americans (displacing the Japanese, who held that position in the 1980s), was a distant third at 9 percent. Although the R&D intensity of the United States put it in eighth place in the Organisation for Economic Co-operation and Development (OECD) rankings, all the countries that had higher ratios (Israel being the highest at 4.7 percent), with the exception of Japan, are considerably smaller than America.[7]

One easily anticipated objection to the data showing the increasing absolute and relative importance of private-sector R&D is that, by the conventional criteria, private R&D is overwhelmingly "applied," whereas federally sponsored research, especially at universities and federal laboratories, is defined to be "basic." In this view, future commercial success and thus economy-wide growth depends most importantly on advances in "basic knowledge"—the fundamentals of science—that will not be funded or pursued by the private sector for the previously stated reason that basic research is a "public good."

This long-held distinction between basic and applied research, reflected in years of official government reports and in academic literature, in fact is no longer so clear, if it ever really was. The massive DOE stimulus spending program illustrates this. For example, some of the DOE grants to private companies are aimed at improving battery technologies, which are critical to the commercial success of the plug-in electric car (and possibly other "clean" uses). It is far from clear whether this kind of research is basic or applied. The same vagueness is increasingly true of all kinds of other research. Indeed, many technology-oriented companies effectively conduct both basic and applied research at the same time: think Google in Internet search, Intel in chip design, and any number of small biotech or pharmaceutical companies (often launched by a university professor) that develop new treatments and are then sold to large pharmaceutical companies with the resources and experience to conduct the required clinical tests and the legal staff to gain the requisite regulatory approvals. Indeed, the remarkable finding of economist William Nordhaus cited in the last chapter—that inventors obviously continue to engage in innovative activity despite the small fraction of the monetary value of their successes that they personally reap, which is the very essence of a public good—is a testament to both the difficulty of drawing a bright line between basic and applied research and the huge economic and social importance of privately conducted and financed R&D.

Even if the increasingly outmoded distinction between the two types of research continues to have some relevance, it does not necessarily follow that the most cost-effective policy for the U.S. government is to spend even more on basic research than is now being spent. As we have noted, the textbook justification for such spending is that it supplies a public good that otherwise would be suboptimally produced. But in an increasingly global economy where other nations' governments continue and even increase such spending, it can make sense for the United States to effectively "free ride" on basic research conducted elsewhere. True, foreign researchers and companies get a head start by conducting such research, but eventually its results "leak out" to the rest of the world through academic publications, and perhaps even more importantly—and quickly—through academic conferences and correspondence, which has become truly global in this age of the Internet. Of course, by this logic, no country would want to provide any funding for basic R&D, preferring instead to free ride on others. But that hardly seems likely, as countries around the world want to upgrade the quality of their universities, and one of the best ways to do that is to attract the very best in research talent—in what has truly become a global market—to their national universities through the availability of research funding.[8]

If the United States wants to play this game, too, as it surely will, then it will also have to continue—and some will say increase—its federal funding of R&D. But it does not follow that the *federal government* should be the source of these additional funds. Private industry, already a source of much university research, can be an even more important source over time if universities are more welcoming and less bureaucratic. Critics will argue that university support typically comes with strings; namely, that the funders can get the first look at the research results. But again, since the lion's share of the gains from innovation ultimately leak out to the larger public, both inside and outside the country where the research is conducted, the fact that some firms may gain a temporary inside track must be weighed against the much larger social benefits that the additional research itself, however it is funded, provides.

Even more cost effective would be a loosening of our nation's immigration laws to make it easier to import skilled scientific knowledge from abroad, and to train those foreign students who want to acquire that knowledge in our country, as we discuss in Chapter 5. It is easy for this generation of Americans to forget the massive contributions of foreign scientists to this nation's effort in World War II. Without these individuals, the United States would never have had the atomic bomb in time to bring the war with Japan to a rapid conclusion. Now, the very best way to ensure that new ideas, wherever they are developed, are quickly brought to the United States is to ensure that our borders remain open to people, goods, and capital (which often comes with ideas) from abroad.

Finally, if the key to much higher economy-wide growth is through the formation of significantly more home run companies, then it is far from clear that more federal spending on R&D is the best way to achieve that objective. Government support admittedly was important in helping get a number of hugely successful high-tech companies such as Intel and Hewlett-Packard off the ground, but this support came in the form of government *purchases,* not R&D funding. The federal government has had a long-standing initiative for funding R&D by small startups, the Small Business Innovation Research (SBIR) program, through which eleven federal agencies provide roughly $2 billion annually in research grants to small businesses. An independent assessment of SBIR by the National Academy of Sciences is largely positive.[9] But even that assessment did not make the claim that the SBIR program was successful because it produced truly home run companies.

In sum, we know we are taking a somewhat heretical and perhaps not politically correct position with respect to suggestions that the federal government up its R&D spending. But for the multiple reasons just outlined, we believe a totally clear-eyed assessment questions the cost-effectiveness of this approach to significantly increasing our national growth rate. A better approach, in our view, is to restructure existing federal tax incentives for private-sector R&D, and thus even more effectively harness market forces in generating new commercially useful knowledge.

Federal Income Tax Policies

Taxes on income would seem presumptively to affect entrepreneurship and innovation because they determine the net, after-tax rewards the market hands out to successful entrepreneurs and innovators. How, if at all, should income taxes be structured to best promote entrepreneurially led growth?[10] This question implicates several different types of income taxes: those on the ordinary income of corporations and individuals, and capital gains taxes on the increased realized value of equity investments in firms, especially new ones.

The relevance of ordinary income taxes on corporations should be obvious since any potential growth enterprise almost certainly will be legally organized as a corporation, primarily to take advantage of limited liability—the legal doctrine that equity investors cannot be held liable under any circumstance for more than the monies they invested. The limited liability concept is perhaps one of the most important legal prerequisites for modern capitalism, for without it, firms would not be able to attract the funds they need to scale their activities. And without scale firms, we would not have "scale economies."

Below, we provide a mixed assessment of taxes on entrepreneurship, scale or growth companies in particular. The one thing that is not mixed, however, is the uncertainty generated by the increasing "temporariness" in the tax code, exemplified most recently by the extension of the 2001 and 2003 federal income tax cuts at the end of 2010 for only two years. Similarly, the R&D tax credit, which we have already discussed, has been permanently "temporary," never really permanent. If there is one single piece of advice we could give policymakers, it is that whatever taxes they decide on to fund government services, stick with the decision and change it infrequently. Too much change makes it difficult for companies and individuals to plan. There is enough uncertainty in business as it is; the government should not add to it by making the tax code not only increasingly complex but temporary. This is yet another argument for reaching a comprehensive federal budget accord that addresses the highly disturbing and rapidly growing federal deficit. Hopefully, some greater permanence in at least the federal tax code will be an important by-product.

Corporate Income Taxes

But there are different kinds of corporations for tax purposes, and entrepreneurs pick one or the other for various reasons. A "C" corporation is the standard corporate form used by any company wanting to "go public"; that is, to have a sufficient number of outside investors that the company's shares can qualify to be traded on public stock exchanges. A C corporation is taxed as a separate legal entity from the individuals who own shares in it, giving rise to what economists call "double taxation": a public or non-public C corporation pays corporate income taxes on the income it earns, while the company's owners pay personal income taxes on the dividends the company pays to them. Since the dividends are derived from corporate earnings that have already been taxed, the shareholders who receive them pay taxes twice on corporate earnings—once at the corporate level, and again at the personal level.

Most economists have long opposed the existence of a separate corporate income tax and have advocated instead taxing shareholders only once, when they receive dividends. Not only is the corporate income tax unfair in this respect, but because the tax code permits companies to deduct interest payments from the debt they issue but not the dividends they pay to shareholders, the corporate tax makes it more difficult for C corporations to grow and biases their financing toward debt. As a result of the current income tax treatment of interest and dividends, the corporate sector is more leveraged and thus more unstable than it would be if interest and dividends both were treated equally for tax purposes.

It actually gets worse: at 35 percent, the top U.S. corporate tax rate is one of the highest of any industrialized country. While many public companies employ a variety of tax-minimization strategies that effectively reduce that rate, these activities introduce friction and biases into economic activity that we would be better off without. The United States took a major step in 2003 to reduce the impact of double taxation when President Bush and Congress agreed to lower the tax rate on dividends (and capital gains, a subject which we will come to shortly) to 15 percent, well below the top marginal income tax rate of roughly 38 percent at that time (which had been reduced from an effective rate of about 42 percent in 2001). In 2011, the Obama administration proposed lowering the top corporate tax rate, funded by ending various corporate tax breaks. At this writing, the idea seems to have considerable support in Congress, but whether it will be adopted depends on how the administration and Congress eventually come together on a comprehensive budget arrangement.

The growing literature on the corporate tax indicates that it clearly has a negative impact on the growth of existing companies, while discouraging the location of corporate activities in high-tax areas.[11] Also, with the assistance of clever tax counsel, companies can—entirely legally—move money around so that it is taxed in the lowest cost location without necessarily moving physical activities, such as plant and personnel. While all this maneuvering imposes extra costs on companies and thereby on the economy, we do not want to overclaim the tax's negative impact on *entrepreneurship, or the formation of new companies, especially those that mature into home runs with large social benefits.* We have already noted that until the modest uptick in 2008–9, the trend in new company formation in the United States had been relatively flat over the previous fifteen years, seemingly impervious to the business cycle. Likewise, the business formation rate showed no noticeable change after 2003 when the major cuts in dividends and capital gains were adopted by Congress.

The larger negative impact of the corporate tax is on already established companies seeking to grow. Investors who have to pay taxes on the income the companies earn are discouraged from providing equity capital for growth in particular. In an ideal world, we, like many other economists, would like to see the corporate tax substantially reduced, if not eliminated, and any lost revenue made up through taxes on consumption. This is one of many major changes in the U.S. tax system that would improve the environment for new and existing companies alike, and for the general economy. As a purely political matter, however, this kind of fundamental tax reform is not likely to be accomplished on its own, but as part of a broader tax reform/deficit reduction initiative (see Chapter 8).

Personal Income Taxes

Although for limited liability reasons most startups are formed as corporations, an increasingly popular form of incorporation is the "limited liability corporation" rather than the traditional C corporation. An LLC, although technically corporate in form, is taxed like a partnership, with the owners' income shares taxed as personal income, and thus only once. This is the great advantage of the LLC relative to the C corporation. The major downside of the LLC is that it is not suitable for going public, and thus entrepreneurs who use it either stay private or at some point convert to C status. Of course, self-employed individuals who operate their businesses personally are also subject to personal income taxes.

Given our interest here in policies conducive to the creation and growth of "home run" companies, most of which are likely to need outside capital at some point and thus are likely to go public, we do not think that changes to the personal income tax system are likely to have significant impacts, one way or other, in affecting the kind of home run entrepreneurship we really need to substantially boost economic growth. We are aware that recent scholarship has shown that progressive income taxes can deter entrepreneurial activity (in contrast to some earlier studies which suggest that higher income tax rates may actually *encourage* people to become self-employed as a way of deducting some personal expenses that otherwise cannot be deducted).[12]

But for founders of future home run companies, or triples or doubles, personal tax rates even somewhat higher than those now or that some "reform" plans have envisioned for the future, are not likely to be a significant factor in the decision to form such enterprises, for at least two reasons. One factor is that entrepreneurs creating those hoped-for large enterprises expect to realize most of their personal financial gains from the sale of some portion of their stock at some distant point in the future. These gains will be taxed at lower capital gains rates, rather than at personal income tax rates.

The other factor has nothing to do with taxes or even financial considerations. Founders of home run companies, in particular, are motivated as much or more so by their desire to "change the world," to be recognized as an important entrepreneur, or by the personal satisfaction of achieving a hugely ambitious goal, as they are by different levels or structures of the personal income tax. Thus, it is not surprising that such contemporary business icons as Bill Gates (Microsoft), the late Steve Jobs (Apple), Gordon Moore and Andy Grove (Intel), Fred Smith (Federal Express), and other 1960s- and 1970s-era founders launched their companies when the highest marginal tax rate was *70 percent*—nearly double the effective rate after the Bush tax cuts of 2001, and approaching the modestly higher top marginal tax rate that previously prevailed on high-income earners to which President Obama had wanted Congress to return.

We do not want to dismiss, of course, the potential though likely modest negative impact of high personal tax rates on the singles, and possibly doubles, launched by entrepreneurs—or conversely, the possibly small positive impact of lower marginal rates that a flatter personal tax system might have on many smaller entrepreneurs. But for the future high-impact entrepreneurs, within a large range, personal income tax rates do not appear to be a material factor one way or the other.

Capital Gains Taxes

Given that entrepreneurs who swing for the fences are looking for their financial reward many years in the future after they launch what they hope to be home run (or triple or double) companies, the capital gains tax rate would seem at first blush to have an important impact on *the entrepreneurs themselves*. But on a closer look, this is unlikely to be the case for two reasons similar to the ones we just reviewed for personal income taxes.

The first reason is that entrepreneurs whose main motivation in starting their companies is nonfinancial, any level of the capital gains tax, within reason, is not likely to have a significant impact on the decision to launch and grow the enterprise.

Second, one of the great benefits of the capital gains tax for buy-and-hold investors such as founders of home run companies is that any tax obligation is deferred until the stock is sold. Because of the time value of money, this "realization" requirement of any capital gains tax regime means that the effective tax rate is discounted more heavily the longer the stock is held. This implies that the nominal capital gains tax rate is not likely to figure heavily into the launch-and-grow decision.

As with the personal tax, we do not ignore the fact that the lower the tax rate on capital gains relative to the top marginal rate on personal income, the more individuals, at the margin, are likely to take the risk of starting a company rather than remain at their current job or to look for one to begin with.[13] This is especially relevant in light of the fact that the median age at which successful entrepreneurs launch their companies is thirty-nine, implying that the difference (rather than the absolute level) between capital gains and personal income tax rates should be especially relevant to workers who already have jobs (although in difficult economic times such as those since the financial crisis, this effect could be attenuated).[14]

Regardless of its impact on the willingness of entrepreneurs to launch companies, the level of the capital gains tax is likely to be far more important for *outside investors in companies*. This is because independent investors are much more likely to want the ability to sell their stock once the enterprise proves successful. This is especially true of angel investors and venture capitalists, whose business model is to make a quick "exit"—either through an initial public offering or the sale of the company—so that they can return their capital to themselves and/or to their investors. With a much shorter time horizon than the entrepreneurs themselves, therefore, outside investors should be much more sensitive to the capital gains tax rate. We draw out the implications of this in a later chapter, on entrepreneurial finance.

Nurturing Entrepreneurial Ecosystems

Many visitors from across the United States and around the world come each year to the Kauffman Foundation. Among other things, they seek the advice and counsel of the officers and staff about entrepreneurship programs at universities and various levels of government. But perhaps no question is more frequently asked than a variation of "How can we create another [or the next] Silicon Valley?" We suspect that firms and government officials in Silicon Valley itself are asked the same question with regularity.

Of course, the reason the question is asked is that there clearly are positive feedback loops between successful companies in particular industry segments (or "verticals"), venture capitalists and angel investors, cashed-out entrepreneurs (who become angel investors and often serial entrepreneurs), accountants, lawyers, suppliers, and skilled workforces, all of whom make up an "entrepreneurial cluster." Once one or more successful companies are founded, they strengthen these networks or feedback loops, and in a virtuous cycle, help create others. It is not surprising, therefore, to see so many state and local efforts aiming to replicate that magic.

Perhaps the most popular vehicle for doing so is the "incubator"—typically a large building (often a converted warehouse)—that rents space to start-up entrepreneurs with some shared or common areas for the entrepreneurs to meet and get to know each other and have access to various forms of administrative support (including in some cases an on-site accountant or lawyer). Most incubators also provide mentors to give general business advice. Consistent with its name, the incubator is meant only to provide temporary "housing," with firms encouraged to graduate to their own quarters once they reach a certain level of success or, if they fail, to move out and make room for new startups. (Later we discuss the notion of an "accelerator," a mechanism or entity that features more mentoring and social networking, generally over a shorter time frame than is the case with incubators as they are conventionally understood).

Incubators come in many forms and are primarily owned or organized by nonprofits (typically economic development organizations or universities), though a small portion are privately owned. According to the National Business Incubation Association, as of 2006, there were more than one thousand such entities in North America and roughly seven thousand worldwide. About half of the North American incubators support start-up companies regardless of industry, while the rest have a specific industry focus (most in high tech). Incubators have been created in thriving communities as well as in depressed areas seeking to make a comeback, hopefully with new firms in different industries.

If the replication of Silicon Valley is their goal, then the incubator movement clearly has failed. To our knowledge, there is no community in America that owes its success by any measure to one or more incubators. But to be fair, that is too high a bar. Is there evidence that incubators have facilitated the formation and growth of more new companies than there otherwise would be?

The literature on this topic is surprisingly thin and inconclusive. A number of reasonably successful companies—many with annual revenues of $50 million or more—got their start in a traditional incubator (we use the term "traditional" here to distinguish these entities from the newer "business accelerators" we discuss later in the chapter).[15] Likewise, several incubators—notably, the Ben Franklin Business Incubator in Philadelphia, Innovation Works in Pittsburgh, Pennsylvania, and IC-Squared of Austin—are well recognized for having successful track records in helping companies get started and grow. But, perhaps because academics do not get rewarded or published for studying or documenting failures, we do not have a complete count of the failures of the surely many thousands of companies that even the "successful" incubators have hosted. Nor do we have well-done studies to determine the extent to which the incubators contributed to or were responsible for the successes of the companies that graduated and went on to bright futures.

Given the thinness of the evidence in support of incubators, we are thus highly skeptical of proposals to have the federal government give some of them more money in an effort to create more clusters. To the contrary, as we noted at the outset of this chapter, there is no evidence indicating that any currently successful high-tech cluster—apart, perhaps, from Research Triangle Park in North Carolina—was deliberately created by affirmative government policies. Rather, when we look at the successful clusters that now dot the American landscape, we see the marks of serendipity, the founding of one or two companies by the accident of fate that later grew to support a much larger ecosystem of other companies, entrepreneurs, and service providers: Dell Computer in Austin; Qualcomm in San Diego; Microsoft, Amazon, and Costco in Seattle; and of course Intel, Hewlett-Packard, and Apple, and later Cisco, Google, eBay, Yahoo!, Sun Microsystems, and Facebook (after it moved from Massachusetts), among many others in Silicon Valley. Each of these companies, now household names, was the creation of one or more daring entrepreneurs who defied the odds and went on to build a highly successful company, which in turn did its part to change the world. No government at any level "planned" these companies.

Even if there were evidence that clusters could be planned—or at the very least, the odds of serendipity significantly increased through deliberate government policy—we have no confidence that a *federal* spending program aimed at launching clusters *where they have greatest chances of being successful* would be cost effective. This even applies to federal programs aimed at boosting existing clusters, such as the jobs and innovation initiative the Obama administration announced in May 2011. For one thing, the way Washington works, it is difficult to prevent the money from being channeled on the basis of political rather than economic criteria. As for the latter, it is also not clear that government officials, acting even with the best of intentions, can target clusters that are truly the most promising. One possible way of finding out is to distribute the money on a matching basis—the time-honored way of following the market and an approach we recommend for allocating funds toward "proof of concept" centers in Chapter 6. But even with a matching requirement, it is not clear to us that the local and state matching sources have any better knowledge about the future success of a cluster. That is like an investor trying to guess what the next Microsoft, Apple, or Google will be before the company goes public. No individual can do that consistently. Third, the amount of money in the Obama cluster initiative, a total of $33 million for the entire country for a single year, is unlikely to be enough to make much of a difference anyhow.

Admittedly, there are countries—such as China and Singapore—that are attempting to prove these propositions wrong, namely they are betting that government officials can pick winners and do so better than the private sector, especially when the private sector may be unaccustomed to doing so itself. Perhaps they will be the exceptions that prove the rule. But keep in mind several things about China and Singapore. For one thing, despite China's rapid growth, it is still well behind the United States in terms of GDP per capita and will take decades to catch up. And while Singapore's GDP per capita has surpassed that of the United States, it is far from clear that continued state guidance in that country will keep it ahead of the United States. As we have pointed out elsewhere, it is much easier to successfully shoot at an already known target than at targets yet to be defined, which is what U.S. firms must do.[16] Indeed, Singapore's leaders recognize this and have been experimenting with ways to instill more of an entrepreneurial culture in the country.

Just as important, China and to a lesser extent Singapore are autocracies that can direct resources free of political and economic opposition in a way that is impossible in any democracy. Benevolent autocracy (in the economic, not political sense) may thus be more able than a democracy to bring greater focus and energy to particular projects for a period of time (the atomic bomb project in the United States was an example of autocracy at its best, directed as it was by the U.S. military out of the public limelight and free of any bureaucratic opposition or knowledge). But only history will judge whether, *once they are at the technological frontier,* autocracies can *consistently* develop and commercialize new technologies more successfully than their democratic and "messy" counterparts in more entrepreneurial environments, such as those found in the United States and Israel, for example. We believe that, over time, market-oriented entrepreneurial economies will win out, although we concede the temporary advantages that state-guided, politically autocratic societies temporarily may have with respect to the successful development of certain technologies.

In any event, back here in the United States, the home of political democracy and entrepreneurial capitalism, our skepticism about federal—or even state and local—governmental attempts to create clusters does not mean that we advocate no role for government at all in fostering entrepreneurial ecosystems. One highly important step is to reinvent the K-12 public school curriculum to include much more entrepreneurial and creative thinking, ideas that we outline in Chapter 9. But there is a simple— almost embarrassingly simple—step that mayors and governors can take that would more immediately generate increased entrepreneurial activity in their jurisdictions.

The idea stems from the innovative research of Ted Zoller, a senior fellow at the Kauffman Foundation, a professor at the University of North Carolina, and a former successful software entrepreneur. Building on insights of other researchers who have identified social networks as an important, and perhaps the most important, factor in determining the success of a startup or any business, Zoller has mapped out the social connections of the most successful "dealmakers" and entrepreneurs in roughly a dozen communities that host successful high-tech companies to determine: Do these individuals know each other somehow? Do they serve or work together on common enterprises, as board members, funders, advisers, and the like?[17] The key insight from Zoller's pathbreaking research is this: while the pictures (and they are worth a thousand words) show much greater density of connections in places like Silicon Valley, and to a lesser extent San Diego, the connections are surprisingly sparse in most of the other clusters widely recognized to be successful—Boulder, Seattle, Austin, the Research Triangle Park, and even Boston. What this means in plain English is that *many of the entrepreneurial "movers and shakers" in even relatively successful high-tech clusters do not know or regularly interact in a work or deal environment with each other.*

This is a crucially important insight because even in the age of the Internet, local social networks—especially among successful entrepreneurs and their financial backers—are critically important for making the virtuous cycle of company creation and growth work best. So here's the simple policy implication: mayors (less so governors because ecosystems tend to form around metro areas and do not extend statewide, except in small states) should form special "mayors' circles" or exclusive clubs of the most successful entrepreneurs and entrepreneurial firm investors that initially meet in informal, dinnerlike settings where these individuals can get to know each other while discussing how to improve the local entrepreneurial climate. It is possible that useful policy suggestions—such as streamlined approval processes for gaining necessary local licenses and permits—may emerge from these meetings. But the real purpose and output of these meetings or dinners is to establish and "thicken" personal networks. Over time, these entrepreneurial dealmakers should become sufficiently comfortable to begin discussing and referring deals to each other or people in each others' networks (in many cases, individuals located elsewhere). That is how new businesses get funded, recruit the personnel they need, and get in touch with key potential customers and suppliers. Even with nearly ubiquitous presence and use of the Internet, personal connections still count. Indeed, Internet-based social networks, such as LinkedIn or Facebook, largely are successful because they make it far easier and less costly for individuals *who already know each other* to stay abreast of each others' activities, while validating the trustworthiness of individuals who are referred to others via the network.

If making more deals generates more firms and jobs, what can government, or the private sector for that matter, do to create opportunities for the many others who may not have the skills, connections, or expertise to fit into the new, often high-tech entrepreneurial ventures? Do they just get left behind in the entrepreneurial economy? This is not an acceptable answer, either on moral or economic grounds. We have thoughts about better answers in Chapter 9.

University-Based Entrepreneurial Ecosystems

Before we turn to the set of ecosystems that we believe could have the best chance of being the game changers that significantly boost the numbers of future home run companies, we want to pause to discuss another group of entrepreneurial ecosystems that also should play a major role in the new entrepreneurial economy. Here, we refer to the various entrepreneurial models developed by or affiliated with universities. We underscore the word "various" because university-based ecosystems come in many different types, which makes them difficult to assess in the aggregate but which are proving through a process of experimentation to be important factors in generating new high-growth firms.

Thus, for example, many universities are promoting entrepreneurship through some variation of the incubator, providing dedicated space on or near the university to host and help mentor—with the help of faculty, alumni, and successful local entrepreneurs—student and faculty startups. Indeed, according to national incubator statistics, 20 percent of all North American startups are university affiliated. The MIT Venture Mentor Service, MIT's own campus-wide student entrepreneurship programs, and The Launch Pad at the University of Miami (discussed in more detail below) promote mentoring and connections with experts in the local community. Other universities, notably Washington University in St. Louis, and the University of Utah, have an incubator and a mentoring program. Some schools (such as Washington University and Duke University) have dorms dedicated to undergraduate entrepreneurs, on the view that proximity breeds new ideas and collaborations that might otherwise not be formed. An increasing number of universities host "business plan" competitions that award prizes to the most innovative and promising plans, some of which even get funded by angel investors or venture firms. Most universities, however, take the more traditional approach to promoting entrepreneurship: teaching it in the classroom. In some universities, students can minor, and even major, in entrepreneurship, most often in the business school or department (although entrepreneurship is frequently taught in engineering schools and departments).[18]

We focus on university ecosystems for several reasons. First, many bold new ideas with commercial potential come out of universities, through graduate student and faculty research as well as classroom teaching. These ideas may not be immediately commercialized, but their seeds may eventually sprout in the form of new products or services introduced to the marketplace by students, faculty members, or corporate sponsors of university research.

Second, universities have their own potential or actual entrepreneurial ecosystems, including not only the faculty or student entrepreneurs themselves, but also mentors and even sources of capital through alumni and local area supporters of the university. This is not to say that universities are the necessary and/or sufficient conditions for a successful city or metropolitan "cluster." We can think of one prominent cluster, the Seattle metro area, where none of the most recognized entrepreneurial successes—Microsoft, Amazon, Starbucks, or Costco—was started because of a link to the local university (the University of Washington). Nonetheless, universities can be important catalysts and facilitators of entrepreneurial growth because of all the assets just mentioned.

The Kauffman Foundation also has had a special interest in university entrepreneurship since its inception, based largely on the premise (which in retrospect we still cannot completely confirm) that the most impressionable time for affecting an individual's decision whether to become an entrepreneur at some point in his or her life is during that person's college years (perhaps more so undergraduate than graduate). Thus, roughly two decades ago, the Kauffman Foundation began giving small grants (mostly less than $100,000) to many universities to develop and provide entrepreneurship courses. Over time, other universities adopted these courses, while philanthropic alumni began endowing chairs in entrepreneurship and providing other kinds of support for the teaching of this subject.

More recently, shortly after the two of us arrived at the Kauffman Foundation (in 2003), it awarded on a competitive basis "Kauffman Campus" matching grants of up to $5 million each over a period of five years to roughly forty universities for the promotion of entrepreneurship "cross-campus," or beyond the business school. The premises of the Campus program were threefold: that most entrepreneurs never attend business school (though they may take individual business courses) and come from a variety of educational backgrounds (engineering and liberal arts in particular); that universities should be free to experiment with how they want to promote entrepreneurship, whether inside or outside of the classroom, or both; and that the Kauffman Foundation would likely get better results by providing fewer, but much larger, grants to the winning universities.

The Campus program encouraged many schools to expand their course offerings in entrepreneurship and to pursue other innovative approaches to promoting entrepreneurship, which have continued even since the Kauffman Foundation's grant formally ended. The program also has confirmed one of the Foundation's assumptions going in: namely that entrepreneurship promotion and training should not be limited to business schools. But perhaps the most important lesson we learned from the Campus program is that we have become even more convinced that entrepreneurship at the university level is best promoted, at least on campus, *outside* the classroom.

Given the way entrepreneurship is conventionally taught, it is unrealistic to expect students—most of whom probably have no idea what business they might want to start before they enter an entrepreneurship class—to come up with not only a business but a reasonable plan for implementing it within the artificial fourteen- to fifteen-week constraints of a typical college class. Moreover, by teaching budding entrepreneurs that the primary objective of their initial activity should be preparing a business plan—which may be easiest for teachers to grade but has little relevance to the vast majority of entrepreneurs, who never seek or obtain outside financing, and in any event is made irrelevant in the first few days a business is actually launched—business plan–focused entrepreneurship courses may actually be doing students who later start a business a disservice. Entrepreneurship courses that put more emphasis on opportunity recognition, customer and market analysis, and the actual mechanics of launching a business hold greater promise.

The best illustration of the limits of conventional classroom-based entrepreneurship instruction, at least to us, is provided by the incredible and immediate success of The Launch Pad program, developed at the University of Miami in 2009 by the senior associate provost (and former provost of one of the initial eight Kauffman Campus schools, the University of Rochester).[19] The Launch Pad is an *out of the classroom* incubator-mentoring program for all student-entrepreneurs at the university that is housed—fittingly, we believe—in the university's career center. Students can enter The Launch Pad at any time by pitching their business idea, gaining immediate feedback, and then taking as much training and mentoring as they want from the program's few employees and many more mentors (entrepreneurs who are Miami alumni or local area supporters of the program). In just its first two years, The Launch Pad has attracted more than a thousand University of Miami students, while facilitating the formation of more than fifty businesses. The Launch Pad model has since spread (primarily with the support of the Blackstone Foundation) to two universities in the Detroit area, and may expand to other locations. Even if postgraduation employment prospects for college graduates were not so poor, there ought to be a Launch Pad–type program at every two- and four-year college across the United States.[20]

As commendable as The Launch Pad program is, there will be, as with any campus-based entrepreneurship program, generally a long lag between student enrollment or participation in the program and entrepreneurial success. The stories of Bill Gates, Steve Jobs, Michael Dell, and Mark Zuckerberg, among other highly successful young entrepreneurs, are the exception rather than the norm. Even in this age of Internet wonders, as we noted earlier, the median age of successful entrepreneurs is almost forty years, not a few years after high school or college. Given the long lead times associated with university-based programs, it is important to look for ways to build and strengthen other types of entrepreneurial ecosystems, especially if we want to begin more quickly to launch those home run companies the U.S. economy will need if it wants (as we do) a sustained permanent increase in its growth rate. That is the subject we take up next.

Moving Beyond University-Based Ecosystems

We see three ways to move beyond university-based entrepreneurial ecosystems. The Kauffman Foundation and other private-sector organizations are supporting these efforts.

One approach uses the Internet to make available at very low cost—literally with a click of a mouse—potential ideas for launching new businesses, some portion of which could grow into substantial enterprises. This is theory behind two Kauffman Foundation initiatives, iBridge and iStart.

iBridge is an Internet-based platform intended to provide transparency and access to innovations developed at universities. Anyone can visit the site (www.ibridge.org), including entrepreneurs, established businesses, and investors. Multiple universities participate through having faculty post their innovations (both patented and unpatented) on the site. As of this writing, over 40 percent of the ongoing traffic to the website comes from outside the United States, illustrating the increasingly global nature of entrepreneurial activity. While very little e-commerce is conducted on the iBridge website, innovations linked to e-commerce are licensed extensively. We believe this validates the notion that lowering the barriers to accessing information about technologies speeds up commercialization of new ideas.

iStart (www.istart.org) provides a platform for implementing and completing a business plan competition, while providing transparency and access to all of the business ideas submitted to the site. In its first three months of operation, thirty-eight university competitions joined the platform. Despite our earlier criticism of business plan–based courses, the Kauffman Foundation has supported iStart as a way of linking the individuals who participate in the competitions more closely with mentors, judges, and other participants. Furthermore, even though many participants never implement their plans, the plans themselves may contain the seeds of worthy ideas that could be successfully implemented by *other entrepreneurs*.

The common element in both the iBridge network and iStart is to help solve one of entrepreneurs' first and most common problems: finding a worthy *idea*. Although success is largely determined by the *execution* of any idea, it helps to have a good idea to begin with. The more information about potential ideas that is available—and at no cost—the easier it will be for future entrepreneurs to get started.

Perhaps the most important ingredient for entrepreneurial success, as we have repeatedly suggested, is the network or ecosystem to which the entrepreneur belongs. Starting and building a firm is one of the loneliest endeavors one can imagine. Even with the best of ideas, it is easy for entrepreneurs and their early partners (including investors) to get discouraged by doubters along the way, and often by themselves. Entrepreneurs who are surrounded by knowledgeable mentors who can help the enterprise avoid mistakes and enhance the prospects for success by putting entrepreneurs in touch with potential sources of financing, customers, suppliers, and employees are much more likely to be successful than those who have no support network or ecosystem to call on.

University-based ecosystems and incubators each may supply qualified mentors, but by definition they are limited and defined by *place*—individuals who generally are within driving distance of the entrepreneur or the firm. Furthermore, as we argue in Chapters 4 and 9, although entrepreneurship has a major role to play at universities, especially in bringing to market innovations developed by university faculty, it is best pursued outside rather than inside the classroom.

As we all know now, one of the great virtues of the Internet is that it reduces (though does not eliminate) the importance of geographic proximity. Might it be possible to harness the power of the Internet to develop new clusters or make existing ones more effective? In Chapter 6, we discuss some innovative new efforts that are trying to prove the viability of this new model.

Various privately owned accelerators also are now thriving and turning out new companies, but mostly in low-capital intensive software and Internet related businesses. Examples include the TechStars network, Y Combinator, DreamIt Ventures, Excelerate Labs, and Capital Factory. One accelerator, the Foundry, has had remarkable success in spawning new medical device companies. These new accelerators typically use "American-Idol" like methods of auditioning entrepreneurs and then mash together those selected for several months in dorm-like settings in the hope that the chosen entrepreneurs will develop entirely new ideas, which the accelerators either will fund themselves or connect to sources of capital. So far, this technique seems to be working in some places, and hopefully more of these success stories will be replicated. Organizations like these can help the nation spawn the future singles, doubles, triples, and perhaps a few home runs that will significantly boost growth.[21]

Conclusion

One of America's great economic challenges is to extend and improve the successful ecosystems that will help launch and nurture the formation and growth of the home run inventive companies required to significantly increase our economy-wide growth rate. Rather than doubling or tripling the number of overall company starts to generate more home runs, we believe that the far more efficient and doable strategy is to vastly improve the odds of success for those roughly six hundred thousand companies that are formed year in and year out. To borrow yet another metaphor—this one from another sport, hockey: we do not need more shots on goal, but *better shots on goal*.

The conventional policy tools—more R&D money and various kinds of tax cuts—while helpful, are not likely in our view to substantially improve the entrepreneurial "hockey team" we put on the ice. Instead, the keys to success lie in the improvement of current entrepreneurial ecosystems and their replication. University-based systems have their advantages and, as we have summarized here, there are some notable experiments going on that will be scaled at other universities and eventually may have large payoffs.

In the meantime, we need and clearly could benefit from ideas and programs that can bring results—more home run companies, consistently and continuously—more quickly. Privately owned incubators that screen carefully for future entrepreneurs, bring them together, and then mentor them, all within a single vertical, are providing one answer to this challenge.

Whatever the mechanism, the formation and growth of these entrepreneurial ecosystems are likely to have more influence on how entrepreneurial the U.S. economy continues to be than variations in the traditional policy levers, such as increases in federal support for basic R&D and tax law changes designed to encourage more innovation. Nothing less than the future of the U.S. economy—and how rapidly it grows—depends on how successful our economy is in consistently and continuously generating more high-growth firms.

4

UNLEASHING AMERICA'S ACADEMIC
ENTREPRENEURS

Among the many miracles of modern medicine are the various methods for releasing drugs in measured amounts, over time, at the right targets. Few of these achievements would be possible without the genius of Robert Langer, a celebrated biomedical engineer at MIT. Langer is responsible for an incredible 750 patents, the author of over 1,000 technical articles, and the most widely cited engineer in history. He has founded numerous companies and his innovations have been licensed to many others.

While Langer may be America's, and possibly the world's, leading "rock star" scientist, the United States fortunately has many more. Stanford University hosts or has been home to many such academic entrepreneurs. In the medical field, they include Dr. John Adler, who can count among his many innovations the CyberKnife system of radiosurgery, which uses focused beams of radiation to destroy cancerous tumors without the need for invasive surgery, and Paul Yock, the founder and cochair of Stanford's bioengineering department. Yock is the inventor of, among other things, the Rapid Exchange angioplasty delivery apparatus, which has become the most widely used angioplasty technique in the world. He also created the Bio-X program at Stanford, which incubates inventions and facilitates the commercialization of medical devices and products.

On the opposite coast, the state of North Carolina is home to other rock star scientists. Dr. Richard Stack, professor emeritus at Duke University, is the founder and president of Synecor, a diversified company whose mission is to incubate startups deploying disruptive medical devices and biotechnologies. As of 2007, the companies he had launched had a combined market value of nearly $700 million. Or consider Dr. Anthony Atala, one of the fathers of regenerative medicine, who moved from Harvard to Wake Forest University. Atala is credited with developing pioneering ways of growing new organs in the body.

These names are just a handful of the many stellar scientists—great teachers, researchers, and entrepreneurs—who populate our nation's universities. Lynne Zucker and Michael Darby of UCLA, two of the leading experts on this subject, have compiled a comprehensive database of such academic entrepreneurs and find that they have been instrumental in promoting the growth of entrepreneurial hot spots around the country.[1]

Admittedly, "rock star entrepreneurship" is not what one usually thinks of when considering the important economic and social role of universities. Instead, our institutions of higher learning are valued for their more traditional research and teaching functions—the processes by which their faculty discover new knowledge and disseminate it through students, their academic peers, and ultimately society at large. But academic publications and teaching are not the only ways new discoveries benefit society, nor are these functions carried out best in isolation. Universities are part of the fabric of the societies in which they are situated, and the research their faculties carry out would not be useful or relevant to helping people unless professors had regular interactions with the private business sector. Indeed, one of the features of the American university system that increasingly is being admired and copied around the world is that our research universities are *not* ivory towers.

If America wants more rapid sustained economic growth in the twenty-first century, therefore, it must depend heavily on the future research output of its universities. In large part, this is because much federally funded basic scientific research is carried out on campuses, not in federal labs. In 2009, for example, the federal government accounted for almost 60 percent of the $53 billion that was channeled from all sources (including state governments, industry, and philanthropic organizations) into university research.[2]

The translation of these research dollars into commercially successful innovations could thus not be more important. The past U.S. record in this regard is enviable, as we will soon demonstrate. But no state of affairs is perfect, even the academic–industry pipeline that has developed in the United States, which other countries are trying to replicate. Indeed, we will argue in this chapter that one important aspect of the commercialization of university innovations—the process governing licensing of intellectual property (IP) rights in innovations developed by faculty inventors—is not working as well as it could or should to facilitate the prompt commercialization of important faculty-discovered innovations. That's the bad news. The good news is that this situation is readily fixed, by enterprising universities acting on their own, or with a helpful nudge from the federal government.[3] Importantly, these fixes should not cost the federal government or taxpayers a dime—an attractive proposition for policymakers looking for costless ways to boost growth.

We suspect that some readers who otherwise believe they are well informed on economic matters may not be familiar with this admittedly obscure corner of the economy. However, academic entrepreneurship not only has been vital to U.S. economic growth in the past, but we believe it will be even more important in the future. As Jonathan Cole states in his impressive history of universities in the United States, *"In the future, virtually every new industry will depend on research conducted at America's universities"* (emphasis added).[4]

The Bayh-Dole Act and the Rise of Commercially Useful Innovation in American Universities

The notion that universities must play an integral role in the commercialization of faculty-generated innovations, however controversial it may still be in some corners of academe and elsewhere,[5] in fact has been national policy for over three decades. In 1980, Congress codified this notion in the Bayh-Dole Act, which among other things explicitly grants inventors in universities, small businesses, or nonprofit institutions rights to retain intellectual property in inventions funded by the federal government. In 2011, the Supreme Court in *Stanford v. Roche* clarified that these rights belong to the *inventors themselves,* although as a practical matter, the typical contracts that scientist-inventors sign with their universities require assignment of those rights to the school (the same contracts also generally require that the scholars assign the rights to *license* the inventions as well, a feature we criticize later this chapter).

While scholars continue to debate the effectiveness of Bayh-Dole, two features of the act are not much in dispute. The act made commercialization policies far more consistent among agencies, reducing the need for costly and protracted case-by-case negotiation. In addition, it set strong default rules for ownership of intellectual property, again reducing transaction costs. The Bayh-Dole Act thus increased the efficiency of commercializing university-developed technologies developed with the assistance of federal funding.

It is also beyond dispute that federal funding of university research has resulted, in one fashion or another, in numerous and important commercial applications, at least some of which have been facilitated or made possible by Bayh-Dole. As just one illustration, consider the list of the fifty most important innovations and discoveries funded by the National Science Foundation in its first fifty years, according to the NSF itself in 2000. Although this "Nifty 50" list includes some huge basic advances—such as the discovery that the universe is expanding at an accelerating rate—most items on the list are innovations that have been commercialized or become platforms for many commercial products and services now widely in use: barcodes, CAD/CAM software, data compression technology used in compact discs, and perhaps most significant of all, the Internet (which the NSF funded along with DARPA, a defense research agency).[6]

Not all of the Nifty 50 innovations are high tech, but their importance, too, is indisputable. These include yellow barrels used on the sides of highways to slow down out-of-control vehicles before they hit barriers and walls, and the American Sign Language Dictionary, which has changed the lives of the deaf and hard-of-hearing.

Another, more recent accounting of the importance of university-generated innovations is reflected in an analysis of the top 100 "most technologically significant new products" listed each year in *R&D* magazine. Fred Block and Matthew Keller report that universities and federal laboratories have become much more important sources of the top 100 innovations over the last thirty-five years.[7] In 1975, for example, they note that private firms accounted for over 70 percent of the "R&D 100," while the academic institution share was only 15 percent. By 2006, just three decades later, these two shares were reversed: academia contributed over 70 percent of the top 100 innovations, while private firms accounted for about 25 percent. It is hard to escape the conclusion that the passage of the Bayh-Dole Act of 1980 had something to do with this remarkable turnaround. Since the act, academic institutions and their faculty clearly have become far more active in research with potential commercial outcomes.

At the same time, some of this commercial innovation likely would have happened anyhow as a consequence of the huge growth of federal funding for research over the six decades since World War II. Given the lags between spending, discovery, and commercialization, it almost surely took a couple of decades for this new devotion to federally supported university research to begin translating into commercially significant innovation. Funding of academic research clearly will continue to be a crucial federal policy affecting the national innovation system.

Yet despite the apparent success of Bayh-Dole in accelerating the commercialization of federally supported academic research, the act has had unintended consequences that, ironically, also slow the commercialization process. Or, put differently, the commercialization process is "suboptimal" and could and should be improved. Nothing less than our nation's pace of future economic growth depends on it.

The Commercialization of University-Generated Innovation: Not All It Can Be

Those who believe the current system is working well and should essentially be left alone very likely will point to the substantial revenue that universities already are earning from the licensing of faculty innovations. According to the Association of University Technology Managers (AUTM), which compiles these data for most universities annually, universities earned $1.9 billion in licensing revenue from faculty-generated IP in 2008, up from just $221 million in 1996 when these data were first available.[8] The top ten university earners over the entire 1996–2008 period are listed in Table 4.1.

But how significant are these figures? One conventional way to answer that question is to compare licensing revenue to invested funds from all sources (not just federal government support) in order to compute a "rate

Table 4.1.   Licensing Incomes and Research Expenditures, Top 10 Universities 1996–2008 (Cumulative)

School name	Licensing income (billions of dollars)	Research expenditure (billions of dollars)	% Return annual average
New York University	1.49	2.67	4.3
University of California System	1.40	33.28	0.3
Northwestern University	0.96	3.81	1.9
Emory University	0.76	3.48	1.7
MIT	0.49	12.23	0.3
University of Minnesota	0.42	6.01	0.5
University of Washington	0.41	9.25	0.3
University of Florida	0.41	4.76	0.7
Florida State University	0.37	2.05	1.4
Wake Forest University	0.36	1.43	3.4

Source: AUTM Licensing Survey, 1996–2008

of return." Table 4.1 also lists these rates of return for the top ten schools for the thirteen-year period, which range from lows of 0.3 percent (for the University of California system and the University of Washington) to a high of 4.3 percent for the top earning school, NYU.[9] Admittedly, these rates of return are imperfect measures because they do not take account of the different *kinds* of research in which the faculty at different universities are engaged. For example, almost by definition, if a school is focused largely on basic research not likely to have any immediate commercial pay-off, then its rate of return will be close to zero. At the other end of the spectrum, if much of the research is concentrated on projects likely to have more immediate commercial uses, then rates of return should be higher. In addition, a university may be engaged largely in basic research but have one or two commercial "big hits" that bump up the reported rate of return for the school as a whole. Only a very few university inventions become financial blockbusters, and the returns are highly skewed; luck plays a large role in these "home run" financial successes. The rates of return shown in Table 4.1 are not adjusted for these differences in research types and outputs, and in the absence of other data it is impossible to do so.

Moreover, in all fairness, licensing revenue certainly is not and should not be the only measure of university research effectiveness and its dissemination. Much of what universities produce are true public goods, and the knowledge from research finds its way into others' research and leads to changes in the way firms and other organizations operate that do not readily show up in market transactions or prices. Even when the knowledge does have some commercial benefit, it is not easily attributable to any particular research finding.

Nonetheless, licensing revenues are still a useful indicator of commercial success; indeed, certainly more useful than some other hard counts of research output such as papers published in prestigious journals (many of which may have no commercial value), or even numbers of patents filed or issued (which do not account for the differential commercial value of different patents or take account of non-patent-related intellectual property, such as copyright or trade secrets which may legally protect certain innovations, or the open channels of communication that are not captured by patent counts or revenues). Ideally, it would also be useful to have measures of the number and performance of companies launched by university faculty members, but such data are generally not available. A well-known study has documented the large number of firms and jobs generated by MIT faculty and alumni, but we know of no similar study for another university (MIT is an unusually productive entrepreneurial institution by any account).[10]

Even with all the foregoing caveats, the rates of return reported in Table 4.1 are abysmally low. Collectively, they indicate either that most research by most universities has very little commercial value, or that the commercial potential is there but far from being fully realized. Both things could be and probably are true. Nonetheless, several factors—in addition to any inferences about suboptimality that may be drawn from the rates of return—indicate that the current system of university commercialization activity is not all it can or should be.

The first indicator is based on a quick look at some other relevant data. Much federal funding of university research is for biomedical research, and so it is appropriate to look at the trends in productivity—namely in the regulatory approvals of new drugs—from all this research. The answer is not a comforting one. Whereas federal funding for health-related research, which is primarily channeled to university faculty through the National Institutes of Health, has increased substantially—from under $20 billion in 1993 to almost $30 billion in 2008—the number of new FDA-approved drugs has dropped fairly consistently since 1996, when it peaked at over fifty, to just fifteen in 2008.[11] There may be a lot of factors discouraging new drug approvals, but overall these two trends clearly suggest that federal research support for the health sciences—the dominant way in which federal university research dollars are spent—has been growing less commercially productive.

Admittedly, this pattern of declining research productivity is just part of the broader story of the pharmaceutical industry, which from 1993 to 2004 increased its R&D spending by 147 percent but increased the number of new drug applications to the FDA annually by only 38 percent.[12] Clearly, there is something at work causing health sciences research, however it is funded and pursued, to turn out fewer valuable drugs. Perhaps the culprit is just a process of diminishing returns. But there also may be underlying inefficiencies in the research and commercialization process in both private industry and on campus, as well as legal and regulatory impediments.

In fact, the most important of these inefficiencies ironically stems from how universities responded after Bayh-Dole was enacted. For various reasons—to realize economies of scale in licensing, to provide advice and assistance to faculty innovators about how to commercialize their innovations, and to sort out legal claims where multiple inventors from different universities were responsible for the commercial opportunity—universities gradually began to centralize their technology licensing activities in a single technology licensing office (TLO) or technology transfer office (TTO). In the typical case, faculty members would agree not only to split any income realized from commercializing innovations developed on university premises or with university resources, but also to give the TTO exclusive rights and responsibility for pursuing commercial opportunities—especially the licensing of any intellectual property rights related to faculty-generated innovations.

While there were and arguably still are good reasons for centralizing these commercial responsibilities, the TTO monopolies—for that is what they have become—on many campuses have frustrated commercialization as often as they have facilitated it. This is a strong and, we admit, controversial statement. But there are also strong reasons backing it up.

For one thing, the TTOs are not all equally well funded or staffed. Most such offices have to ration the attention they give to university faculty. Furthermore, in principle, a successful TTO employee should have the same skill set as a partner in a private venture capital firm. In practice, this is rarely possible because VCs are able to (and do) pay their staff and partners much more than a university could afford or justify. As a result, faculty innovators must stand in a proverbial line at many TTOs, trying to get the staff to give their full attention to commercializing innovations whose market value the staff may have less expertise in judging than the faculty innovators themselves—or certainly than the market. The monopoly position of the TTOs with respect to their university faculty reinforces this conclusion, as we elaborate shortly.

In addition, in part for the reason just stated, and also because TTOs themselves have their own bureaucratic tendencies, some university faculty do not technically comply with their employment contracts requiring them to use the TTO for licensing, and instead commercialize their innovations "through the back door." Indeed, the extent to which this occurs is an indicator of the suboptimality of the current university commercialization system.

How much "backdoor" activity takes place? This is difficult to answer with precision, since many faculty innovators are reluctant to admit this is what they are doing, and universities may have difficulty finding out. Nonetheless, the best research on this subject, by Jerry Thursby, Anne Fuller, and Marie Thursby, suggests that the volume of backdoor patenting, and by implication commercialization, is substantial. The university can elect to forego patent rights, leaving them to the faculty inventor, or research may have taken place abroad or under terms giving faculty ownership rights, so not all such cases represent backdoor commercialization. The frequency of apparent backdoor commercialization seems high enough, however, to suggest that it is a very real phenomenon. In their study of eighty-seven research universities, this research team found that almost 38 percent of the more than 5,800 patents in their sample were not assigned solely to the university, which the authors note is surprising in light of the standard faculty employment contract that expressly requires that universities gain ownership rights to faculty inventions when university resources are used in the research.[13]

In effect, backdoor commercialization acts as a safety valve for a less-than-ideal system, but it is an inefficient one. Not every faculty innovator who is frustrated with the university's TTO will take the risk or go to the effort of commercializing "in the dark" and instead will simply take his or her place in the queue at the TTO. When this happens, useful commercialization activity may be slowed or halted.

Finally (and arguably most important), because the monopoly position of the TTO leaves faculty inventors with little choice about how, to whom, and at what pace to license or otherwise commercialize their innovations, the TTO structure is inherently inconsistent with the kind of robust competition one sees in most markets elsewhere in the economy. Consider this: if universities applied the same model to faculty research, it would mean that all faculty members would be required, by contract, to first obtain the approval of a (purely hypothetical) central "faculty publications office" that would coordinate the submission of articles to journals and books to publishers. It almost goes without saying that faculty would not stand for such an approach to their publications, nor would universities voluntarily adopt it for fear of frustrating the dissemination of research results to the academic community and the wider public. Yet when it comes to commercial activity, universities have taken a very different approach.

It has not always been this way. Prior to the passage of Bayh-Dole in 1980, few academic institutions—Wisconsin's independent Wisconsin Alumni Research Foundation (WARF), established in 1925, being the notable exception—had a formal TTO, either inside or independent of the university. Only after Bayh-Dole was enacted did universities gradually begin to centralize the commercialization functions which the act legitimated. Now, as noted, virtually all research universities have a TTO, which in the typical case has exclusive control over the licensing and commercialization activities related to innovations developed by university faculty.

In theory, of course, TTOs can be structured or operate in such a way as to facilitate rather than hinder licensing and commercialization. There are examples where this, in fact, is the case. But monopolies, especially those wielding legal rights to that status by virtue of university employment contracts, also have well-known incentives to behave suboptimally.

Perhaps most recognized is the incentive for monopolies to reduce output. In the university commercialization context, this tendency manifests itself in the limited attention, within limited resources, that TTOs have to give to all faculty-developed innovations, and the inherent need therefore to focus on only a few potential "winners." But with no more talent and experience than private venture firms, and without the same or similar gain-sharing incentives for success that motivate VC firm general partners (who typically take 20 percent of the profits of the enterprise), there is no reason to believe that the TTOs can be any more effective than the market itself in determining the true winners. This potentially leaves many innovations not given favored treatment by the TTO staff in bureaucratic limbo until someone in that office can give them proper attention—if ever. Indeed, the well-known tendency toward bureaucracy and inefficiency of monopolies, to which TTOs certainly are not immune, aggravates this problem.

The monopoly that each TTO has over its university's licensing and commercialization of faculty inventions also leads to a potentially even more significant *systemwide* flaw. Given their exclusive control over licensing, TTOs are required to be jacks-of-all-trades and thus cannot, without ignoring innovations across many technologies by many different faculty members, specialize in one or a few technologies. Even in cases where TTOs choose to specialize in their search for "home runs," they cannot exploit any economies of scale, since with all research universities relying on their own TTOs for licensing there is no opportunity for them to offer their services to faculty of other academic institutions (a situation that can be remedied under at least one of the reform options outlined below). The net result is that the market for licensing of university-developed technologies is highly fragmented and almost certainly inefficient.

In sum, despite the clear progress universities have made since 1980 in commercializing innovations by their faculty, there are several reasons for believing they could do even better. Rates of return on research investment, however imperfect as a measure of success, are disappointingly low. Research productivity in one particular field where university research is amply supported by the federal government—pharmaceuticals—has been declining.[14] Most technology licensing offices are underresourced, and cannot effectively compete in the market for talent in identifying promising commercial opportunities. And perhaps most important, the university technology licensing market is structured to inhibit competition, which almost certainly leaves some commercial opportunities on the shelf while slowing others from reaching the marketplace and consumers.

Possible Reforms

The suboptimal performance of the university commercialization process keeps the economy from growing as rapidly as it can, while also incidentally harming universities and faculty innovators. A more efficient system would generate more commercially useful products more quickly, which not only would accelerate advances in living standards, but also bring greater revenue faster to universities and to faculty innovators whose employment contracts typically give them some share in the royalties or revenues when their technologies are commercialized. University faculty are not in a position to change the status quo, however, since no single faculty member has a strong enough bargaining position to compel his or her university employers to change the system in any meaningful way. Why, then, do university leaders follow a path that seemingly is not in their own interest?

This important question is not well addressed in the literature, so it is possible here only to speculate on the reasons. One plausible answer is that, at least for universities that have had some commercialization successes, such as those listed in Table 4.1, university presidents and trustees are probably pleased with their performance and thus unlikely aware that they could do even better. This is true even though there is no evidence that a university's ranking on the top ten list of cumulative licensing revenue has anything to do with the effectiveness of its TTO. One or a few blockbuster innovations may account for most of the revenue, and these events are more likely to be random than the result of successful staff work at the TTO. Nonetheless, for reasons already given, the current monopoly TTO structure is not well suited to quickly identifying and speeding the commercialization of even these random successful innovations.

Universities with far less success at commercial licensing may also be unaware of how much better they might do under different arrangements.

While perhaps disappointed by their relative (and absolute) lack of success at commercialization, their leaders may attribute this result to randomness of a different sort: their faculty, either because of disinterest in commercially relevant research or because they have just been unlucky and have not yet had the big hits that drive commercial success.

Another factor at work may be that technology transfer officials have no interest in calling attention to university presidents or other leaders the suboptimality of the current system, assuming they believe this to be the case. Indeed, there is little evidence that technology transfer officials even believe the current system is suboptimal in any way. But for those few who might recognize this to be true, it is still not in their self-interest to disturb the status quo, especially in any way that might compel them to compete against other licensing agents.

The Great Recession and its aftermath, however, may eventually induce some university leaders and/or trustees to begin searching for ways to improve commercialization outcomes. With the drop in university endowments caused by the decline in equity and real estate values, the corresponding falloffs in wealth among alumni donors, and the potential decline in federal research monies post-stimulus due to continuing budget pressures, universities will be looking even harder for ways to raise funds (other than by raising tuition even more than already would be the case). One obvious target is to increase revenue from technology commercialization.

An intensified focus on commercialization could be a mixed blessing. On the one hand, it could reinforce TTOs' incentives and tendencies to concentrate their time and efforts on what they believe are home run opportunities, to the detriment of perhaps many other singles and doubles. Certain licensing agents in a freer market can be expected to behave in the same fashion, but at least they would be competing against each other for deals; thus, some agents who might not have access to the true home runs would be content to work on the doubles and singles if they had the chance. Given the difficult economic circumstances confronting universities, it is possible that leaders of some would recognize the advantages of harnessing free market forces in licensing, or at the very least be open to fundamental rethinking about the ways they want to commercialize their faculties' inventions in the future.

In that spirit, we now offer some ways to improve upon the current university technology licensing system. We focus on licensing even though we recognize the potential benefits to universities of granting their faculty the rights to the intellectual property in their inventions, hoping that successful faculty members will later give back a portion of their profits in gratitude—a very realistic alternative strategy in our view. The case for faculty ownership of IP was strengthened by the Supreme Court's decision in *Stanford v. Roche* in June 2011, in which the Court held that the Bayh-Dole Act does not automatically confer IP rights on universities. As we noted earlier in the chapter, universities either have anticipated or reacted to that decision by making it clear in faculty employment agreements that faculty members preassign their IP rights in any future inventions to the university (which Stanford had not done in the *Roche* case, which is why the school lost). Thus, we are not hopeful that many (or any) universities will try the IP experiment just outlined.[15]

The arena where we hope change eventually will be more likely is the *licensing* of faculty-generated IP. Each of the ideas we now present can be implemented by universities on their own, primarily through changes in their relationships and legal agreements with faculty. Admittedly, most of these ideas so far have not been welcomed or even recognized by other reports that have addressed this subject.[16] We continue to hope, however, that eventually reason will prevail and some or all of these proposals, especially free agency, will attract the attention they deserve. Toward that end, we close this chapter with some thoughts on how the federal government, as a significant funder of university research and the originator of the concept that inventors/universities have a right to commercialize federally funded research (under the Bayh-Dole Act), might encourage universities to adopt one or more of these ideas.

Standardized or "Express" Licensing

Perhaps the most straightforward way to make licensing more efficient and provide stronger incentives to faculty innovators (who may be closer to market opportunities than less-specialized TTO staff) to explore commercially relevant opportunities is to standardize the license agreements themselves. This would eliminate the need for potentially time-consuming and costly negotiations between university TTO staff, potential licensees, and faculty inventors.

The Universities of North Carolina and Washington have implemented a form of this idea for startup company licensees only though an "Express License Agreement." The Express License can be chosen by any faculty member, student, or staff member who is a founder of a company using IP rights owned solely by the university, and after a detailed business plan is reviewed and approved by the TTO. Key provisions of the standard agreement include a 1 percent royalty on products requiring FDA approval and 2 percent for all other products. In addition, the standard agreement at North Carolina requires the licensee to make a cash payout of 0.75 percent of the company's fair market value upon its merger, stock or asset sale, or initial public offering. The license also encourages the licensee to make products available for humanitarian purposes in developing countries.[17]

Something like an Express License should be easily replicated at other universities and at federal labs. Admittedly, one limitation of the idea is that it presumes capability within the university's TTO to evaluate the innovator's business plan. Not all TTOs are equally well equipped to do this. One way to address this potential problem is for universities wanting to use the Express License approach to establish an outside panel of experienced entrepreneurs (composed of alumni and local residents with interest in the university) to review these plans.

One other possible objection, which on closer inspection may be an advantage, is that since the standard license would be available only for startups, it might bias university faculty, staff, and students toward launching new companies (which is likely to be a riskier source of revenue) rather than licensing existing companies. The advantage of such a bias, however, is that the payoff from a new business launch, if it succeeds, may be much larger than any royalty that might be realized from a license to an already established company.

To help ensure the best possible outcome for the university, innovators, and society, it therefore is in universities' best interest—regardless of which, if any, of the reform ideas outlined here (or others) they wish to adopt—to provide entrepreneurial training and mentoring to faculty and students who want to launch a business around their innovations. There are successful models of this idea at many universities—MIT, Washington University in St. Louis, the University of Miami, and the University of North Carolina, among others—that can and should be replicated.

Multi-University Technology Commercialization Consortiums

TTOs have inherent difficulties in realizing economies of scale, both because of resource limits at their universities and also because of the broad range of technologies developed by their universities' faculty. Licensing and commercialization activity thus cries out for specialized providers, those who can serve a sufficient volume of similar innovations to develop expertise and realize some economies of scale.

One way of doing this would be for university TTOs to join forces, either in full-scale mergers or less-than-full-scale joint ventures. Such consortia could be developed along regional lines, within specific technological fields, or both. A single consortium could replace an individual TTO, or a single TTO might join multiple consortia. Obviously, there are many possible combinations of these alternatives.

While participation in one or more consortia would enable universities to better realize economies of scale and the advantages of specialization, this option has its drawbacks. It may be difficult to specify *ex ante* rules for distributing the gains from various royalty or equity participation arrangements, and possibly also for splitting expenses. Likewise, there may be disputes over these matters *ex post* in individual cases where faculty members from different universities in a consortium are involved in creating the innovation. At the same time, these issues may be no more difficult than is the case now where faculty from multiple universities share in the invention and the universities involved have to decide how to split the IP rights and any related gains.

The advantages of the consortium option(s) may be enhanced if the consortia also adopt a standardized license for startups. This would combine the benefits of both approaches while eliminating at the outset some potential disputes or negotiating difficulties that otherwise could later arise.

iBridge, the invention platform we discussed in the last chapter, bears some resemblance to this consortium idea but is much broader, with many more universities participating than would likely participate in a consortium of university TTOs. Nonetheless, we mention it here because the success of iBridge demonstrates the power of cooperation, which smaller universities without the resources of their larger counterparts may wish to harness.

Choice in Licensing (or "Free Agency")

As meritorious as they may be, neither consortia nor the standardized license get at the root cause of the likely underperformance of university commercialization efforts. That is because neither option would break up the monopoly control each university TTO has over its own faculty, which as we have argued has led to excessive bureaucracy and slowed or inhibited the commercialization of innovations that TTOs deem not to be potential home runs.

The best solution to these problems is to let the *market* decide—more than it does now—which innovations should be commercialized and at what pace, rather than gatekeeper TTOs. In particular, this third reform option would grant faculty (or staff and student) innovators the same freedom in choosing the licensing agent for their innovations that they now have in choosing where to publish their research. The "free agency" option would require, of course, a change in the standard university-faculty employment agreement, but it would extend only to the licensing decision and not affect the university's financial and reporting arrangements with respect to faculty innovations and, if adopted by universities on their own, would not require statutory change or altering the fundamentals of the Bayh-Dole framework.

Freeing up the market in technology licensing should bring big benefits to all parties concerned. It would provide much stronger incentives for faculty to commercialize their discoveries more quickly, eliminating the potentially long waits at the TTO to get recognition. This would generate benefits for society, faculty innovators, and the universities that will share in their success. Choice in licensing would also encourage specialization and thus economies of scale among licensing agents, whether or not they are affiliated with universities. Some universities might even decide to drop their TTOs, merge or pool them with other research institutions, or significantly reduce their TTO staff as a result and thereby save money and generate better returns. Or, universities could decide to keep their TTOs to compete with other licensing agents and/or transform them into technology consulting offices that would advise faculty about the commercialization and licensing process.

Several objections to the free agency model in technology commercialization can be anticipated. One question that may arise relates to who will pay for patent filing fees in a system of free agency. Under the current system, a faculty or staff innovator who can persuade the university TTO that a patent should be filed will have that cost underwritten by the university itself. But under free agency, might faculty inventors have no way other than digging into their own pockets to fund their patent filings, in which case, might IP be underprotected?

There is an easy answer to this question. Markets would (and should) determine how patent filings are funded. Non-university licensing agents or attorneys may compete by taking royalties or a small equity interest in the innovator's company as payment for patent filings that innovators cannot fund themselves. Since there are many such potential agents, competition among them can be counted on to protect innovators. Alternatively, even under free agency, faculty innovators would retain the right to choose their own university's TTO or any new commercialization consortia that may be formed in a freer and more competitive environment, and any one of these entities could front the patent filing costs. Moreover, in many cases, the university does not pay patent prosecution costs even now, but rather the licensing firm pays them.

Another possible objection to free agency is the belief that many faculty innovators need the guidance of their TTOs since they are unlikely to have significant experience in this area or as entrepreneurs more broadly. It is precisely for this reason, however, that universities more generally should help train and mentor entrepreneurial faculty. But this training need not be done by the TTO. Indeed, there should be a presumption against this since TTO staff members are not likely to have the requisite entrepreneurial experience.

Furthermore, the notion that many faculty innovators need the helping hand of TTOs in licensing is wrong often enough that an alternative is prudent policy. There are cases where faculty innovators do need the expertise of TTO staff, but other cases when faculty expertise far outstrips TTO capacity. Current policy only makes sense in the situation where the TTO adds value. Consistent with the "80/20" rule applicable in so many other realms of life, a relatively small group of the most successful serial faculty innovators are probably responsible for most of the successful innovations university TTOs are now licensing. Indeed, as we noted at the outset of this chapter, such "rock star" scientists have been demonstrated to be critical to the economic success of the local areas where they live and work. These individuals are not likely to be in need of the counseling that TTO staff may provide. On the contrary, many of these innovators are likely to have more experience and a stronger social network than TTO staff members. As for other faculty members with less commercial experience, in a free market many almost surely would do what consumers who are looking for a doctor, a repair specialist, or an auto mechanic routinely do: ask others (in the university case, most likely more senior or experienced faculty innovators). In addition, in a freer market, information providers would likely build Internet-accessible databases and rating services of the most effective licensing agents, in general and in particular technological fields.

A third potential concern is whether free agency complicates the commercialization of innovations developed by faculty from multiple laboratories within a university, or from multiple universities. In particular, with innovators having the right to choose their licensing agents, will this lead to more disputes over ownership of the IP, which would slow commercialization? Although it is difficult to know the answer to this question with any precision, there are reasons to doubt that free agency would lead to significantly more intra- or interuniversity disputes. Problems of attributing IP to different inventors and universities already exist under the current system, with TTO offices and university general counsel having to resolve them. Indeed, the nature of research is evolving to bigger teams and more institutions involved in invention and its commercialization. The problem of multiagency is very real and likely to intensify, but it is not necessarily a problem solved by centralization at the university level, which is the current default framework.[18]

Of course, if free agency were to lead to more cross-university faculty collaborations—some of which may result in IP ownership disputes—this is not necessarily a bad outcome. To the contrary, the more cross-fertilization of ideas takes place, the more innovative the entire university ecosystem is likely to be. Having to resolve some increased level of IP disputes seems a price worth paying for more commercialized innovation.

In the end, opponents of free agency have a difficult question to answer: why only in the particular case of technology licensing, but not in research, should faculty members be unable to choose the best method for advancing their innovation—especially when the exercise of choice does not disturb in any way the university's royalty or gain-sharing arrangement in the faculty member's contract? To be more precise, on what grounds can monopoly in this narrow sphere of activity be justified, when the presumption in virtually every other sphere of economic activity favors competition? At the very least, opponents of free agency would seem to have the burden of proof in carrying the day on each of these questions.

Inventor IP Ownership

The final and arguably most extreme option for accelerating the university commercialization process is for universities to give up their IP rights in faculty inventions, or at least not pursue them so aggressively (as has been the norm in a number of universities). This could easily be accomplished by revising the standard university faculty employment contract so that any university rights to inventions under Bayh-Dole would be automatically assigned on a royalty-free basis to faculty (or staff or students).

Letting faculty inventors have full rights in their innovations clearly would provide them the maximum possible incentive to rapidly commercialize innovations, and for that reason the idea should be seriously considered, though perhaps initially on an experimental basis. The major reason for proceeding incrementally is that universities need to test both whether giving up their IP does in fact lead to more commercialization—which is a social good—but also whether faculty inventors, so legally empowered, would feel morally obligated to share with their universities some of their private gains from commercializing their innovations. This has happened already under the existing system, and it is likely that loyal faculty would continue sharing their wealth if they had full rights to the IP. Even if, on a per-transaction basis, faculty givebacks were not as generous as the current standard royalty arrangements, if university assignment of IP rights to faculty led to more commercialization, the "pie" would grow, and universities—individually and collectively—would be better off. Only by experimenting with this option, however, can universities learn whether this would be true.

There are some powerful counterarguments to taking faculty free agency to the level of ownership that we must acknowledge. Probably the most significant concern is that some faculty would selfishly abuse such a system. Most faculty members, however, are likely to want to remain part of their university and must meet many other performance evaluation criteria. Another objection is that the university itself is responsible for creating the environment in which innovation takes place, and therefore deserves part of the reward. This argument could be accommodated, however, through faculty employment contracts that give universities some share of the royalties or revenues earned on the innovations.

State officials can adopt or push university innovation licensing reforms. Governors can persuade their state boards of regents that oversee state universities to take one or more of the steps outlined here—ideally free agency, or at least the express license—or, if necessary, begin by replacing current regents with those more amenable to licensing reform. Change at private universities, meanwhile, will require initiative from their presidents, or failing that, from their trustees. Governors and national authorities, elected and appointed, can and should use their bully pulpits to encourage all universities where research with commercial potential is conducted to move as rapidly as possible to change the status quo.

Role of Federal Policy

Given the broad social interest in more rapid commercialization of faculty-generated innovation, coupled with the substantial federal taxpayer commitment to university research, the federal government also has good reasons for wanting to encourage universities to adopt one or more of these (or perhaps other) reforms.

There are several possible ways for the government to go about this, in cooperation with or parallel to actions by state officials. One "soft" option would be for the funding agencies, in consultation with the Department of Commerce, to issue guidance about the implementation and interpretation of licensing procedures and terms. The National Institutes of Health has done this, in effect, for research tools and for genomic inventions. Perhaps the broadest approach would be for the Commerce Department, which has rule-making authority in implementing the provisions of Bayh-Dole, to issue a proposed rule—meant to apply to all federally funded research—to encourage more effective commercialization of faculty-generated innovations. That rule might outline a "default" standardized license that universities could decide to adopt, while making clear that although Bayh-Dole gave universities the rights to the IP from faculty innovations, it does not confer on universities the exclusive rights to control licensing. Admittedly, this might be a stretch and the Commerce Department would need new legislative authority to issue such a rule, in which case it should ask for it.

Alternatively, individual federal agencies that fund university research—notably the Department of Energy, the National Science Foundation, and the National Institutes of Health—could go further and condition their grants on universities adopting any one of the first three proposals (the notion that the government would condition a grant on universities giving up their IP rights is almost certainly too extreme). Of course, Congress could impose similar conditions on its annual appropriations to these and other funding agencies. But it is possible, if not likely, that the agencies currently have the authority to do this on their own.

One promising reform at the federal level is already under way. During the summer of 2011, the National Science Foundation announced an innovative competitive program that will fund 100 "Innovation Corps" scholar-scientist teams per year to support commercialization of their technologies. The training will be provided by the technology commercialization program at Stanford University, and will treat the commercialization process as a research-based extension of the scientific work these teams have already undertaken. In particular, the Stanford model pushes entrepreneurs with an idea to first identify what *customer uses* it has, and then to refine the product or technology to fit those uses and develop a profitable business strategy around it. With some hard work, luck, and hope, the NSF's "I-Corps" may be to technology commercialization on (and off) campus what the Peace Corps has been for its participants and those around the world who have benefited from their commitment and efforts.

Conclusion

Universities are critical to economic growth in a number of ways: through the students they teach and equip with skills; through the production of new knowledge, both basic and applied; and through the commercialization of research by some faculty members.

The Bayh-Dole Act was enacted in 1980 explicitly to promote economic growth through the last of these channels. It appears to have been effective in stimulating universities to pay more attention to commercialization opportunities. At the time, the act unintentionally led to the centralization of commercialization decisions in licensing offices that have gained *de facto* monopoly control over the licensing of faculty-developed innovations.

This chapter has outlined several reasons that this system is not as effective as it could and should be in bringing to market innovations developed at universities. We also have identified several reforms that individually or in combination could speed commercialization of new technologies, thereby accelerating economic growth and benefiting society, innovators, and the universities that employ them.

IMPORTING ENTREPRENEURS

"Give me your tired, your poor, your huddled masses yearning to breathe free"—famous words by Emma Lazarus that are engraved on the pedestal of the Statue of Liberty and which are cited repeatedly as evidence of America's welcoming attitude toward immigrants. In recent years, however, those attitudes have shifted significantly and depend on who those immigrants are.

Legal immigrants, who are heavily restricted in number by law, are still for the most part accepted here, especially (although not universally) if they are coming to the United States to study or already have skills. Yet the welcome mat is largely a temporary one. Unless even these skilled immigrants have a rare talent and can prove they are qualified for a job no American can fill (the conditions for an EB-3 visa), have $1 million to bring to this country to invest in a business (the condition for an EB-5 visa), or can find a great immigration lawyer perhaps to exploit some other loophole, even skilled foreign-born workers must return to their home countries after earning their degrees or completing their work assignments under limited H-1B visas.[1]

Americans are much more skeptical—if not downright hostile—to illegal immigrants, especially those with few skills, however hard they work when they get here or however much American families benefit from the low-paid jobs they fill as housekeepers, lawn care service workers, or dishwashers in restaurants. Any such benefits seem to be easily trumped by the fears that illegal immigrants bring with them drugs, crime, and heavy demands for public services, not to mention perceived security risks (in the case of immigrants from countries with large Muslim populations), a concern which has been aggravated since the 9/11 terrorist attacks. Even those who disclaim any nativist impulses are still bothered by illegal immigrants simply because they are *illegal*—they have circumvented the principle which defines for Americans what America is all about: that only if you play by the rules will we give you an opportunity to succeed.

As we write this, immigration policy is as much a third rail in American politics as Social Security and Medicare, perhaps even more so. Feelings about illegal immigration in particular have been at fever pitch ever since the state of Arizona in 2010 enacted legislation—widely supported by the state's citizens and clearly many Americans—making it a crime to be an illegal alien and giving the police the authority, if not the duty, to arrest anyone they even suspect to be illegally in this country. The Obama administration challenged the Arizona statute in court, asserting that federal immigration law preempts attempts by Arizona or other states to enact laws that conflict with federal policy. In July 2010, a federal district court issued a preliminary injunction against enforcement of parts of the Arizona law. Meanwhile, other states continue to experiment with their own versions of the Arizona legislation.

However the Arizona litigation ultimately turns out, and however many states take similar (perhaps more legally sound) steps to restrict immigration, reform will remain a hot political issue. Conceivably, the climate will stay too hot for a logical compromise—one that toughens border security and at the same time provides a legal path for currently illegal, mostly low-skilled immigrants to work here and eventually become citizens. In the meantime, there so far has been little appetite for either the Obama administration or Congress to take the equally logical and far less politically controversial step of revamping the nation's immigration policies toward *highly skilled* immigrants.

At one level, the case for doing so would seem to be straightforward. Significant achievements in U.S. history are directly tied to skilled immigrants. The Manhattan Project, which helped win World War II, would not have been possible without a wave of European immigrants, including Albert Einstein, Niels Bohr, Enrico Fermi, Leo Szilard, Eugene Wigner, and Edward Teller. The first viable helicopter was built by Igor Sikorsky, who came to the United States from Russia, while the first nuclear submarine was developed under the tutelage of Admiral Hyman Rickover, who was born in Poland.

Likewise, the U.S. economy was literally built by a series of famous immigrant entrepreneurs and inventors, whose companies went on to become American icons. Readers will surely recognize the names of these outstanding immigrants and the companies they founded or helped launch, but we'll bet not many realize that these individuals all were born in other countries: Alexander Graham Bell (AT&T), Levi Strauss (Levi Strauss & Co.), Andrew Carnegie (U.S. Steel), Herbert Dow (Dow Chemical Company), E. I. du Pont (DuPont), Charles Pfizer (Pfizer), David Buick (Buick Motors, later purchased by General Motors), Adolph Coors (Coors Beer), Henry Heinz (H. J. Heinz Company), James Kraft (Kraft Foods), William Procter and James Gamble (Procter & Gamble), Eberhard Anheuser and Adolphus Busch (Anheuser-Busch), Samuel Goldwyn and Louis Mayer (MGM), Marcus Goldman (cofounder of Goldman Sachs), and even Ettore Boiardi (Chef Boyardee). In all, 18 percent of the Fortune 500 companies in 2010 were launched by immigrants, and fully 40 percent were founded by immigrants or their children.[2]

Successful immigrant entrepreneurs are not just ancient names in history books. Living immigrant superstars include Sergey Brin (Google), Andrew Grove (Intel), Jerry Yang (Yahoo!), Pierre Omidyar (eBay), Elon Musk (PayPal, Tesla Motors, and SpaceX), Jawed Karim (YouTube), and Gururaj "Desh" Deshpande (Cascade Communications, Sycamore Networks, Airvana, and A123Systems). Social scientists are fond of saying that the plural of anecdotes is data. The names just recited should provide enough data to satisfy even the hardiest skeptic that immigrants have played and continue to play a crucial role in shaping and improving the American economy and society. But for those who want numbers, consider some hard facts. For one, according to U.S. government data, immigrants have consistently started new businesses at a substantially higher rate than native-born Americans.[3] Immigrants have been especially important to the founding of highly successful companies and the making of important new discoveries while they are in this country. Between 1995 and 2005, for example, immigrants started or cofounded about one-quarter of successful U.S. firms engaged in technology and engineering—those with at least $1 million in sales and over twenty employees—which collectively generated an estimated $52 *billion* in revenue and employed 450,000 American workers in 2005.[4] Other research studies have corroborated this one-quarter ratio—of companies founded in Silicon Valley between 1980 and 1998,[5] of biotech companies launched in New England,[6] and of publicly traded companies that were started between 1990 and 2007 and were financed at least in part by venture capital.[7] Currently, immigrants make up only about 12.5 percent of the U.S. population, which means that, as a group, immigrants are punching well above their weight in terms of starting new businesses (and certainly even higher if one looked only at skilled immigrants).

Perhaps not so coincidentally, the hard numbers show that immigrants have been equally successful in patenting new inventions, especially in recent years. The U.S. immigrant share of globally recognized patents (those filed with the World Intellectual Property Organization) was just 7 percent in 1998. By 2006, that share had climbed to 24 percent, about the same share found in entrepreneurship data.[8] Indeed, immigrants with at least a college degree obtained patents at twice the rate of similarly educated native-born Americans, and for those with a graduate degree, at three times the native rate.[9]

In short, if America wants and needs more innovation and entrepreneurship, one obvious way to do that would be not only to accept more skilled immigrants into the country, but to do all that we can *to recruit them*. Although this idea can be found in some op-eds and blog postings on the Internet, it has not yet been part of mainstream political discussion. The reason, of course, is that the potential benefits of importing more skilled immigrants—potential entrepreneurs in particular—have been totally overshadowed by the controversy and concerns surrounding illegal immigrants. Elected officials understandably are especially reluctant to be seen as favoring immigration—of any type—when the overall economy is fragile and unemployment rates are persistently high and projected to remain that way for years to come.

America nonetheless cannot afford this political timidity. Since consistent and more rapid economic growth is necessary to defuse Americans' anxieties about their economic and financial futures, and it is clear from the recent past that skilled immigrants in particular are ideally equipped to help achieve these outcomes, it is time for logic and reason to prevail. Accordingly, we outline in this chapter a range of concrete reforms to U.S. immigration policy that would bring in more skilled immigrants, followed by a discussion of how the language of immigration can and should be changed so that any one or more of these proposed reforms can become politically acceptable. But first, we take a short step back to briefly review how our immigration policies came to be.

America's Hot and Cold Immigration Policies

Although it is widely taught that the United States is a "melting pot" of different peoples who have been welcomed into this country, the reality is far more complicated. In truth, Americans have been moody when it comes to immigration—sometimes hot, sometimes cold. Public policies and sentiments toward immigrants have fluctuated dramatically over the last century in particular, though this pattern only recently has extended to immigrants who come here with skills. As we will argue, America's recent hard times call for a more welcoming attitude, toward skilled immigrants especially, than we have seen in political discourse over the past few years.

Until the late 1800s, the annual flow of new migrants was relatively constant, though the source stemmed from two distinct groups with two different stories: one of despair for Africans, and one of relative ease for Europeans.

It goes without saying that the forced migration of African slaves to the United States is a dark stain on our nation's past. But the economic motivation behind the migration—the desire for cheap labor—is a theme that has been repeated throughout American history. Sadly, the racist justification for the slave trade is representative of other often discriminatory U.S. immigration policies as well.

For other immigrants arriving by choice (mostly Europeans), the route to America was fairly simple and welcoming. As the territories and states in the Midwest and on the West Coast needed people to settle them, the American public and Congress remained relatively open to immigrants. With a few exceptions, new arrivals could travel and live wherever they wanted. Indeed, not until the opening of Ellis Island in 1892 was there much official screening of immigrants.[10]

The open-arms policy toward immigrants began to change, however, during the late nineteenth century. One ethnic group in particular, the Chinese, became the focal point of public dissent. Chinese immigrants were recruited several decades earlier as cheap labor for America's monumental railroad construction projects. Many Chinese immigrants eventually settled on the West Coast, which was buzzing with activity during the gold rush. As more immigrants poured in, competing with already established Americans for the new pots of gold (literally), much of the public turned sour on Chinese immigrants.[11] Eventually, in 1882, the United States adopted its first explicitly anti-immigration statute, the Chinese Exclusion Act, which barred all Chinese from entering the U.S. legally thereafter.

The story of Chinese immigration through the 1880s is representative of what would become a pattern in U.S. immigration policy—that it is heavily tied to the economic and social conditions of the time. The cycle goes like this: businesses desire cheap reliable labor and immigrants are willing to work at rock bottom wages. Businesses begin to hire immigrant workers, who continue to arrive en masse. As the number of foreigners from a given nationality increases, natives become anxious about the newcomers' ability and willingness to assimilate into existing culture. These fears are often fueled by disproportionately negative media coverage of immigrants. When the growing fear of immigrants combines with a down economy and unemployment, especially when these events are aggravated by fears of foreigners stoked before or during a major war (World Wars I and II), policy toward immigrants turns much more restrictive.

This narrative has repeated itself most notably since the late 1890s until the present day. Indeed, recent research has shown that people grow more fearful about immigrants during periods of economic difficulty. Over the past decade, views about immigration were highly correlated with the unemployment rate. When unemployment rose, more Americans thought immigration should be cut back; when it declined, fewer felt that way.[12]

Take, for example, the largest wave of immigrants until that time, who arrived here between the 1880s and 1920s. These immigrants came almost exclusively from places in Europe—Ireland, Italy, and southern and (what is now) eastern Europe—which had not before been major source countries

(England, France, Germany, and Holland, or "Old Europe"). As millions of new Irish and Italian immigrants settled in, public opinion toward them eventually turned negative based on perceptions of their failure to assimilate into existing American culture. Not by coincidence, nativist resentment toward new immigrants spiked during the Panic of 1893 and resulting recession. Various acts of Congress were passed throughout the early 1900s, culminating in the National Origins Act of 1924, which restricted the annual quota of new arrivals to three hundred thousand and proportioned them to nationalities based on the 1890 census (thereby discriminating against the new Irish and Italian immigrants, as well as Asians). Unsurprisingly, the restrictive attitude and policy toward immigrants continued right through the Great Depression and World War II.

Until the 1960s, the one exception to this hot-and-cold pattern of immigration policy was the attitude of citizens and their leaders toward skilled foreign workers. Public outrage against immigrants, when it has arisen, has been limited to immigrants perceived—fairly or not—as lazy, unkempt, and uneducated, perceptions (and facts) that clearly do not apply to those who are highly skilled. For example, the National Origins Act just mentioned explicitly exempted skilled workers (at that time specifically in agriculture) from counting against the immigration quota.

Returning to our narrative, as the U.S. economy picked up in the 1950s and 1960s and the civil rights movement reached full force, national embarrassment arose over the unfairness of the existing country-based quota system for immigration. President Kennedy labeled it "nearly intolerable."[13] The resulting Immigration Act of 1965 aimed to make the system more just. The bill's original intent was to abolish the quota system and focus on bringing workers with desirable skills in short supply to the United States. Although the final bill recognized skills as a factor, the main focus of the 1965 liberalization became family reunification, because of broad lobbying by religious organizations and ethnic groups already represented in this country, who stressed the social importance of family ties. Labor union opposition actually, for the first time, limited the reach of the skills-based provisions, fearing competition for what they believed were scarce jobs. This was the first time in American history that skilled immigrants, as a group, faced significant domestic opposition.

The focus on family reunification in the 1965 act marked a dramatic shift in U.S. immigration policy, creating lasting impacts on new migrant demographic trends. Under the new law, migrants hailed not from Europe as expected, but mostly from Asia and Latin America, joining their relatives already in this country. Critics came to call the family-based policy "chain migration." The new trend showed up in immigration data fairly quickly. In 1970, five years after the new family-oriented policy had been put in place, entry linked to occupational preferences accounted for 60 percent of the quota ceiling. But by 1978, "chain migration" had already started to dominate (especially after the Vietnam War), with the skills-based share of new migrants dropping to 17 percent of the total.[14]

The most significant change to immigration policy since 1965 came in 1990, and was again skills related and economically motivated, with the establishment of the temporary (six-year) H-1B visa. H-1B visas would help fuel the information technology boom of the 1990s as companies such as Microsoft, Intel, and IBM persuaded Congress that they could not satisfy all their employment needs with Americans alone. The introduction of the H-1B thus brought skilled programmers and technicians from abroad, a good number from India, to the United States.

In the past decade, immigration policy's tie to economic and social events has not diminished. The public and policymakers still react to emotional events, notably the crackdown on immigration resulting from the USA PATRIOT Act, a response to the September 11, 2001, terrorist attacks. Likewise, as noted in the introduction to this chapter, concern about the influx of illegal immigrants has mounted and is now at an all-time high.

Even skilled immigrants have been caught up in the anti-immigrant fervor. After increasing the H-1B quota to 115,000 in 1999 and 2000, and further raising it to 195,000 for the years 2001–3, Congress reduced the cap in 2004 to 65,000, where it has since remained. The reduction was motivated in part by the fact that U.S. companies did not fully utilize the permitted visas during the 2001–3 period, but the large reduction in the gap itself even during the expansion years clearly reflected a shift in public mood toward even skilled immigrants.

Likewise, the number of immigrant student F-1 visas plummeted after 9/11, dropping from 293,000 in 2001 to 234,000 the following year and to a fifteen-year low of 216,000 in 2003. Since then, however, the number of issued student visas has been on the rise, with roughly 331,000 granted in 2009.[15]

Given what are likely to be above-trend unemployment rates through much of this decade, it is unlikely given the history that U.S. policymakers will do much to liberalize legal entry of low-skilled immigrants, let alone address in a meaningful way the nagging problem of the more than 10 million illegal immigrants already here. But as this brief review of U.S. immigration policy should demonstrate, history should also give comfort to elected officials that Americans are much more likely to be accepting of skilled immigrants. As we noted at the outset of this chapter, this group of immigrants is more likely to be entrepreneurial than Americans born here, and for this reason alone, we believe it is long overdue that U.S. immigration policies be designed to welcome and indeed recruit such individuals.

Importing Entrepreneurs: The Options

The option for bringing in more skilled immigrants currently getting the most attention is to expand the numbers permitted temporary entry under the H-1B program. Thus, as policymakers have done before, they could again raise the "global cap"—the total number of immigrants granted H-1Bs—and also certain country-specific caps for countries with the greatest supply of skilled IT and scientific workers that U.S. employers need but cannot fill with U.S. citizens alone (India, China, and countries in Eastern Europe, for example).

However useful H-1B immigrants may be for large existing employers, they are of little or no use for entrepreneurial firms, which typically either don't have the economies of scale to pay for the legal expenses associated with bringing in temporary foreign workers or, more problematically, don't have the comfort or luxury of being able to plan sufficiently ahead to wait for them to arrive. Of even more importance to the subjects addressed here, H-1Bs are essentially useless for immigrants who want to start and grow a business in this country since the visas are tied to the particular employers who sponsor the visa recipients and, in any event, lapse after six years, making it virtually impossible for temporary residents to launch a new firm here—especially one with significant growth potential.

Accordingly, any immigration reform that will meaningfully add to the pool of entrepreneurs here must overhaul the granting of *permanent* visas, not temporary ones. The most ambitious of these options, which has attracted attention in some quarters of Congress and among some analysts, venture capitalists, and other interested parties, would be simply to staple green cards to all diplomas from U.S. universities handed out to foreign students.[16] There are variations of this idea. Green cards could be attached to any kind of diploma in any subject, to undergraduate and/or graduate degrees, or to degrees in certain fields (science, technology, engineering, and math, or "STEM") which are likely to generate many, if not most, of the next big innovations.

Current foreign student enrollments give some idea of the minimum numbers involved with variations of this "diploma visa." We say minimum because the prospect of gaining a green card with a U.S. university no doubt would attract more foreign students to study and obtain their degrees in the United States, an outcome that should be welcomed. A starting number for the diploma visa discussion is the approximately 125,000 foreign residents earning university degrees (undergraduate and graduate) in the United States annually, of which roughly 60,000 are in science and engineering.[17]

If any version of the "diploma" green card is viewed to be too politically risky, there is an obvious fallback that should not be: a new visa for entrepreneurs. There are variations of this idea as well. In 2010, Senators John Kerry and Richard Lugar introduced the "Startup Visa Act," which would have granted a temporary visa to entrepreneurs who receive at least $250,000 in outside financing and hire at least one nonfamily member, and then a green card once their enterprises employ at least five nonfamily members or earn at least $1 million in revenue. The following year, the two senators introduced a more expansive version of their bill that offered three different "doors" to entry into the United States: one tied to third-party capital (at least $100,000); a second for immigrants already here on a temporary H-1B visa or who have graduated with a STEM degree from an American university and meet minimum income ($30,000) or asset thresholds ($60,000), with a much lower third-party capital requirement ($20,000); and a third for foreign company owners whose business has generated at least $100,000 in U.S. sales. The various income, capital, and revenue thresholds are included in the bill to screen out individuals who might simply open a sham business in the United States as a way of getting into the country. Permanent residence in the United States under each of the three options is tied to meeting a minimum job generation number (ranging between three and five nonfamily members) after two years.

The 2011 version of the Kerry-Lugar proposal is a major improvement over the earlier one, and clearly much better than the current EB-5 visa that is available to individuals who bring at least $1 million into the country and invest it in companies here (the threshold is $500,000 if the investment is in an economically distressed area). Only about half of the EB-5 quota of ten thousand immigrants per year is used. The new startup visa (EB-6) would use up the rest of the EB-5 allocation, which is good, but also is a significant limitation.[18]

We see no reason that there should be *any* quota on something like the EB-6 visa, because those who qualify by launching a business in this country *create new jobs* that did not previously exist. Moreover, since immigrants who attend college or graduate school here or are already highly skilled when they arrive in the United States are also well educated, the new businesses they launch are likely to be more technology intensive than the typical business. This outcome is consistent with the need to accelerate the development and commercialization of innovation in this country.

There is an ample supply of immigrants who might qualify for an employment-based entrepreneurship visa: the roughly one million skilled foreign workers here now on temporary H-1B visas who otherwise must go home after six years,[19] as well as the roughly sixty thousand foreign students who each year earn a science or engineering degree at an American university. To be sure, not all of these individuals have the income, assets, or outside investment to qualify for any of the EB-6 "doors" even if there were no quota. This shortcoming could be overcome by dropping the outside investment requirement altogether for the EB-6 and providing instead a phased-in system for immigrants who launch businesses here to receive a one- to two-year temporary visa, then qualify for permanent status once they employ a certain minimum number of nonfamily U.S. workers.

A true "entrepreneur's visa" would create a substantial number of new jobs *without any government or taxpayer expenditure*. For illustrative purposes, if roughly one in ten of the H-1Bs and foreign students launches a U.S. business—about the share of self-employed in this country among all workers—and each hires one employee, a true "job creators" visa could generate at least one hundred thousand new jobs. The number could be higher given immigrants' propensity to launch firms at a greater rate than native-born Americans, or the fact that the typical employer firm has more than one employee.

To its credit, the Obama administration took some administrative steps in August 2011 to liberalize several entrepreneurship-related visas without seeking legislation, which as discussed next has thus far run into a political buzz saw. The notable regulatory changes include a clarification that holders of H-1B visas can work for themselves as well as others (but still this visa is a temporary one); an easing of the labor certification requirements surrounding the EB-2 visas, which some immigrant entrepreneurs with "exceptional ability in the sciences, arts, or business" have used in the past; and improvements in the process for approving the existing entrepreneur's visa, the EB-5. But each of these visa categories still has a numerical cap, and thus fails to take full advantage of the brainpower and energy from around the world that ideally the United States could harness by letting a lot more immigrant entrepreneurs into this country. For this to happen, Congress must approve legislative changes to our broken immigration system.

The Politics of Immigration

It almost goes without saying that the key impediment to constructive improvement of U.S. immigration law and policy is purely political. Elected officials, who may readily understand the virtues of not only letting in more highly skilled immigrants but actively recruiting them, fear being tarred as supporting measures to give scarce U.S. jobs to foreign residents.

At bottom, this is a marketing problem that can be overcome. In politics, as in markets, the key to "selling" a particular change in policy is couching it in the right words. An entire industry of political consultants has grown up to advise politicians on how to do this. Perhaps the best example of a small change in wording—from the "estate tax" to the "death tax"—persuaded Congress and a large majority of the American people to support a major rate reduction and a steady increase in the deductible for the estate tax in 2001.[20] It is somewhat remarkable to us that no political consultant appears to have yet provided an equally effective way of changing the terms of the immigration debate.

At the risk of invading a field beyond our expertise, but at the same time believing that political marketing is not exactly rocket science, we think that a healthy majority of Americans would support liberalized immigration policies for highly skilled immigrants if those policies were sold as a way to *create more jobs for Americans* and/or *outcompete other countries*. This ties in directly to the current political mantra of "jobs, jobs, jobs."

The job creation argument is easiest to make for any visa program targeted specifically at entrepreneurs, especially if the visa is linked directly to job creation. Elected officials should be able easily to explain to voters that under such a program, immigrants are only let into the country on a more-than-temporary basis if they actually hire Americans (or immigrants already here with permanent work permits). Indeed, such a visa for this reason might be better labeled a "job creator's visa" rather than an "entrepreneur's" or "startup" visa.

A broader visa reform linking work permits to the completion of a degree at a U.S. university is a bit more difficult to sell as a job creation program, even though the data establish that immigrants found new businesses at a higher rate than native-born Americans, and that immigrant founders tend to have more education than natives.[21] Nonetheless, Americans admire the hard work it takes to complete a course of education, especially a graduate degree. And so it should be possible to sell a broader degree-based visa program as a way of boosting innovation and thus economic growth.

A second but not mutually exclusive way to market the immigration proposals is to highlight the fact that if we fail to loosen our restrictions on visas for highly skilled immigrants, *we will be outcompeted by other countries* that already have been vying for this talent, including some of the home countries from which many of the skilled workers temporarily here have emigrated. As economists, we have some hesitancy in advancing this "competitiveness" argument, since economic growth is not a zero-sum game. All countries benefit when each one grows. Likewise, the world is better off regardless of where talented individuals choose to work or start a business.

Nonetheless, there is a good economic case to be made that the world *and the United States* are both better off if talented individuals wanting to start or work for a company or organization on the cutting edge of technology can pursue these opportunities in the United States rather than other countries more welcoming to highly skilled immigrants (such as Canada), including their home countries. Although a few other countries may rank more highly in the World Bank's "Doing Business" reports that grade the regulatory costs of starting and running a business, none has the economic heft and market size of the United States. In addition, even taking account of the flaws we discuss in Chapter 6, no other country has as well developed a system for financing startups as the United States. And while universities in other countries are catching up, as we discuss shortly, the United States still leads the world by a large margin in university education and research.

In short, the United States still has the best overall entrepreneurial ecosystem of any country in the world, which means that all else being equal, a skilled entrepreneur is more likely to be successful starting his or her company in the United States than in any other country. From a global welfare perspective, therefore, this argues strongly for having skilled immigrants with entrepreneurial inclinations launch their enterprises in the United States rather than in their home countries (or in third countries). The U.S. venue would also be better for the entrepreneurs themselves, as well as for the United States, even if not all the workers hired by such firms were based in the United States. Any additional employment would be a plus for the country, in addition to profits generated by these firms.

Whatever steps U.S. policymakers take to secure these outcomes, other nations are not sitting idly by. On the contrary: some are already actively competing for talent. Australia, for example, has long welcomed and indeed sought out skilled immigrants. Canada has a point system based largely on skills. Two of the leading source countries for U.S. immigrant entrepreneurs—India and China—are now increasingly and successfully wooing their best and brightest who have come to the United States, often on temporary H-1B visas, to return home to pursue their ventures. Indeed, increasing numbers of U.S.-based venture capital firms have financed startups in those two countries and some even have opened offices in India and China, staffed heavily by locals who have strong networks within on-site entrepreneurial ecosystems.

The global competition for brains—and ultimately for entrepreneurial fervor—is being fought on the educational front as well. As our colleague Ben Wildavsky painstakingly documents in his book *The Great Brain Race,* university education is rapidly being globalized. U.S. universities are expanding with satellite campuses to other countries, while universities abroad are actively competing for both students and faculty from any location. Countries that enable university graduates to remain and work after they complete their degrees are obviously much better positioned than those, like the United States currently, that only permit immigrant students to finish their studies and then force them to return home.

Certainly the boldest experiment in immigration going on right now is the new Start-Up Chile program, which is actually *paying three hundred immigrant entrepreneurs $40,000 each* to come to Chile each year for a six-month trial period to launch their businesses in the country, after which they can stay if they want. The program is highly competitive. Chile is looking for individuals who can start scale companies with a global reach, using Chile as a physical platform. We are told that over half of the successful immigrants who have qualified for the program through late 2011 were Americans. This is a canary in the coal mine if there ever was one. As other countries introduce some form of Chile's idea—and we bet that many eventually will—the United States will be losing some of its best entrepreneurs to other countries. Although U.S. consumers eventually will benefit from the new commercial ideas these individuals introduce into the global marketplace, the companies themselves, at least initially, will generate jobs in foreign lands that could have been generated here. Perhaps it will take a jolt like this to break the political logjam that so far has prevented meaningful immigration reform that brings more job creators and innovation to the United States and lets them stay.

Conclusion

Even though immigration policy in general may be the new third rail in American politics, it should not, and indeed need not, impede constructive reform of U.S. immigration laws that will promote innovation and growth. Americans understand the language of jobs and outcompeting other countries. Welcoming and even recruiting skilled immigrants, especially those wanting to launch a business in the United States, can be—and is—both good economics and good politics.

6

IMPROVING ENTREPRENEURIAL FINANCE

Ask most entrepreneurs what one thing they want and think they need most, and the answer you will probably get is simple: money— preferably not their own, ideally at a low price (a low rate of interest if a loan, or only a small piece of their company if equity). Our experience and academic research indicate that this is wrong. As we discussed in Chapter 3, what is most important for entrepreneurs is having the right *network*— which may *lead* them to sources of money, but equally if not more important, to potential partners, mentors, employees, suppliers, and customers.

Still, money is important for almost all startups and young growing companies—to pay for legal expenses, market research, hiring the right people, and so on—and so it is not coincidental that in writing this book about "Better Capitalism" after the nation's worst financial crisis in over seven decades, we address whether and how the financing of high-growth companies in America can be improved.

This is not an easy issue to address because of a major data problem: we only know high-growth companies in retrospect. What data exist refer to all small business, and what data we have for high-growth companies in particular, such as those on the Inc. 500 list of the most rapidly growing companies in America, suffer from the problem of selection bias: we don't know or can't observe the financing patterns of *would-be* growth companies that didn't make it. So we must make inferences, using our judgment and experience and that of our Kauffman Foundation colleagues with entrepreneurial backgrounds, and drawing on our reading of the relevant literature (much of it authored by the Kauffman Foundation's research grantees).

This book was written largely during the aftermath of the 2007–8 financial crisis and the slow recovery, during which the lack of capital—both debt and equity—for small and especially new business has been a major economic and political issue. Overall business lending by banks fell or was stagnant through 2011, but we have no good breakouts on lending to new businesses at their launch and during their early years. All of this is complicated by the fact that much bank lending acquired by new and small business is not classified as such, but is carried out through personal credit card borrowing (and before the real estate bust, by residential mortgages and home equity lines of credit) that does not show up in business loan statistics.

The data for equity injected into new businesses are little better. Most firms are launched with the entrepreneurs' own funds, investments from friends and family, and as we discuss shortly, with bank credit. But still there are no good data sources that track all of these fund flows into new business.

The best data relating to investments in new companies cover equity injections made by venture capital firms, but this activity represents only a tiny share (much less than 1 percent) of the roughly six hundred thousand businesses formed each year. This is especially true since the Internet bust, which has caused venture firms to be far more gun-shy about making "seed" investments, or those that help form companies. As shown in Figures 6.1 and 6.2, what venture money is going into new firms has drastically declined over the last decade, and is shifting into later, less-risky rounds of financing.[1] We have much more to say about venture finance, its importance, and its future, later in this chapter.

Many startups—how many is uncertain—also receive equity infusions from "angel investors," third parties they may or may not have known previously who want to get in on the ground floor of promising businesses. There are many definitions of this term, which makes the money they invest virtually impossible to track reliably. Indeed, there is no official time series for angel investment, although various federal surveys and some academic scholars have attempted to measure these flows at different points in time. Nonetheless, the conventional definition covers wealthy

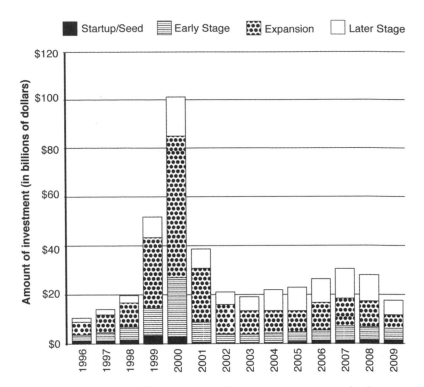

Figure 6.1 Total Amount of Venture Capital Investments 1996–2009 by Stage
Source: National Venture Capital Association 2010 Yearbook

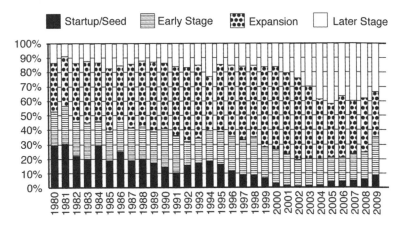

Figure 6.2 Ratio of Venture Capital Investments 1980–2009 by Stage
Source: National Venture Capital Association 2010 Yearbook

individuals, most often successful entrepreneurs themselves, who provide both money and counsel to new firms in their early stages.[2]

However the term is defined, it is widely accepted that angel investment also dropped, most likely sharply, during the recession and has yet to fully recover.[3] This is both because angel investors themselves suffered a loss of wealth during the financial crisis (and again in the stock market drop over the summer of 2011) and because their appetite for risk—along with that of investors generally—has diminished in the slow economy since the Great Recession. Likewise, entrepreneurs themselves suffered losses during the crisis, which reduced their financial capacity to launch new businesses (although, as discussed in Chapter 2, the number of new businesses launched actually increased after 2008, it is likely that this increase reflected an unusual influx of "necessity" entrepreneurs, or unemployed individuals who couldn't find stable new jobs).

A key question, of course, is whether all these downtrends are temporary or permanent. Surely, some parts are temporary and related to the business cycle. As the recovery—slow as it is—continues, some wealth and appetite for risk taking will be restored. But there also seem to be some significant changes in the market for entrepreneurial capital that are likely to be lasting. After all, total venture capital committed to new businesses even before the crisis began in 2007 was down significantly from several years before. Likewise, as we will discuss shortly, the returns from venture investments to the suppliers of these funds—their limited partners—also, with a few exceptions, were poor throughout the preceding decade. Although venture capital is only the tip of the entrepreneurial financial iceberg, we suspect that if something is amiss in this tip, it reflects something deeper going on with seed financing more broadly.

It is not a coincidence, for example, that in the entrepreneurial world one constantly hears about the "Valley of Death"—the inability of innovative companies, once started, to raise the several hundred thousand or million dollars that could enable them to prove the commercial viability of their concept. Or a common refrain from startups between the two coasts complaining of the "flyover problem" in venture or angel capital financing—that money sources too frequently and unfairly ignore many worthy deals launched beyond the zip codes of Silicon Valley, Route 128 around Boston, the nation's heartland, or the South. In short, many entrepreneurs and policymakers believe, rightly or wrongly, that as successful as the market for entrepreneurial capital has been in this country, it still fails to connect worthy ideas and entrepreneurs with the money they need to get started and grow.

The often-heard answer to this sort of problem, of course, is for government to step in with funds of its own, hence the increase in the number of states providing some sort of income tax credit for angel investment in companies in their states. Other states even have launched venture funds of their own. And, of course, the largest governmental experiment in venture capital in recent years has been the Department of Energy's multi-billion-dollar investment in various clean-tech projects and companies, a program that was included in the 2009 federal stimulus package.

These efforts are too new to have been subjected to rigorous evaluation, although the highly publicized failure of the $500 million-plus loan guarantee for Solyndra, a topic we return to later in the chapter, certainly has cast doubt on the whole effort. Even if other government-assisted projects prove worthy, we remain skeptical of the long-run usefulness of government funding for clean tech or entrepreneurship more generally. The state angel tax credits and the few state venture funds are too small to have a material effect on overall entrepreneurial activity. The DOE program is much larger, but a large share of its funding has been doled out in small amounts to particular firms to support employment rather than fund breakthrough technologies. In any event, the DOE venture capital experiment is a one-off event unlikely to be repeated, not only because of the change in the political environment since the stimulus bill was enacted, but more importantly because of the downward pressure on federal spending that will be exerted for the foreseeable future by large and expanding federal budget deficits.

But just because government *financing* may—and we believe should—play a limited role in funding entrepreneurial ventures doesn't mean either that *private* financing is sufficient to support a new wave of worthy entrepreneurial ventures, or that government *policies* are irrelevant to *private-sector* financing decisions (they are not). As we will show in this chapter, the business of entrepreneurial finance—especially for new, potentially high-growth companies—is undergoing a major and necessary transformation. Once the growing pains associated with that reinvention subside, the United States will have a new and vibrant financial engine for financing new growth companies. That engine will work even better, especially for new companies requiring significant capital commitments, if federal research financing policies are changed while the rules governing the raising of equity capital are modernized and made more friendly to financing new growth companies (as happened as this book was being completed, discussed shortly).

The Stages of Entrepreneurial Finance

Companies are like human beings in many ways—they have births, growing stages and pains, and mature adulthood—and if the successors to their founders are smart and lucky, companies can live on (unlike humans) under different management teams and boards of directors (if they are public). The financing needs of companies are very different at each of these stages as well. Before turning to the propositions about the current and potential future changes in entrepreneurial finance that we have just previewed, we first step back to provide an overview of how new companies generally are funded.

In particular, we find it constructive to distinguish three separate financing stages: at the start of the enterprise, during its early growth, and if the firm is highly successful, during its rapid growth phase (the steep upward slope of an "S" curve). For data we draw on the Kauffman Firm Survey (KFS), the nation's only longitudinal database of new firms, and an extensive analysis by Alicia Robb and David Robinson of the financing of these firms. KFS is based on roughly five thousand firms that were launched in 2004 (a good year in retrospect because it was during the middle of the last expansion, and thus not an unusually "down" or "up" year), with an oversample for high-technology firms as a way of capturing potential high-growth firms.[4]

Most entrepreneurs begin their enterprises with their own money, saved or borrowed. Each of these sources has suffered in the wake of the financial crisis. Financial and housing wealth are down (though equities have bounced back since the bottom in early 2009), while borrowing lines for credit cards and home equity have been cut back or eliminated. Indeed, at this writing, roughly one in four homes in America are "underwater"—

that is, the market value of the house doesn't cover the mortgage. Still, many entrepreneurs can and do tap their credit card lines as an important source of start-up capital. According to Robb and Robinson, one-fourth of new firms are funded to some degree by the entrepreneurs' personal debt, and this overwhelmingly tends to come from credit card borrowing.

More important, and perhaps contrary to conventional wisdom, the KFS survey documents that new company founders rely mostly on other, more formal bank loans and lines of credit to fund their enterprises.[5] They do this to a greater extent than tapping friends and family for start-up funds. Indeed, seven times as many firms report accepting debt from third parties as from outside equity. This finding implies that only a very small fraction of new firms are funded by angel investment, and an even lower proportion (surely less than 1 percent) are financed by venture capital (even this fraction, for reasons already indicated, is itself down since the bursting of the Internet and tech bubble of the late 1990s).

The successful firms that grow and eventually hire employees to help meet the demand for their products or services finance that growth in various ways. Formal bank loans start becoming available to firms that have both revenues and hard assets, such as inventories of parts and final products, to pledge as collateral. The KFS survey shows that, in fact, firms launched with either equity, debt, or some combination, on average continue to rely on some debt as they mature.[6] At the same time, some firms "bootstrap" by using revenues to finance growth without going to outside sources, thus diluting the equity of the founders and their backers or incurring debt. The rare few, mostly in software- or Internet-related businesses that promise "early exits" at substantial multiples for their investors, attract formal venture capital in so-called "Series A, B, or C" rounds (the letters denote the stages at which outside equity is sought and the company revalued).

The third stage of new company financing is relevant only to the very few companies whose products or services, or both, are in such explosive demand that they must grow very rapidly, or die. Such companies have three choices: borrowing; issuing stock either in a private offering (which until April 2012 meant that the total number of shareholders had to remain below five hundred, a limitation that has since been raised to two thousand) or in a public offering (the much more common route); or selling out to a larger company capable of taking the firm to the next level. With the exception of the handful of capital-intensive companies in businesses such as energy supply, few companies experiencing rapid growth would be able or want to borrow for expansion. The only realistic alternatives are to issue more equity, preferably in a public offering where demand for new stock is likely to be the greatest, or sell out. Yet if significant expansion is the true goal of the company's founders rather than instant liquid wealth, a sale of the company is not really an option either, since there is no guarantee that the buyer would expand the business at all, or in ways that the founders would prefer. That is why properly functioning securities markets—which are necessary for private companies to "go public"—are critical for fostering the growth of the home run companies (or even doubles or triples) that the broad economy needs to sustain and increase its rate of growth.

The Transformation in Finance for High-Growth Startups

Even before the financial crisis, two concerns about entrepreneurial finance—especially the funding of potential high-growth companies—were much in the public consciousness. As highlighted at the outset of this chapter, one worry was that venture capital investment—especially for startups—was down significantly, portending to some a decline in the risk appetite of investors, a drop in the number of worthy deals, or both. The second complaint focused on the decade-long slump (with some moderate rebound) in initial public stock offerings by private companies wanting to access the public capital markets.

We have some unconventional views on each of these matters. In this section, we address the concerns surrounding venture capital, which we believe to be largely misplaced. In the next section, we examine the more serious concerns relating to the drop in IPOs, but offer a different explanation and remedies than are commonly found in discussions of this topic.

We focus on venture capital because, in many minds, it is coincident with entrepreneurship itself, especially high-growth entrepreneurship. In perhaps the most comprehensive analysis of the subject to date, Harvard Business School professors Paul Gompers and Joshua Lerner documented that between 1972 and 2000, venture capital helped fund more than two thousand companies that eventually went public and, by the end of that period, had an aggregate market capitalization exceeding $2.7 trillion, or 32 percent of the total value of all public companies at that date.[7] The trade association of venture capital firms, the National Venture Capital Association, has since expanded on this work, claiming that in 2008, venture-backed firms collectively accounted for over $2.9 trillion in revenues and 11 percent of the economy's private-sector employment.[8] The strong implication of reported statistics like these is that the initial venture financing was somehow responsible for all of the beneficent results later generated by these companies.

This, of course, is a gross exaggeration. Any such contention disregards the effectiveness of hiring, product development, marketing, subsequent financing, and other company decision making by founders or their managerial successors in validating the venture investors' initial growth expectations. Likewise, the broad claim of the importance of venture capital ignores any number of other "but for" causes, including but not limited to the idea behind the company, the education of the founders, and so on, that could claim to be just as important as any initial venture investment. Moreover, venture firms and their limited partners typically sell their shares once their companies go public, which weakens any claim that venture financing is responsible for the *subsequent* success of those firms.

We do not mean by this to minimize the important role of venture capital in facilitating the rise and success of entrepreneurial capitalism—and thereby fueling the U.S. economy—especially in information technology (IT) and Internet-related companies that were able to promise quick payoffs to the limited partners of venture firms. Yet as important as it has become, IT is not the only driving force behind the growth of the American economy. Far more companies have launched and displayed rapid growth in the much more mundane sectors of construction, manufacturing, finance, retail, health care, and other service endeavors, which collectively generate most of the output of the U.S. economy. And the lion's share of the new high-growth companies in these sectors *did not* start with venture capital. To the contrary, the best count we know of suggests that just 16 percent of them were financed this way.[9]

Moreover, however important venture capital was to many successful IT and Internet *startups* in the 1980s and 1990s, the Internet bust changed all that. As noted at the outset of this chapter, both the total amount of venture funds raised and the total amount invested have plummeted since then, and of the venture monies committed this past decade, far greater proportions have gone to later financing rounds for companies that have already proven their mettle.

With venture capital firms taking less risk, one would expect their rewards, or rates of return to limited partner investors, to have fallen. And that is exactly what has happened. According to the best data available, the venture industry yielded returns in the decade following the Internet bust of just sixty basis points above the S&P 500, which itself provided no net returns to investors over the same period.[10] Moreover, what positive returns have been recorded by the industry as a whole can be attributed to a very limited number of venture capital firms. Based on the Kauffman Foundation's experience with venture investing—and true to the entrepreneurial roots of the foundation's creator, Ewing Kauffman, the foundation has been among the nation's leading investors in this "asset class"—virtually all of the positive returns in the industry over the past decade have been generated by just the top 10 percent of venture firms. The rest of the industry—or nearly all of it—has been a net drag for investors during this period.

There is a view that the drop in venture fundraising and investments is an expected cyclical event. If this perspective is correct, then as the economy recovers, so too will the volume of venture capital raised and the number of companies funded.[11] We disagree. The inability of roughly 90 percent of venture firms to earn a positive return even in a decade, especially with fewer risks taken in their financing decisions, is a damning indictment of the current venture financial model's viability. This is especially true for seed funding, from which, as we have indicated, venture firms already have largely disappeared.

In fact, the venture finance model itself seems ripe for change. Venture funds are established by general partners who raise money from limited partners, and charge management fees for doing so. The typical fee structure is "two and twenty." The "two" refers to the 2 percent of asset fee that the general partners charge regardless of the fund's performance. The "20" denotes the 20 percent "carry" of any annual profits. The carry provisions, on the surface, seem to align incentives of the funds' general partners with those of their limited partner investors. But a closer look reveals that this is not necessarily the case.

Under the typical venture arrangement, the general partners receive their 20 percent bonus *annually,* often on a per-deal basis, which means that they can take home big winnings in the one or two years their fund has strong exits, even though over the lifetime of the fund (typically ten years), exits and the profits earned on them may fall. This is a perverse outcome, and one that unfortunately is all too real.[12] The Kauffman Foundation's experience with the venture funds in which it has invested (with more than forty different general partners in nearly one hundred different funds over the years) is that, on average, venture funds record their highest returns to investors in the first two years of the fund, with returns in subsequent years falling off sharply—often negative in absolute value. This pattern reflects the likelihood that the general partners have already identified the most successful target companies before their funds are actually established, and then essentially throw darts in years after that. This would account for the well-known fact that fund managers are pleased if they can "bat .200," or hit home runs on two out of every ten investments. That batting average seems to be earned entirely with the first two annual "pitches," with strikeouts thereafter. Given that fund managers make much, if not most, of their money from the 2 percent annual management fee, this gives them a powerful incentive to post strong early returns from the funds they currently are managing in order to demonstrate their investment prowess to investors in the general partners' *next* funds. On the strength of their early returns, the partners do what the 2 percent of asset management fee structure encourages them to do: raise more money so they can earn even more fees.

These features represent to us a deep structural flaw in the current venture model that is not cyclical and not likely to disappear as the economy recovers. To be sure, limited partners have pressured some funds to drop the absolute amount of their fees, given the firms' disappointing investment performance. But we have yet to see major changes in the investment patterns of most funds—that is, the initial positive spike in performance followed by subpar returns thereafter.

Likewise, it is a mistake to confuse the general partners of venture firms with the entrepreneurs themselves. Venture GPs have unique skills which clearly deserve some reward, not so much in identifying winners (many would even admit to that), but in using their networks to help fledgling but potentially high-growth companies realize that potential by linking them with executive leaders, suppliers, advisers (accountants and lawyers), and customers, among other important parties. This is entrepreneurship of a sort, but it should not be equated with the innovations of the companies they support and which the economy requires to maintain and ideally increase its rate of growth.

Looking ahead, then, the real issue confronting the economy is not whether the venture capital industry will return to its former status, but instead where the seed money for high-growth enterprises will come from as the recovery continues. In particular, has the Great Recession permanently downshifted the risk appetites of angel investors and serial entrepreneurs? If so, is there a way to change these attitudes?

We have some tentative answers to these questions, and they are surprisingly positive. As early as the summer of 2010, we and our colleagues at the Kauffman Foundation began to detect a new "seed capital industry" developing out of a rising number of successful cashed-out entrepreneurs turned angel investors. This new class of "super-angels," formalized as part of a new network, AngelList, is posing strong competition to traditional venture capital firms that rely on general partners to manage other peoples' money. The new super-angel seed model of finance instead consists of successful entrepreneurs *using their own money* to fund new companies, often investing in the ventures launched by other successful serial entrepreneurs they know, and frequently in many others in small amounts, hoping that a few of these "lottery tickets" really pay off. Because they are using their own funds, super angels do not need to pay a management fee or carry to someone else, but instead earn their returns directly. Moreover, these super angels as a group have just as much, if not more, networking power than the venture firms, and certainly more direct entrepreneurial experience. The new super angels use trusted third parties to screen deals, or, because of their personal networks, many deals come directly to them.

There are no publicly available data yet on the amounts of money committed by the members of AngelList, but given the prominence of the members, it is likely to be a large and growing figure. By one unpublished account, the impact of AngelList is already substantial. Through May 2011, about 500 of the group's 850 total investors had individually and collectively financed 310 startups.[13] To this must be added the monies committed by individual angels and the growing number of angel groups (now roughly 200) that belong to and are assisted by the Angel Capital Alliance (an organization birthed at the Kauffman Foundation several years ago).

Given the advantages of the super angels, we strongly suspect they and others like them will eventually (if they have not already) replace much formal venture capital as the primary source of seed equity for many new high-growth companies, especially those that require limited capital and promise relatively rapid scaling and thus potentially quick exits, such as new Internet-related firms. Indeed, because of the size of organizations such as AngelList, the companies they fund may not need to go to other venture firms for later rounds of financing, but instead—once having proved themselves—can tap the AngelList members for these additional funds. This implies a shrinking role for the more traditional venture firms in the future. Furthermore, the returns from venture backing of later financing rounds almost surely will be lower than from successful seed investing, as the past decade has demonstrated. Indeed, we would not be surprised to see the most successful venture capitalists of the recent past join their wealthy brethren in AngelList or branch out on their own by investing their wealth directly in new companies.

At the same time, just as relatively few high-growth companies in the past were launched with venture capital, we suspect the same will be true in the future even with a more effective angel structure in place. That is, the majority of new high-growth companies will continue to be financed by entrepreneurs themselves, with some help from friends, family, and banks, however successful the new super-angel model of seed finance turns out to be.

One natural question to ask is whether we might see money begin to flow to entrepreneurs via social or matching networks. Already, for example, there are stories of some companies being funded through entrepreneurs' contacts on LinkedIn, a prominent business-oriented social network. Might the Internet do for equity and debt investing what it has done for social networking?

For a long time, we were dubious. Although Internet platforms such as Prosper.com, Kiva, and Kickstarter, which enable those with funds to provide loans and grants to new ventures in limited quantities, have been growing rapidly in popularity, we are among those who questioned whether individuals, even wealthy ones, would invest *equity* in new companies they would know about only by looking at a web page. After all, unlike a loan, whose performance can be easily monitored by the lender, who is entitled to receive regular interest payments, the equity investor must wait for some "liquidity event"—a sale of the company or an initial public offering—or for some third party to buy their shares, which are likely to be difficult to resell. Our minds began to change, however, during the debate over the "crowdsourcing" provisions of the JOBS Act, which quickly passed by large bipartisan majorities in the House and Senate and was signed into law by President Obama in early April 2012 (we discuss other features of this important legislation shortly). As that debate was under way, Facebook announced that it was creating a place on its website where companies might be able to raise funds, a strong indication that there will be a market for crowdfunding and the platforms that facilitate it. Our conversations with entrepreneurs have only reinforced this judgment.

Critics of crowdfunding, which the JOBS Act essentially exempted from the securities laws, believe it is an invitation to fraud. This is a legitimate concern, but one which we believe has been minimized through a number of restrictions written into the JOBS Act (mostly added by the Senate). For one thing, there are limits, tied to investors' income and assets, to how much they can invest in a crowdfunded company. The company itself may raise only $1 million per year in this manner, and do so only through a third-party platform that is registered with the SEC. Companies that raise funds this way also are subject to liability for misrepresentation, like public companies. Finally, and most important in our view, the crowdfunding platforms have their reputations to protect and will want to make efforts to screen out fraudsters, while entrepreneurs will have strong market-driven incentives to develop methods for assuring investors of the companies' trustworthiness, as will the companies themselves.

Should Government Step Into the Financing Breach? If So, How?

A critical question remains, however: Who is going to finance the launch of new science-heavy but also capital-intensive companies—in pharmaceuticals, medical devices, or clean energy, to name a few—which angel investors may not be willing or able to finance? One knee-jerk answer to this "Valley of Death" financing problem is that either or both federal and state government should step in to fill the void. In fact, many states already have established venture funds for this purpose. We already expressed our skepticism about any level of government being able to pick winning companies and ideas any more successfully than even the imperfect market. One potential way around this problem is to limit government venture funding only to ideas that are backed by an equivalent or larger amount of private money. But even this idea, which Israel successfully used to help attract U.S. venture funds to the country, has its limits. How is the government to choose between projects if it has more applications for funds than money? Moreover, unlike Israel in the 1980s, which did not then have a thriving venture industry and used the matching requirement to help stimulate one, the United States' venture industry is well established (although for reasons we have just discussed, it is probably in secular decline). The danger of establishing matching requirements in such environments is that venture funds will seek government support for their least promising projects, keeping their most likely "winners" entirely to themselves. Even Israel avoided this problem by ending its matching program once a venture industry had been established in the country.[14]

Government venture funding or loan guarantees for specific companies have had an even more checkered history in the United States. These programs seem to have been especially attractive for backing companies in the energy industry, with some dismal results. The billion-dollar government loans for synthetic fuels in the late 1970s were debacles. Forty years later, the government's $535 million loan guarantee in 2009 for Solyndra, a solar energy company, turned sour. The guarantee was made with much fanfare at its announcement in 2009 (by both the president and vice president), yet only two years later, in September 2011, the company declared bankruptcy.

We believe there is a more effective way that government can help solve the financing problems of potentially high-growth but capital-intensive companies, without the political controversy and doubtful effectiveness of direct government subsidies. That answer is either to eliminate capital gains taxes for investments in new companies that are held for a minimum number of years, as the Obama administration proposed in 2011, or to restructure capital gains taxes so they phase out for early-stage investments in new companies held after some substantial time period. So, for example, an investment held for six years might be taxed at 17.5 percent (modestly below the current 20 percent rate, at this writing), one held for seven years at 15 percent, and so on, until the tax rate is zero for investments held for twelve years. We are not wedded to this precise formula, but the idea of lower tax rates on committed investments in early-stage companies would specifically address the problems faced by companies requiring more capital for longer periods than the typical Internet startup.[15] By one estimate, a capital gains exemption for investments held in startups held for at least five years would induce more new seed investment in startups ($750 million annually) than the revenue lost to the Treasury ($500 million per year).[16] A more general tax incentive helps guide the market without pretending to pick specific winners, which is difficult enough as it is for private investors, and even more difficult for government officials who may lack the necessary expertise or inevitably will be subject to political pressures to channel funds to favored firms.

One particular class of investors that may benefit from a permanent capital gains incentive for startups (in addition to the conventional list of entrepreneurs, angel investors, and partners of venture firms) includes large corporations that either have a venture arm or seek to spin off new companies. We believe spinoffs should be encouraged because, by its nature, the bureaucratic management structure at many large firms is incapable of spawning or supporting individuals within the organization who have bright ideas for new ventures. Endless layers of committees or the desire of an existing business not to render obsolete its existing product or service line may stop a good idea and the "intrepreneur" behind it dead in their tracks. As a result, frustrated originators of new business ideas must often leave their company if they want to turn the ideas into reality. This helps explain the surprising finding that the median age of technology and engineering enterprise founders is thirty-nine and not the proverbial twenty-something college dropout.[17] There are exceptions to this apparent need for would-be entrepreneurs to leave their employers in order to launch their businesses—notably 3M, which famously gives intrepreneurs seed capital, an operating budget, and a new division to try out their ideas (reportedly this is how Post-it® notes were invented)—but these models are not the rule.

A zero or limited capital gains tax for new ventures could help change this pattern and make it the norm for many existing companies. These enterprises can give experienced employees who know their business and have excellent social networks the missing ingredient—sufficient start-up capital to get going—that many may not have. The companies can also lend their own networks to make the new ventures successful. Such "strategic" venture starts have a leg up on the stand-alone venture firms or angel investors, who often are not as likely to be as deeply knowledgeable or networked as the existing competitors. Launching spinoffs can also be an important way of keeping valuable employees "in the fold" of large enterprises, whether they succeed (in which case the company's initial and any subsequent investments can pay off big) or fail (in which case the individual may have the option of returning to his or her corporate home). In short, encouraging corporate spinoffs can be good for the firms spun off and for the economy as a whole by facilitating the launch and growth of more successful startups by individuals with industry-specific expertise.

We are acutely aware, of course, of the deep structural federal deficits plaguing the United States, and thus the possibility that lower capital gains rates might add to them. In Chapter 8, we discuss the deficit problem in much greater detail and note that a recent presidential deficit reduction commission has recommended the elimination of all capital gains preferences as one of many ways to bring the structural deficit under control. We would not be opposed to that idea if it was truly part of a package that really did solve the structural deficit problem, given its preeminent importance. However, we also believe that, even then, there is a case for singling out only investments in new enterprises for special capital gains treatment, which would significantly reduce any impact on the deficit. Although we are hesitant to make this claim, since most "tax cuts pay for themselves" arguments are without basis, we nonetheless believe it is conceivable. A targeted capital gains preference only for investments in new companies could really pay for itself over the long run, or come close, if it significantly increased the number of successful growth companies in the process and if proper account is taken of the external benefits of the innovations introduced by those companies, for other firms and for consumers.

The Decline in IPOs and What to Do about It

While the concerns about the decline in venture capital raised and invested are misdirected, those centered on the decline in initial public offerings over the past decade are not. Admittedly, many of the companies at the end of the 1990s that went public shouldn't have. They simply were not ready. But the number of IPOs in recent years has been well below the IPO levels of the mid-1990s when the Internet frenzy had not reached fever pitch, and even many IPOs of late have been foreign firms accessing our capital markets rather than companies born in the United States. As a task force reported to the Treasury in October 2011, IPOs averaged 547 per year in the 1990s, but only 192 since then.[18] Even if there is no decline in the number of IPOs, it will be necessary for more growth companies to go public in the future if the U.S. economy is to significantly increase the annual formation of high-growth companies. Those "home run" companies may never get launched without the prospect of a later equity offering, or many of the new companies that are started are not likely to grow to their potential without being able to tap the public equity markets. We thus need a thriving capital market that does its best to facilitate the growth of future home run companies. We think it is fair to say that few entrepreneurs, investment professionals, or academic scholars believe that the current system meets that test.

For almost a decade, the discussion of this topic has concentrated on the impact of the Sarbanes-Oxley Act (SOX) of 2002 on IPOs. SOX was enacted in the wake of the financial reporting scandals of the late 1990s and early 2000s—Enron and WorldCom in particular. The act added more penalties for misreporting, placed responsibility for the accuracy of financial statements squarely on the shoulders of company CEOs, and, most controversially, added new auditing requirements for public companies, especially those relating to their "internal controls" (a broad term covering a range of procedures and methods companies use to make sure their cash is not going to the wrong places, or worse, being illegally diverted).

SOX has unleashed a torrent of debate and a growing academic literature. Some large companies, and of course the auditing firms that have
benefited from the additional work mandated by the act, defend the law
and say that, even with some of its warts, the legislation brought much-
needed reform to financial reporting. Critics respond that the law was
overkill and in any event largely ineffective because securities laws already
had punished financial fraud for years. More recently, some critics have
noted that SOX failed to prevent the financial crisis that followed only a
few years later, which in part resulted from the ability of large banks to
lawfully hide their toxic mortgage assets in off–balance sheet affiliates.

This debate will surely go on. But one fact about the impact of the law
is uncontested: its internal controls auditing requirement proved to be far
more expensive than originally envisioned. Touted by congressional sponsors to cost companies no more than $100,000 per year, subsequent stud-
ies have found that just this one part of the law costs companies well in
excess of $1 million annually, although the initial costs may have come
down a bit as companies and their auditors have become more familiar
with the requirements.[19]

In 2011, the SEC Office of the Chief Accountant issued a report on the
costs of Section 404 of SOX for smaller public companies (those with
market caps between $75 million and $250 million), claiming compliance
costs had come down.[20] But nowhere in this document did the commission
attempt to weigh the benefits of that section of the act, let alone the rest of
the act, against its benefits. Even though that would have been a worthy
exercise—if at all possible, no legislation should pass nor regulations be
issued unless their benefits are likely to exceed their costs—it is not one
whose outcome will be the same for each and every company. Nor would
such an analysis be conducted by those who really count: those who have
"skin in the game," namely, shareholders of the companies subject to the act.

In any event, to large public companies, $1 million a year is a rounding
error, but to privately held companies seeking to go public, this is a lot of
money. Assuming this is an after-tax cost (that is, the gross cost is roughly
$1.5 million minus about $500,000 for corporate taxes), a $1 million annual
cost translates at a price-to-earnings ratio of 20 into a market valuation of
$20 million (the P/E for new, growing companies could be considerably
higher than 20, implying a much higher market cap equivalent cost than

$20 million). For companies with $100 million in market capitalization seeking to go public, shaving off at least $20 million due to SOX compliance costs is indeed significant.

For this reason, we favor a simple change to SOX. Since SOX was enacted to protect shareholders, why not give shareholders of newly public companies, and perhaps those with a market cap under $1 billion, *the choice* whether to comply with SOX in its entirety, or at a minimum, whether to comply with just its unexpectedly expensive internal controls auditing requirements? If a majority of shareholders believe these requirements enhance investor interest in the company and its stock, they will vote to continue compliance. If not, they will opt out.

Congress took a modestly different course in enacting the JOBS Act. Instead of giving shareholders choice, it established a SOX "on-ramp" by essentially exempting from most SOX rules newly public companies, or those within five years of their IPO, with market capitalization under $700 million or sales less than $1 billion. The Act went further, by raising the "Regulation A" offering exemption for privately held companies wanting to raise equity capital without going public from $5 million to $50 million, and by allowing more public communication before an IPO for companies choosing to go public.

But the Act has not eliminated all of the barriers confronting growing companies seeking to raise more funds, especially those on the verge of wanting to go public. Here we draw on Kauffman Foundation research published in late 2010 painting an unlikely culprit inhibiting some private companies from going public: The rapid growth of certain types of exchange traded funds (ETFs).[21]

ETFs are securities whose values are tied to other underlying financial instruments, initially indexes of stocks, bonds, or commodities, and more recently, baskets of actively traded instruments of this sort, including derivatives such as futures contracts, options, and swaps. Unlike mutual funds, whose net asset values are computed only once a day, after the markets have closed, ETFs are traded like stocks throughout the day, on and off exchanges.

ETFs have two other advantages that have made them increasingly popular with investors. First, their operating expenses tend to be lower than those of mutual funds.[22] Second, because ETFs trade like stocks, investors only pay capital gains taxes if they recognize a gain on the sale of the ETFs themselves. In contrast, mutual fund investors have no control over the timing of purchases or sales of the securities that make up the fund; these decisions are made by the fund managers. As a result, many mutual fund investors were compelled to pay capital gains tax during the financial crisis when stocks generally plummeted, because their fund managers had sold more "winners" than "losers" and the net gains automatically passed through to the investors.

For all these reasons, ETFs have grown in spectacular fashion. In a little more than a decade, their assets under management have skyrocketed from virtually nothing to over $1 trillion. There are now more than 1,100 ETFs to choose from, a number that has continued to grow, while the number of actual stocks traded in the public markets has steadily declined.[23]

But as is so often the case in life, there can be too much of a good thing, and we fear that ETFs, especially those that consist of baskets of newer, small cap stocks, have fallen into this category. Over time, as ETFs have grown in popularity, they have also become more heavily traded. As of late 2010, ETF trades accounted for the majority of all trades on SEC-registered exchanges![24] This is an astounding development, and helps account for another fact: stock prices, even after the financial crisis when "all correlations were expected to go to one," remain highly correlated by historical standards.[25] There can be only one reason for this trend. Stocks are moving together because they are increasingly being packaged and traded into common baskets that are themselves traded—namely into ETFs. Put another way, ETFs are becoming the tail that wags the stock dog, especially for newer companies or those with relatively small total market capitalizations. As money pours into and out of ETFs composed of relatively illiquid underlying stocks, ETF prices effectively determine or heavily influence the prices of those stocks (or other financial instruments), not the other way around.

To illustrate the implications of all this, imagine you are the owner of a rapidly growing company that seeks public financing to keep growing. In addition to the costs of complying with the various securities laws that govern public companies (including SOX), exposing your company to shareholder lawsuits if things go wrong, and being subject to the whims of Wall Street that obsessively focus on your projected and actual quarterly earnings, you now have to consider the impact of being included in one or more ETFs that, *without your company's permission,* nonetheless can add the stock of your company to their portfolios. In a world where the prices of other small cap stocks are being driven by the demand and supply of the ETFs to which they may belong, this means that when your company goes public, your stock price will be driven more by these larger macro factors—especially by rapid-fire, high-frequency traders rather than long-term investors—than by matters specific to your company. It is as if you were about to launch your small boat of a company onto an ocean of capital whose forces you have no hope of ever controlling. Wouldn't you think twice about doing that, or at least give greater consideration to some alternatives—like raising money in a private placement, growing at the pace at which your earnings allow, or perhaps, even more likely, borrowing a bit of money to finance some additional growth? When one of us conducted (with the Kauffman Foundation's chief investment officer, Harold Bradley) some private interviews of company executives and investment professionals, this is exactly what we found.

To be fair, we have no other hard data to confirm or refute the hypothesis that small cap ETFs are discouraging private companies from going public, but the circumstantial evidence we have just highlighted certainly raises suspicions. To put these fears to rest (without, we believe, causing significant harm), we endorse several ideas that would clearly reduce any negative impacts of ETFs on IPOs.

At a minimum, shareholders of new public companies and those below a certain threshold, such as $1 billion in market capitalization, should be given an opt-out right to choose whether their company's stock should belong to an ETF. This effectively would vest a property right in small cap companies—namely in the use of their stock in a broader trading vehicle. A more expansive alternative would be simply to prohibit ETFs from including small cap stocks (new companies and those below a certain size threshold) in their portfolios. Either reform would leave ETFs of more widely and deeply traded financial instruments untouched. In those situations, the markets for the underlying securities, by definition, are sufficiently deep not to generate the "small boat on the ocean" problem that small cap stocks now confront in an investment environment increasingly influenced, if not dominated, by the creation and trading of ETFs.

So far, neither the SEC nor any other federal agency has recognized the connection between small cap ETFs and IPOs. But in early 2011, the SEC was beginning to take notice of the IPO problem more broadly by considering an increase in the number of shareholders (above the then threshold of 499) permitted for privately held companies. Eventually that ceiling was raised (to two thousand) in the JOBS Act, as we have discussed. The higher threshold for defining what it means to be privately held will permit more growing companies to access the capital markets without having to meet costly SEC and other public reporting requirements.

Taken together, the various provisions of the JOBS Act should substantially reduce the costs of raising equity capital for companies seeking to launch and grow their enterprises. The Act represents an important fix to our capital markets laws and one that could make significant advances toward financing the future singles, doubles, triples, and home runs that will be required to permanently lift the nation's economic growth rate. A permanent exemption from capital gains taxes for startup investments held for five years would be an important complement to the securities laws reforms in the JOBS Act.

Removing Other Barriers to Financing High-Growth Entrepreneurship

Earlier we suggested that the most comprehensive way for the government to address the so-called "Valley of Death" problem confronted by founders of businesses that require substantial capital to prove their commercial value, or because the businesses themselves are capital-intensive, would be to gradually phase out or eliminate altogether the capital gains tax for early but long-held equity investments in these enterprises. That commendable reform may not be sufficiently targeted, however, to the very specific kinds of companies that have this financing problem—mostly in the life sciences and clean energy sectors where much trial and error may be involved to prove the merit of an idea.

One type of institution has developed to address this particular problem: the "proof of concept" center (POCC). Variations of this idea have sprung up at different universities. Some are supported by federal money, but private-sector funds also play an important role. In brief, the POCC provides research support for originators of promising scientific break-throughs with broad commercial potential to prove the commercial via-bility of their innovations. These are generally long-shot bets and thus not attractive to venture capital or angel investment. But with enough funds and supporting personnel, the managers of a POCC can make enough bets to produce the few home runs that more than justify the effort.

The Deshpande Center at MIT and the von Liebig Center at the Uni-versity of California, San Diego, are two well-known POCCs that have proven their early mettle and serve as role models for similar centers at other universities. Founded in 2002, the von Liebig Center has funded sixty-six projects and already spun out sixteen startups, four licenses, and over $71 million in investments in spinouts. Similarly, the Deshpande Center has realized twenty new startups that have acquired over $180 mil-lion in capital, from among the eighty projects it has funded. These two centers do far more than just give faculty and researchers money. At their core are mentoring and advisory services that pair university faculty and research staff with experienced entrepreneurs and innovators. Their suc-cess in this approach again demonstrates the importance of networks, not just money, for entrepreneurs and startups.

Given the limits on federal spending for the foreseeable future, we do not advocate unconditional additional federal spending on POCCs. Rather, a more realistic alternative is for the government to *reallocate* some portion of its scientific spending now going to pure basic research to more proof of concept centers capable of attracting matching state government or pri-vate monies. More modestly, there is also a case for some additional real-location of federal monies toward SBIR grants, which, as we discussed in Chapter 3, also have a positive track record. If forced to choose between the two ideas, however, we would put our chips on reallocations for more POCCs.

Conclusion

All business ventures require start-up capital, and growth ven-tures typically require additional financing to catch up to and get ahead of demand. The recent downtrend in venture capital, which on the surface would appear to be troublesome, in fact more likely represents a transition toward a new, potentially more effective way of funding high-potential startups—through the direct investments made by successful entrepreneurs themselves. The more worrisome financing trend is the drop in initial public offerings, because upping the number of high-growth firms will require easier access to the public equity markets. The 2012 JOBS Act is an important step in the right direction. Measures that would reduce the impact of ETFs—an otherwise important financial innovation—on IPOs would also help.

Government can assist the financing of new companies in two other respects: by increasing the after-tax rewards to long-term equity investments in new companies, and by targeted reallocation of federal funds toward proof of concept centers and perhaps some additional research support of new companies.

The Great Recession may have temporarily dulled the risk appetite of some investors, but at the same time it seems to have ushered along a new means of financing new companies. If the federal government can avoid getting in the way of this process, and instead nudge it along with the ideas suggested here, the money to finance ongoing future entrepreneurial revolutions will be there.

7

TOWARD SUSTAINABLE GROWTH

The history of economic growth is heavily intertwined with the history of energy. Our modern way of life, not to mention continued improvements in our well-being, would not be possible without being able to harness nature's fuels in ever more sophisticated ways. To "make things go," to make it possible for increasingly innovative machines and computer chips to do the work of human beings, we must also advance our utilization of energy resources.

More precisely, the transportation sectors throughout most of the world are totally dependent on one single oil-based fuel, gasoline. People in developed societies in particular—their homes, their places of work, and their production facilities—are also entirely dependent on electricity, powered predominantly by coal, natural gas, and, in some countries, nuclear power. Other than electricity generated by falling water (hydropower), so-called renewable sources of energy, like solar, geothermal, and wind power, account for small fractions of electric power—so far.

The more advanced—technologically, socially, economically—we become, the more energy of all types we will use and need. This trend will be true even as we learn to become more energy efficient; that is, to use less energy per unit of output or GDP. Over the past three decades, higher prices plus efficiency standards are responsible for improved efficiency in the U.S. economy. But the global need for energy will grow as developed countries become richer, and even more so as the less-developed countries transform into developed societies.

Precisely because of its importance, controversies and concerns have always surrounded energy, and specifically oil. Does any society have enough of it, and if not, how do we secure it? The quest for oil security led Japan on an expansionist drive throughout the Pacific that ultimately led to its attack on Pearl Harbor and entry into World War II. Lack of oil was one of many factors that led to Germany's defeat in that war.

Almost four decades ago, in the United States in particular, concerns about oil sufficiency surfaced with the publication of *Limits to Growth* by a team of scientists at MIT and the first oil embargo by the oil-producing countries of the Organization of Petroleum Exporting Countries (OPEC).[1] The embargo triggered short-run concerns, but the MIT report implied that one day not only the United States, but the entire world, would run out of oil, bringing modern life as we know it to a halt. Those fears diminished in 1980s and 1990s with the decline in oil prices due to efficiency improvements and the discovery of more oil in both OPEC and non-OPEC countries. However, the worries resurfaced just prior to the 2008 financial crisis when oil prices hit $150 a barrel. Again a chorus claimed that oil production in the United States was nearing or may have passed its "peak." Whatever one thinks about this argument, and there are good reasons given continuing discoveries using advanced drilling and recovery methods to believe it is too pessimistic, the fact remains that the United States is importing oil and will continue to do so, mostly from countries that are autocratically ruled, unfriendly toward the United States, or at best, unreliable allies.[2] There is a broad consensus that the continuing U.S. dependence on oil imports from such countries is increasingly a potential source of economic instability.

Foreign dependence is not the only major concern about energy use. The consensus among scientists is that man-made carbon emissions are contributing to climate change, and that rising carbon levels in the atmosphere will eventually cause higher temperatures that may result in a myriad of ecological shifts. There is a difference in views about how serious these impacts will be, but they could include permanent flooding of many low-lying land areas and changes in weather patterns that could produce droughts and irrevocably alter ecosystems for animals and other living organisms. Some of the projected impacts of climate change, especially warming in many areas, may be benign or even beneficial. Still, widespread concerns exist that the negative effects will outweigh the positive.

There is a conventional set of policy proposals for addressing both these energy policy challenges by reducing the demand for energy (oil in particular) while increasing energy supply. The demand side remedies included higher energy taxes and stiffer conservation standards. The supply side answers include more research and development on alternatives to carbon fuels and relaxed rules on oil drilling.

We outline later in this chapter a very different policy agenda. We ask readers in the meantime to suspend judgment while we first quickly address one important fact about energy that is common to other industries: the critical role of entrepreneurs. It was entrepreneurial risk taking that led to our modern energy-intensive economy, and it will take the same kind of entrepreneurial zeal, guided by the appropriate rules and incentives, to address the energy challenges our society now faces.

The Early Energy Entrepreneurs

Many entrepreneurs have created our modern "energy economy" and any fair accounting would recognize them all. We do so implicitly here. But we believe it is appropriate to single out four giants in particular, two of whom discovered and organized key sources of energy production while the other two pioneered the commercialization of the automobile, the central driver of the demand for oil.

Although he was not the first individual to successfully drill for crude oil—Edwin Drake accomplished this feat in 1859—John D. Rockefeller is by all accounts the pioneer of the modern oil industry. He was the first to establish the nation's (and the world's) first fully integrated oil company, the Standard Oil Company. Founded in 1870, Standard would become by the early 1900s a behemoth, by some estimates controlling upwards of 85 percent of the American oil industry.[3] But the company's business practices, which included price-fixing schemes and other anticompetitive practices, would prompt a backlash from the public and the government. The government's antitrust lawsuit against the company culminated in a famous Supreme Court decision in 1911, finding Standard guilty of various abuses of its monopoly power that led to its dissolution into thirty-four separate companies, among them the "Seven Sisters," many of which have since been merged into other companies. Even today, roughly a century after the Court's decision, the remnants of the Standard Oil decision persist and flourish. ExxonMobil and Chevron, both born of Standard Oil, are among the largest and most profitable companies in the world. By any account, John D. Rockefeller clearly changed the world with his company and was hugely responsible for many of our modern conveniences that have been enabled or powered by oil-based products.

Rockefeller and his many imitators were not long confined to searching for and refining oil in the United States. In the early twentieth century, Standard Oil and its new competitors began searching for oil abroad. The most notable find was in 1938 in Dhahran, Saudi Arabia, which was followed by discoveries of huge reserves—much larger than those found previously in the United States—in other Middle Eastern countries. For decades, host governments passively took royalties while the oil companies exported what they found and searched for more. The beginning of the end to that arrangement happened in 1933 when Saudi Arabia formed Aramco, a joint venture between oil companies active in the area and the Saudi government. As other countries in the region realized the economic power their oil reserves gave them, the tables eventually turned. OPEC was formed in 1960 and made its first real show of power in the fall of 1973 when its members sharply lowered production in response to American support of Israel against Egypt, Jordan, and Syria in the Six-Day War. OPEC has continued to play a large role on the world political and economic stage and is the main reason America's large and growing dependence on oil imports from OPEC countries has played a central role in U.S. foreign and military policy.[4]

The second energy entrepreneur we highlight, Samuel Insull, is less well known than Rockefeller, but he had an equally important impact on the energy industry and, in turn, on the global economy. Although much of what he is remembered for are the accusations of antitrust violations and mail fraud in the 1930s (of which he was acquitted), Insull's main contribution to society was the assembly of the nation's first integrated electricity generation, transmission, and distribution company, Commonwealth Edison.[5] Like many other successful entrepreneurs, Insull did not invent electric power; scientists like Thomas Edison and George Westinghouse take credit for that. But Insull's genius was in his ability to put together electric power generation and distribution into a large commercial apparatus, similar to what Sam Walton and Bill Gates did many decades later for retailing and personal computer operating systems. The organization and mass production of goods and services is an innovation that is often as important as, and perhaps even more vital than, the original invention.

The two other energy entrepreneurs we briefly mention here actually had no hand in discovering or producing energy, but instead were forerunners in commercializing the single innovation that has, more than anything else, made one particular energy source—oil—hugely popular and indeed indispensable. We speak, of course, of the two giants of the auto industry, Henry Ford and Alfred P. Sloan.

Ford, for all his eccentricities and biases, was a genius of manufacturing. He built a huge vertically integrated company that gave consumers the first low-cost car, the black Model-T, the only color in which it was offered. Ford's company is the only one of the thousands of U.S. auto firms since Karl Benz invented the first true automobile in 1885 that has lasted to this day without any government bailouts. Sloan had a different genius: inventing and popularizing annual style changes in automobiles through his company General Motors. His philosophy was the antithesis of Ford's and demonstrated that in autos, as in so many markets, there is room for diverse competitors meeting a wide range of consumer demands.

The cars produced by Ford and General Motors, along with other competitors like American Motors, Studebaker, Chrysler, and Dodge, all ran on gasoline refined from the crude oil discovered by Standard Oil and thousands of other, mostly independent (non-integrated) oil producers. Interestingly, for reasons to be elaborated next, the Ford Model-T was the first commercial "flex-fuel" automobile capable of running on either gasoline or alcohol or any mix of the two, though at the time and for the next century, such a quality was an anomaly.[6] Also of modern interest, numerous entrepreneurs tried their hand at making and selling electric cars, but they all failed due to the main problem still plaguing all electric cars today: limited battery life and therefore limited range.

Toward True Energy Independence: Choice in Transportation Fuels

In the almost four decades since OPEC began to flex its muscles, oil importing nations and their consumers have been wrestling over the appropriate policy responses. Those few countries lucky enough to discover sufficient oil within their own borders or close offshore to satisfy their own needs—such as Norway and Great Britain—are certainly breathing easier. But even they, along with the rest of the oil-consuming world, are still hostages to OPEC because the OPEC producers can vary their production, either in existing wells or in deciding the pace of future drilling. As long as its members maintain unity, which they have done in varying degrees throughout these four decades, OPEC can determine the price of oil by deciding on their collective production. Regardless of how much additional oil the United States may find or how successful it is in conserving oil through taxes or efficiency mandates, this fact will remain true. In short, neither of the main recommendations on energy public policy agenda—conservation or more production or both—would do much, if anything, to curtail OPEC's pricing power as long as it has plenty of excess capacity (already drilled or capable of being drilled), which it does.

That being the case, is there any hope for oil-importing countries trying to become less dependent on OPEC? Fortunately, the answer is yes. The reason lies in the basis of the great market power of OPEC producers: in the United States and almost all other oil-importing countries, *there are no effective substitutes for oil-based fuels* for their most important use—transportation, primarily cars and trucks, but also airplanes. If OPEC instead had a monopoly over, say, butter, its "power" would be far diminished. Why? Because there are substitutes for butter, not only margarine but the wide range of butterlike spreads that are widely available at any major grocery store. In this hypothetical world, if OPEC were to raise its price for butter, many and perhaps most of its customers would switch to these substitutes. Not so with oil-based fuels. OPEC is safe knowing that it is likely to take decades for developed and developing countries alike to rebuild their expanding numbers of cars and trucks to run on other fuels.

The key insight from this butter-margarine analogy is that nations, or any jurisdictional unit, can be *functionally independent of even a monopolist and at the same time consume much of its product* as long as their consumers have ready substitutes for that product. Technically, some economists might say that in such a circumstance, OPEC really wouldn't even have a monopoly over "butter," since because of the ease of substitution, the true "relevant market" is not butter but one for "edible butterlike spreads," which in this hypothetical case OPEC would not monopolize. This technical issue aside, the key point is that *market power comes from not having an effective substitute* to which consumers can easily turn if relative prices of the monopolized product or any other reasonably close substitute change.

Gal Luft and Anne Korin make this simple but powerful point and use it to offer a straightforward way for non-OPEC countries, including the United States, *eventually* to escape from OPEC's power in their compelling book, *Turning Oil into Salt.*[7] The solution is to require the principal oil-consuming devices on the planet—automobiles—to be "fuel flexible." At a minimum, this means that cars and trucks should be able to run on a variety of liquid fuels, namely gasoline, alcohol, ethanol, and methanol. Each of the latter fuels can be manufactured from a number of raw materials, including many waste products, natural gas, and even carbon dioxide (thereby attacking the climate change problem at the same time). Luft and Korin estimate that for new vehicles the additional cost of manufacturing this "open fuels platform" would be approximately $100 per vehicle. Once fully phased in for all new cars, the total cost for an entire annual new fleet of, say, 12 million cars, would be just $1.2 billion. The cost of retrofitting cannot be that much greater since the technology for flex fuels is relatively simple. As the authors state, "All it takes to turn a regular car into a fuel flexible one is a fuel sensor and a corrosion-resistant fuel line."[8]

A more ambitious open platform mandate would require that, in addition to flexible liquid fuels, new vehicles and possibly later existing vehicles operate on electric power, ideally using both hybrid and plug-in technologies. From recent experience, the cost of the hybrid option alone appears to be at least $3,000 per car.[9] Adding a plug-in feature would be much more expensive. Luft and Korin indirectly suggest how much this would cost when they point to the additional $8,000 cost (in 2008 dollars) of including both the plug-in and hybrid features in the world's first mass-produced plug-in hybrid electric vehicle (PHEV) manufactured by China's battery maker, BYD.[10] If the $8,000 figure for both features is correct, and the hybrid feature alone costs $3,000, then the current incremental cost of the plug-in capability alone is around $5,000.

The additional costs of electrification are so substantial, at least with current technologies, that we are reluctant to endorse a mandate for either or both hybrids and plug-ins as part of the required open fuels platform. But two fallback options seem worth exploring. At a minimum, if no oil price floor is established, an idea we will discuss shortly, some kind of tax incentive for buying electric vehicles of either type could be temporarily maintained to assure strong demand. Such a measure would enable manufacturers to run down their learning curves to include these features at steadily lower per-unit costs. Alternatively, the secretary of transportation could be given the authority to include electric options as part of the mandated fuel platform once certain cost thresholds are achieved. For example, if the secretary determines that the additional cost of hybrid technology has fallen to $500, that feature could be added to the mandate. A similar marginal cost figure for a battery life of, say, at least 200 miles could trigger the electric mandate. Similarly, once the marginal cost of the plug-in feature (relative to hybrid technology) also falls to something like $500, that technology also could be phased in on the mandatory open platform. At a minimum, the secretary of defense should be able, under existing law, to mandate choice of fuels for new ground military vehicles, and perhaps to retrofit existing vehicles so they can at least run on alternative liquids.

These figures are illustrative and they are not unduly large. A combined hybrid/plug-in technology with a marginal cost of $1,000, for example, would cost the nation annually on its new fleet of 12 million vehicles roughly $12 billion; with the flex liquid fuel mandate, the total would be just above $13 billion. In comparison to the conservative estimate of $40 billion in subsidies the U.S. oil industry receives each year,[11] these incremental costs are relatively low.

Furthermore, by establishing that additional requirements like hybrid and plug-in capabilities would be triggered by achievement of certain efficiency and cost thresholds by manufacturers, the mandates would bear strong similarities to prizes, but with much larger payoffs. By lowering costs below the threshold for any mandate, the "winning producers" would immediately have the inside track to gaining market share on the expanded open fuels platform. Given the huge size of the U.S. auto market, the profits earned from the sale of vehicles with the new mandated electric options on their fuel platforms, or from the licensing revenue to developers of the technology, not only could be much larger than any single prize, but would also not be one-time events and instead continue as long as the vehicles using these technologies were demanded by consumers.

One obvious question is why auto manufacturers have not voluntarily produced flex-fuel cars on their own, or at least struck deals with dealers who offer multiple fuels. There are at least two answers to this question. One is that no single manufacturer can capture the positive benefits to the country and the economy of reducing the pricing power of the OPEC producers, and for this reason the market provides insufficient incentives for manufacturers to adopt a flex-fuel platform. In addition, a coordination or "chicken-and-egg" problem impedes the adoption of this standard. Given the economies of scale in auto production, manufacturers are not likely to produce cars under the cost projections cited here unless they can be assured that alternative fuels are widely available. Conversely, fuel retailers are not likely to offer a choice in fuels unless they know there is a large volume of flex-fuel cars capable of using them. In short, each side of the market needs the other but won't take the first step unless all parties on both sides take the plunge. A flex-fuel mandate would solve this coordination problem by assuring a plentiful supply of flex-fuel vehicles, which in turn would give fuel retailers incentives to offer alternatives.

An open fuels platform in the United States alone would have huge economic and national security benefits. It would vastly reduce the economy's downside exposure to suddenly higher oil prices triggered by OPEC production cutbacks. Further, for this reason, it would also expand the freedom of U.S. presidents and their foreign policy representatives in dealing with OPEC member governments on a wide range of matters, not just Middle East peace. At the same time, it would not mean the United States would need to foreswear the need for oil, even imported oil. In short, true "energy independence" is *choice* rather than abstinence or autarky.

An open platform would also nip the power of any *future* energy cartels in the bud. For example, as the demand expands for electric cars and their batteries, so will the demand for lithium, the key ingredient for new, lighter-weight, longer-lasting batteries. Yet lithium is concentrated in a handful of countries—Afghanistan, Bolivia, China, Russia, and Chile—not all of which are reliable trading partners, at least for the United States. An open fuels platform that includes both liquid fuels and the electric alternatives would constrain any future lithium-producing countries' potential cartel.

Luft and Korin do not spell this out, but because the world market for oil is global, the impact of open platforms on OPEC's pricing power will depend on the total world volume of vehicles to which it applies. Since much of the developing world uses secondhand cars and lacks the funds to retrofit a significant share of its cars, even cheaply, OPEC will always have some control over global oil prices as long as oil is required for transportation and other uses. But the United States and other developed economies purchase the majority of new vehicles and have the resources to equip them with flexible-fuel platforms, initially with liquid fuels and, as the costs of electrification come down, with electric power as well. Accordingly, the more rapidly the developed world moves toward open fuels platforms and is capable of utilizing alternative fuels in response to higher prices, the less vulnerable *all* economies, developed and less developed alike, will be to OPEC's production decisions and the pricing that results.

Ironically, several emerging market economies are well ahead of the developed world in these respects. In 2004, Brazil began mandating flex fuels for new vehicles sold there, and now a majority of the cars there can burn any combination of gasoline or alcohol. China is working hard on developing methanol fuels, and several of its manufacturers are turning out cars that run on it. Even oil-producing members of OPEC are in on the act. Iran is encouraging the production of cars that run on natural gas so that it will not be as dependent on gasoline, since that country lacks refinery capacity and even as a major OPEC oil producer must import gasoline. And perhaps even more unbelievably, Venezuela is pushing new cars sold in its country to run on both natural gas and gasoline, presumably for similar reasons.[12]

Surely, if these lesser-developed and oil-rich economies are moving toward flex fuels, the United States, as the world's largest consumer of oil at roughly 22 percent of the global market,[13] can do the same.

Open Fuels Platform: Transition Issues

Some transition to a flex-fuel transportation sector, of course, is necessary. The U.S. vehicle stock turns over completely roughly every ten years, so once an open fuels mandate is fully phased in it will take about a decade for the U.S. fleet to be completely converted to an open fuels platform.

As it turns out, a decade also should be plenty of time for U.S. producers of other liquid fuels to build ample capacity to supply a substantial portion of U.S. demand for alternative fuels (they need not supply the entire market in order for consumers to have sufficient alternatives to turn to should gasoline prices increase significantly). One way to accelerate the development of this alternative fuels capacity is for the federal government to establish a price floor for oil at a level at which one or more of the next-best liquid alternatives are reasonably competitive with gasoline refined from oil, perhaps in the $60–$70/barrel range. The price floor could be implemented through a variable tax on both domestically produced and imported oil, set at the difference between the market price (perhaps averaged over some period, say a month or a quarter) and the price floor. When the market price is above the floor, there would be no tax; on the less-frequent occasions when the market price falls below the floor, the tax would lift the effective price up to the floor level.

The price floor has two advantages. Most importantly it provides price certainty to the developers and manufacturers of alternative liquid fuels and protects them against the risk that a sustained drop in oil prices below the floor could put them out of business. A price floor also would modestly encourage conservation, although as we have noted, this is not an outcome that should materially affect OPEC's production decisions.[14]

Other transition issues also should be manageable. One question is whether there will be sufficient electricity generation and transmission capacity as plug-in electric power gets added to the mandatory fuels platform. This should not be a significant problem until the distant future so long as plug-in vehicle owners recharge their cars' batteries at night, when demand for electricity is low and there is sufficient excess generation and transmission capacity that can be tapped.

Indeed, the business model of one innovative electric car startup, Better Place, assumes plenty of unused capacity on the grid for at least some significant period. Better Place does not intend to build electric cars, but rather to build and charge for the infrastructure required to recharge and replace their batteries. For short trips—commutes to work or the store— electric car owners either would recharge at home at night or "top off" their batteries in charging stations at their workplace and shopping areas. For longer trips, Better Place would establish a network of battery-swapping stations at which car owners could exchange their depleted batteries for fully recharged ones.

We don't know whether Better Place will be successful in solving the classic chicken-and-egg problem of having enough charging stations installed and at the same time generating sufficient demand for the cars themselves on a large scale. At this writing, the company has a good start, having rolled out its network in Israel, Denmark, and an initial network in Hawaii with further plans for expansion in the United States. The company also has paired with China's largest independent auto manufacturer to crack that country's market, while running a pilot program in Tokyo. In principle, the infrastructure business model of Better Place should be attractive even if, as expected, battery lives are extended and the weight of the batteries themselves comes down. Time will tell whether this innovative approach to the electric vehicle market proves successful.

Of course, other car companies will be needed to manufacture the electric cars themselves. Consistent with the notion that truly disruptive technologies come from new companies, the first lithium ion–based car to hit the market was not developed or marketed by one of the established incumbents, but by Tesla Motors, a Silicon Valley startup that has since entered into a joint venture with one of the world's most innovative automotive companies, Toyota.

Presumably, this corporate marriage will lead to refinements that will both extend battery life and generate models that are priced under the six figures of the initial Tesla models. Other established companies that have since entered the plug-in market are Chevrolet with its Volt and Nissan with its Leaf.

Clearly, adding a plug-in feature to the mandated open fuels platform would greatly expand the market for plug-ins of all types and thus enhance the staying power of both the manufacturers and their support companies like Better Place and A123 Systems. Whether or not this happens, however, policy should encourage battery recharging at night to make maximum use of the existing grid without requiring excessive new construction of generating plants and transmission lines. The best way to do that is through time-of-day pricing of electricity, which is in place in some states but not all. If states do not quickly move in this direction, Congress should require all state utility commissions to implement time-of-day pricing and direct the Federal Energy Regulatory Commission (FERC) to develop minimum standards to this effect. The states could avoid this outcome if they agreed on such standards themselves. In the next section, we discuss other ways in which joint action by states in the electricity transmission arena would be helpful.

The final transition issue is whether existing or new gasoline stations will have sufficient capacity to provide other liquid fuels or mixes that consumers will demand in response to fluctuating relative fuel prices. Luft and Korin address this question by noting that fuel stations have incentives to offer multiple fuels once 15–20 percent of the vehicles on the road are flex-fuel capable.[15] They calculate that the Unites States would reach this threshold in just three years if 50 percent of new cars sold were liquid fuels flexible. This is a much shorter time frame than the decade it will take for the auto fleet to completely turn over.

We cannot leave this discussion of the advantages of and transition issues relating to an open fuels platform without addressing why such an obvious solution has not yet been adopted by the U.S. Congress. It is not for want of trying. Some type of flex-fuel bill has been introduced in every Congress since 2005. A bill with bipartisan sponsorship was introduced in the 2009–10 congressional session, that would have required that half of new cars sold have liquid fuels flexibility, and 80 percent by 2015. Yet so far no action has been taken on these proposals. Energy Secretary Chu, President Obama, and Interior Secretary Salazar have all supported the flex-fuels concept previous to their current offices.

We can only speculate why broader enthusiasm for a mandated open fuels platform has not materialized thus far. It may stem either from a lack of understanding of how oil markets work, or from continued adherence to traditional thinking about energy solutions that is difficult to abandon. For example, those who stress conservation as the answer to the nation's energy challenge will reject legislation that simply allows car owners to drive all they want. Likewise, legislation that relies on *other* fuels, and not oil, is of little interest to congressional representatives from oil-producing states. To be sure, some states could host the production of alternative liquid fuels or more advanced electric technologies and benefit from an open platform. But like the dog that doesn't bark, it is difficult to generate support for activity that does not yet exist but could if appropriate legislation were enacted.

At some point this issue will require presidential leadership. The bills, or the ideas themselves, may benefit from a different marketing strategy. Rather than stress the openness of the fuel platform—an idea more familiar to computer techies than the population at large—why not simply frame the issue as one of choice? It should be argued that for roughly $100 per car, why not require the auto manufacturers to give consumers a choice of what kind of fuel they want to use? Buyers of computers would revolt if they knew that applications and programs would work only on Microsoft's Windows computer platform. It's about time that our elected officials explain fuel choice in the same way, not only to U.S. citizens but to citizens and elected officials of other countries. The more countries that adopt the flexible fuel standard, the more quickly the world will be able to declare true *economic independence* from OPEC.

Toward Cleaner Electricity Generation

The second great energy challenge is how to avert the potential worrisome and possibly cataclysmic effects of man-made climate change. Although, as we have noted, this subject remains highly controversial, there are at least three reasons that the United States and other countries, with or without global or regional agreements, will do something to reduce carbon emissions, whether by using alternative "cleaner" fuels or by "cleaning up" coal, the principal carbon-based fuel.

First, and perhaps most importantly, in developed economies there is demand by consumers for cleaner forms of energy. One need not look further than U.S. television commercials for evidence. Even the major oil companies advertise how "green" they are becoming. The same is true of consumer products and retail companies. Walmart, for example, has committed to a major campaign to buy "greener" products.

There is an important truth in advertising issue raised by the "green" campaigns of so many companies. There are no commonly accepted standards for measuring the full carbon footprint of products. One needs to consider not just the emissions of the products themselves, but the carbon-intensive energy that goes into the transportation of the supplies and services that make them, as well as the carbon content of transporting products from their places of manufacture to wholesale centers and ultimately to consumers. Although it may be tempting to call for more government regulation to police these "green" claims, the explosive power of the web—bloggers, consumer watchdogs, social networking sites, and the like—should be capable of monitoring "green-worthiness" without the need for government intervention.

The growing demand for a cleaner environment is evident not only in developed economies but in less-developed ones as well. Economists have found that the demand for a better environment begins rising once an economy's GDP per capita has crossed some level of per-capita income, roughly $6,000. Recent history bears this out. Citizens in Taiwan and Japan have demanded greater environmental protections to reduce heavy smog in their capital cities. A proto-environmental movement is even under way in China, pushed along in the run-up to the 2008 Summer Olympics when Beijing had to make huge efforts to reduce air pollution, not only to enable the athletes to perform at peak levels but also to demonstrate to the rest of the world that the Chinese government was taking pollution reduction seriously. Chinese industries are also seeking to play major roles in "green industries" such as battery production and clean coal technologies.

Second, even some electric utility executives in the United States have expressed support for measures that would address the carbon emissions problem. Certain executives may want the tougher emissions standards, assuming their companies already meet them, in order to make it more difficult for new entrants to provide competition. But the quest for certainty is probably also a major driving factor. Right now, utility executives know there is strong consumer demand for cleaner energy, but at the same time there is a political stalemate over what to do about it (reflected most recently in the failure of any type of "cap and trade" bill or carbon tax to gain any traction within Congress). These executives suspect there eventually may be some limits on carbon dioxide emissions and/or some kind of requirement to use cleaner coal but don't know when. To these decision makers, the sooner the "cleaner energy" rules are put in place, the easier it will be for them to choose what kinds of investments to make, which will have the side benefit of speeding along the recovery.

Third, virtually every state has laws governing the absolute amount of electricity sourced from, or the share of electricity generated by, alternatives to carbon-based fuels. So far utilities have been able to fully meet these mandates as they exist. But one significant problem in shifting toward cleaner electricity is insufficient transmission lines from solar or wind sources to the grid, both within and across states. Another problem is that most state laws or regulations do not count renewable energy sourced from *other states* toward meeting the efficiency mandates. Thus, for example, utilities in states where the sun does not shine consistently throughout the year do not have the incentive or capacity to seek out solar power from southern states with ample potential supplies of solar power. The same is true of states that are infrequently windy compared to the much windier states of the Midwest, Texas, and portions of California.

Professor Frank Wolak of Stanford University has suggested ingenious solutions to both these problems without requiring federal intervention or preemption.[16] Despite the advantages of having a single federal decision maker determine the optimal locations of electricity generation plants and transmission lines from a national perspective, federal preemption is very unlikely to be authorized given the strong tradition of state and local decision making in these arenas.

First, to make the renewable mandates more cost-effective, Wolak suggests that the states voluntarily agree with one another to permit utilities to meet mandates by buying renewable "credits" from other states. Thus, utilities in states with a lot of wind or solar power could exceed their minimum mandated levels for renewable energy and sell the excess in the form of credits to utilities in other states. To facilitate the pricing of these credits, the states could set up an exchange to be administered by a third party. Such a system of tradable credits is already in place for emitters of sulfur dioxide. Moreover, the notion that states can modify their laws to accept reciprocal behavior from other states is not a radical one. The precedent is present in state laws enacted in the 1980s that permitted entry by out-of-state banks holding companies from other states that did likewise (these reciprocal laws were later made unnecessary when Congress mandated interstate banking unless states specifically opted out, which none have). As for the renewable credits idea itself, it has been in place and working in the United Kingdom since 2002, Sweden and Denmark since 2003, and Norway since 2006. The idea is well tested and certainly can be made to work in the United States.

Second, with respect to insufficient transmission capacity, Wolak notes that many localities or states require proponents of expanded transmission capacity to pass a benefit-cost test, but restrict the definition of benefits to only those reaped locally. No account is taken in many states of the broader benefit that new transmission lines would confer, namely use of the power by recipients in other localities. This result is clearly at odds with the very notion of the United States of America, which defines a common economic market throughout the country. If cars, trucks, oil, and natural gas can move between states without significant impediments, then so could electrons. Of course, many do now through the existing transmission system. The *national* electricity grid must continue to evolve to keep pace with the growth of electric demand, even as its growth rate is reduced by price- or non-price-induced conservation measures.

There are only two ways to assure this result. In principle, Congress could recognize the "one nation" premise of electricity transmission and give FERC the authority to preempt any state or local laws and regulations relating to the location and construction of new *local* transmission lines (FERC already has that authority for "strategic transmission corridors," effectively, interstate lines, under the Energy Policy Act of 2005). That would be the logical approach, but also the least politically probable. The other approach, suggested by Wolak, is for states (individually or in groups) to declare that the calculation of benefits from any proposed transmission facility must include the gains accrued by all electricity consumers who will use power from the added lines. By expanding the geographic area over which benefits are calculated, approval of the additional capacity will be made more likely.[17]

What about additional electricity generation facilities to go along with the expanded transmission lines? The states' minimum renewable mandates provide only limited help here. Given the lengthy regulatory hurdles at all levels of government associated with the construction of nuclear power plants, it is best for the nation not to count on many additional such facilities being built—especially in the wake of the nuclear plant meltdowns following the huge earthquake in Japan in early 2011, and as nuclear waste continues to be a contentious issue. The discoveries of potentially huge natural gas reserves in the vast Marcellus shale reserve of West Virginia, Pennsylvania, and New York, and in other states around the country, should lift the share of electricity generated by natural gas from its current 24 percent[18] and clearly would be ideal from a greenhouse gas perspective since natural gas burns cleanly (although there are environmental issues associated with the hydraulic "fracking" required to release gas from shale, we believe these can be resolved without impairing the recovery of these massive gas reserves). Our reading indicates that most experts conclude that the dominant source of fuel for electricity generation for the foreseeable future still will be coal, which is also a major source of carbon emissions. This is especially the case in the United States, which has the largest coal reserves in the world.

Fortunately, coal can be burned more cleanly, and its carbon emissions thus can be reduced, and to a limited extent "sequestered" or put back underground. It is conceivable that carbon dioxide may also be recycled as part of a process of making liquid fuels that can be burnt in cars and trucks. The leading edge of cleaner coal innovation, if not now then in the future, is likely to be in China, where the voracious appetite for more electricity produced by continuous rapid economic and population growth is driving the most rapid construction of coal-fired generating plants on earth. In part, the Chinese are relying on the best of U.S. technical advice to construct plants that burn coal more cleanly. But over time, it is a fair bet that the Chinese will not only absorb the very best of what U.S. engineers know but surpass them to become the world experts in this area.[19]

Should the United States worry about this possibility, or for that matter, the importation of other clean energy technologies from other countries? After all, besides the coal sector, the Dutch and possibly the Chinese are already experts in manufacturing blades for windmills. The Germans have become experts in solar technologies.

Other things being equal, U.S. incomes would benefit more if most of this clean energy innovation originated and was commercialized in the United States. The same statement could also be made, of course, about any other sector in the economy. But even if the United States has absolute advantage in every technology—which is increasingly impossible in a global economy where other nations are rapidly catching up to us at the technological frontier—it clearly cannot be true that American firms would have a *comparative advantage* in all technologies, or in clean energy technologies in particular. It makes sense in a global economy to make and deliver the goods and services your country is best at producing in exchange for importing other goods and services. In the grand scheme of things, it is possible that cleaner, less-carbon-intensive energy or energy-related products and materials will be on the import side of the ledger, just as oil has been for multiple decades.

Under the circumstances, then, it is certainly an acceptable second-best outcome if the United States ends up importing some or many energy technologies of the future. The key to a cleaner economy is to be able to *use* these technologies. Further, Americans have consistently displayed a genius for building on the advances of others. So even if certain basic technologies are invented abroad, that does not preclude them from being combined in new ways with other advances, or the next iterations of these technologies from being developed or commercialized here. That is the way science and economic development work. In short, the fact of clean energy innovation is more important than its provenance.

Even as the United States takes advantage of foreign clean energy technology and materials, entrepreneurs in this country will certainly continue to contribute their own innovations as they have in so many other areas of economic life. For example, First Solar is the largest global manufacturer of thin film solar modules and has the lowest cost per watt in the solar module industry. Companies like Rentech Inc. and the Basin Electric Power Cooperative are engineering cleaner ways to burn fuel through coal liquidation and gasification.

Another promising alternative energy development is the first stored-heat solar plant, being developed in Arizona by Abengoa Solar of Spain. This $2 billion facility will use daytime sunlight to heat saltwater tanks that can store the heat for a good portion of the evening and thus address a major problem of solar electric power plants up to now: their uneven activity. By releasing stored energy overnight, this facility, and hopefully others in the future using the same or similar technology, will permit solar power to be used more for base load than was ever thought possible. Equally significant, the Abengoa investment is a perfect demonstration of how the United States can benefit greatly from clean energy technologies developed elsewhere.

Finally, we cannot resist commenting on one seemingly costless way out of the greenhouse problem: some form of "geo-engineering" or modification of the environment *after carbon already has been emitted* to offset its effects. For example, interest has been growing in variations of the notion that sulfur or some other substance could be continuously placed in the upper atmosphere to reflect enough sunlight to offset any impact of global warming or climate change generated by man-made carbon emissions. The costs of doing this run in the low billions of dollars a year, a drop in the bucket compared to the much larger costs of even the lowest-cost policies for lowering carbon emissions.

There are large uncertainties, however, over the non-carbon-related impacts of various geo-engineering technologies so far—specifically the concern that they could significantly reduce rainfall and thus cause or intensify drought in various parts of the world, or that they could acidify the oceans, killing off many fish and other species and disturbing the global ecosystem in unforeseen ways. We believe that these problems are not insurmountable for geo-engineering methods, but are instead cause for further research to see if the potential side effects can be reduced to acceptable levels. Even so, few scientists believe that geo-engineering is likely to be the "magic bullet" that will obviate the need for any further measures to reduce carbon emissions. Geo-engineering technologies could provide some constructive transition relief, however, if a consensus eventually forms that there is a feasible, safe way to do so while carbon reduction policies are being phased in.

What about More Energy R&D?

The seemingly safe political answer to America's energy challenge always seems to be more federal research dollars. That answer has been bipartisan. For years we have been promised that more research would produce the hydrogen car, longer battery lives and thus the completely battery-powered electric car, and other wonders. President Obama considerably upped the ante in his first year in office when he persuaded Congress to include authorization for roughly $30 billion in new spending on clean technologies administered by the Department of Energy, not only representing an extraordinary increase in that agency's budget but also giving it a major grant-making job that it previously had not been equipped to handle.

One would think that on top of all this, the calls for more government research funding would quiet down, at least for a while. But that hasn't happened. In June 2010, one year after the stimulus, a blue-ribbon panel of America's leading executives, the American Energy Innovation Council (AEIC), called for yet further increases in federally supported "clean energy" R&D from $11 billion to $16 billion a year. John Doerr, one of the nation's most prominent venture capitalists and a designated spokesperson for AEIC, said in support of the increase, "When our company shifted our attention to clean energy, we found the innovation cupboard was close to bare. America has simply neglected to support serious energy innovation. My partners and I found the best fuel cells, the best energy storage, and the best wind technologies were all born outside of the United States. Other countries are investing huge amounts in these fields. Without innovation, we cannot build great energy companies. We need to restock the cupboard, or be left behind."[20]

The urge for more federal energy research money is not confined to just these business leaders. Even the president's own Council of Advisors on Science and Technology in November 2010 mirrored the AEIC's call for increased federal energy R&D funding.[21] We have already expressed in Chapter 3 our skepticism in general about more government R&D as the main answer to our billion dollar company challenge. There are too many things in the post-R&D commercialization process that need fixing first. Those same reservations apply with equal force to the calls for more energy R&D, especially at a time when, in general, more budget austerity than spending is in order, as will be discussed in the next chapter.

After all, a $5 billion increase in *annual* R&D spending raises baseline spending potentially forever, or at least for a long while. Thus, this additional spending, in our view, should not be the first resort for policymakers when there are, as already outlined in this chapter, better "first-best" options available that *cost no extra taxpayer money:* fuel choice for automotive vehicles and reforms to electricity generation and transmission. In combination, these changes in the rules governing private-sector activity should provide sufficient incentives for companies, old and new, to conduct their own R&D aimed at substituting for oil and generating electricity through less carbon-intensive means. In this regard, it is useful to recall that hybrid cars, one of the biggest clean-energy breakthroughs of recent years, were introduced by two companies—Honda and Toyota—that, to our knowledge, never received a dime of federal research aid (though they did benefit from temporary tax incentives for consumers purchasing such cars *after* they had already been developed).

Conclusion

Measures to raise the national economic growth rate need not and should not conflict with national security and environmental objectives. This is true of energy use and production. As in other sectors of the economy, it is only necessary to get the rules and incentives right. Already, entrepreneurs are leading the way toward the commercialization of alternative transportation fuels and less carbon-intensive ways of generating electricity. Given the changes suggested in this chapter, even more entrepreneurial activity of this type is likely to follow. Let the race for cleaner energy and more choice begin.

8

AVERTING FUTURE ECONOMIC CRISES

In 1911, the brand-new passenger liner the *Olympic,* sister of the ill-fated *Titanic* and the only one of the trio of sister ships that did not sink, was steaming out of her home port of Southampton, England, bound for New York. It was a bright, sunny day, and the sea was glassy and calm. The busy port teemed with ships, but that was nothing new for an experienced captain and crew. The great liner crept along at a glacial five knots, in keeping with maritime regulations. *Olympic*'s crew kept their eyes on the one other really large vessel in the harbor, the Royal Navy cruiser HMS *Hawke.* For an hour the two ships drew closer and closer. Amazingly, neither crew altered its course, and so the two behemoths collided.

This maritime tragedy is an apt metaphor for American federal fiscal policy, at least as it applies to the so-called "big three" entitlement programs: Social Security, Medicare, and Medicaid. We have been cruising for some time toward a crisis—a cataclysm, in fact. Our politicians, those at the helm of the ship of state, can see the danger clearly and yet they refuse to really turn the wheel. Until 2011, in actions we are about to describe, if they took any action at all, it was to add more steam. For instance, the Medicare prescription drug benefit that was added in 2003 and health care "reform" in 2010, which despite official assurances is widely expected to add to the deficit over the long run, further chart our course toward fiscal disaster. Try as we might to avoid this difficult if not depressing subject, in a book about how to ensure sustained growth, we simply cannot do that. To do so would be put to our heads in the sand.

It is not as if our political leaders are unaware of the trends. The official congressional scorekeepers of the federal government's budget, the Congressional Budget Office (CBO) and the Government Accountability Office (GAO), have been issuing long-term fiscal forecasts for at least the past decade warning of the explosive deficits that are in store if policymakers do not change course. Yet so far, elected officials from both political parties shrink from real reform because they are afraid of powerful special interests—not surprisingly, all those on the receiving end of the entitlement promises. But to simply blame "special interests" casts the problem too narrowly. The fact is that decades of lavish government spending have spread the benefits of government largesse across virtually every sector of society. American political culture broadly resists any attempt to rein in entitlement spending because nearly everyone thinks of himself or herself as a beneficiary. Even the bitterly fought compromise deficit reduction package agreed to by Congress and the administration during the summer of 2011 and the scheduled follow-on measures to be triggered at the end of 2012 do not fundamentally change the long-run upward trend in federal deficits (more about this later in the chapter).

In one sense, it should not be surprising why elected officials have not yet tackled the costs of the entitlement programs. Most of the voting public receives benefits from the government, some in the form of direct cash through Social Security and the Earned Income Tax Credit, some in the form of health benefits through Medicare, Medicaid, and new subsidies under the health care reform legislation enacted in 2010, and some in the form of subsidies to the traditional accoutrements of middle class life, like the home mortgage interest deduction and low-interest student loans. Many Americans are not aware of the breadth and cost of these programs, even as they may call for a smaller federal government.

Yet the fact remains that all this spending, overwhelmingly driven by rising government expenses for health care, continues to rack up America's debt. The spiraling debt, in turn, exposes our economy and perhaps others around the world (who still depend on Americans to buy their goods and services) to the mounting danger that one day (or perhaps gradually over some period), those who buy our debt—both American and foreign creditors (who currently hold about 50 percent of it)—will no longer be so willing to do so, at least at the prices (interest rates) offered. At some point, if current trends continue, the dollar no longer will be the "safe haven" for investors that it has long been, and creditors will demand ever higher interest rates, plunging the economy into another great recession. It is possible a future deficit-induced downturn will be followed by yet another financial crisis—depending on the financial condition of banks and other financial institutions—which would further deepen and prolong the recession.

It could easily be worse. As the nation was discovering during late 2011, with large government deficits and near-zero interest rates, neither fiscal nor monetary stimulus can be counted on to help turn the economy around if it plunges again. More deficit spending will not help because by definition, a deficit-induced crisis will have been triggered by market fears of explosive deficits. And "loose money" would be unlikely to help much either, since it would validate fears that all this debt would be "monetized," laying the foundation for a period of "Great Inflation." Indeed, to head off such fears, it is conceivable that the central bank might even be forced to tighten monetary policy, or at least keep it tighter than it otherwise would be. Politicians may be tempted to react to deficit fears by immediately raising taxes or curtailing government spending—the very opposite of Keynesian stimulus—but this course, too, would only aggravate the economic downturn. Only with clear steps to curtail *future deficits* would policymakers have any chance of convincing the buyers of U.S. government debt to again purchase it at reasonable rates that would not further depress the economy.

We cannot say when a debt-driven economic crisis will happen, presuming current trends continue, although others have tried. Most notably, in their widely admired book *This Time Is Different,* professors Carmen Reinhardt and Kenneth Rogoff divine from the history of past financial crises that a flash point exists when a nation's government debt surpasses 90 percent of GDP.[1] As of year-end 2010, the U.S. federal debt-to-GDP ratio stood at roughly 62 percent, and by every reasonable account is projected to climb steeply thereafter. With the dollar as the world's reserve currency, the United States may have a bit more freedom to run up its debt without a crisis than other countries, but even with our central (though diminished) economic status, the market for the U.S. government's debt is not immune to the laws of supply and demand. At some point, the continuing supply of U.S. Treasury debt will outstrip the willingness of creditors at home and abroad to buy it at the sufficiently low interest rates that have prevailed over the past decade.

Consider the sobering deficit projections made by the CBO in 2011. The CBO's "baseline" forecast is that the gap between federal annual revenues and outlays will exceed 4 percent of GDP throughout the next twenty-five years. The agency's more realistic "alternative" scenario envisions a much worse outcome, with even larger deficits causing the ratio of total U.S. debt to annual GDP to reach an unheard-of 190 percent by 2035. With that debt level and the much higher interest rates it would bring, the CBO projects that by that year, GDP would be 7–18 percent lower than it otherwise would be, a massive shortfall as these estimates go.[2]

The CBO has been putting out numbers like these for at least a decade and until 2010 or so, relatively little attention was given to them. As part of the legislation lifting the federal debt ceiling in August 2011, Congress put some small dent in the trends by enacting a package of cuts in discretionary spending programs amounting to about $2 trillion over a ten-year period. That legislation also established a bipartisan congressional panel charged with identifying by the end of 2011 another $1.2 trillion in savings over the same decade, through changes in the tax code and entitlement programs. Failing to reach a $1.2 trillion deficit reduction target would trigger automatic cuts, primarily in defense and Medicare, but not Social Security, totaling $1.5 trillion, scheduled to take effect after the end of 2012.

In the event, the super-committee gambit failed and so the automatic cuts that no one likes are slated to become effective—assuming that Congress does not override or delay them before 2013. But even if the default deficit-reduction package is implemented, it will make only a modest dent in the long-term deficit projections. As former Senator Alan Simpson, co-chair of the commission that President Obama appointed to come up with a meaningful plan (but then later ignored), incisively put it after the summer 2011 package was enacted: "Those savings [referring to the second installment of $1.2 trillion in cuts] will not be nearly enough to prevent things from getting worse. That's a big drawback to this whole gimmicky agreement. *It solves a political problem, not a fiscal one*" (emphasis added).[3]

The United States is not alone in its deficit woes. At this writing, Greece, Ireland, Italy, and even France have been in the midst of their own sovereign debt crises since the broader financial crisis began. Western European countries also have rapidly aging populations and generous safety net programs, and thus have even greater fiscal challenges ahead than the United States. Japan's social safety net is somewhat less generous than that of Europe, but its population is aging even more rapidly, has a birth rate below replacement level, and unlike Europe, has hardly any immigration. Even China's one-child policy is catching up with it, as its population is leveling off and aging while a growing middle class is likely to demand some semblance of a safety net not currently provided. All these trends imply that the rest of the world, having its own financing challenges, cannot forever finance U.S. deficits simply because U.S. Treasuries (though downgraded a notch by one ratings agency) historically have been safe assets.

Faster growth, while it is inherently desirable, will only delay the day of reckoning (as the 2011–12 deficit reduction packages have done). More rapid growth will not prevent our population from aging, nor will it restrain health care inflation. To the contrary, the richer Americans are, the *more* health care they are likely to demand and be willing to pay for, driving up health care costs even faster. More rapid growth will generate more tax receipts, but much of the additional revenue is likely to be offset by the higher salaries that government workers will demand—and get—in a labor market where private-sector jobs, by virtue of higher and rapidly growing productivity, will be paying more too. Outside of the entitlement programs that are the focus of most of this chapter, labor costs account for most federal "discretionary" spending. The agencies in Washington, D.C., are full of people delivering services but not generally buying things (purchases of military hardware and grants for highways being notable exceptions). For these reasons, it is not surprising that the Pew Foundation calculated that to lower the U.S. federal debt-to-GDP ratio to 60 percent by 2025 (not a particularly ambitious objective since the most challenging fiscal problems, absent offsetting policy actions, come to fruition in the years after that) would require GDP growth to be fully two percentage points higher than it is otherwise projected to be—a bold objective which we agree with Pew to be nearly impossible.[4]

A slowing of health care inflation clearly would help ease future fiscal burdens; however, this too would only delay the inevitable. There are two principal ways to achieve such a desirable outcome, nevertheless. One approach to "bending the health care cost curve" would be to rely more heavily on market incentives, primarily through higher deductibles for health insurance (which could be made progressive) that would provide consumers with greater incentive to shop around for the most cost-effective options. Thus, providers and entrepreneurs would be encouraged to accelerate the development of cost-saving health care technologies and methods of delivery. The Affordable Care Act has one provision—higher taxes on more expensive health care plans scheduled to take effect in 2018—that seeks to harness market incentives. If this aspect of the law actually becomes effective, it should encourage employers to be more sensitive to health care costs and thus encourage cost-saving innovations. Unfortunately, we have to wait for seven more years (at the time of this writing) for such incentives even to take hold.

The Affordable Care Act also embraces a second, alternative approach to reducing health care cost growth: through government edict, delivered under the guise of something less harsh, such as "comparative effectiveness analysis" (CEA). We will return to the concept of CEA later in this chapter, arguing that there is a good chance the government's experiment in mandating cost control eventually will give way to a market-oriented approach. We realize this may seem counterintuitive in the wake of enactment of legislation that creates an Independent Payment Advisory Board that, beginning in 2014, can reduce physician reimbursements and in 2019 can do the same for hospitals to help achieve projected savings in future Medicare costs. However, it is our view that, for political reasons, mandates are unlikely to be effective at bending the cost curve; or, if they are, they will prove highly unpopular in the same way that health care maintenance organizations (HMOs) were vilified in the 1990s—for rationing care. Faced with the growing economic threat posed by health care–driven fiscal deficits, we believe that eventually policymakers will reject direct government controls in favor of market-like incentives, such as vouchers (dressed up as "premium support") or progressive deductibles.

Regardless of how health care cost growth is tackled, we believe the cost reductions are unlikely to be of sufficient magnitude or achieved in time to make a significant dent in future deficit forecasts. At the very least, policymakers certainly should not count on a "bent" health care cost curve bailing us out of the deficit problem. This leaves only three other ways to bring down federal deficits to more sustainable levels: dramatically higher taxes, cuts in entitlement benefits, or, most realistically, through some combination of the first two. We will have more to say soon on what mix of these options is most likely.

Will It Take a Crisis?

The critical question, of course, is whether our government leaders will be able to muster the political will to really get long-term deficits under control—and convince voters that the steps are necessary. The conventional wisdom is that elected officials will only do something about tough problems when they are confronting a crisis (such as the looming accounting insolvency of the Social Security trust fund in 1983), or after one already has occurred (banking and financial reform after the banking and savings-and-loan crises of the 1980s and, more recently, after the 2007–8 financial crisis). The 2011 deficit reduction package, such as it was, also can be viewed as a response to a crisis: one that in part was manufactured (by the threat of one political party not to raise the debt ceiling, up to then a routine act) and in part was due to concerns of bond investors (and the ratings agencies), who, it was feared, could run from Treasuries if major steps were not taken to address the long-term deficit.

Fortunately, history also provides some counterexamples, or cases in which federal policymakers have taken major actions without being pressed by a crisis. In 1993, Congress enacted (by one vote in the Senate) a comprehensive budget bill that helped reverse the mounting deficits of the years before and put the federal budget on a more sustainable path. While these deficits were large, there was no immediate threat at the time that bond investors would "run from Treasuries" if deficits were not brought under control. In 1997, again without confronting a pressing economic crisis, Congress reinforced its earlier deficit reduction package by enacting another one. And whatever one may think about the substance of the health care reform package Congress enacted in early 2010—and like many others, we do not believe it will end up controlling health care costs—the elected officials who voted for the bill claimed that they were at least trying to do so while extending coverage to the uninsured.

Still, none of these previous measures, as comprehensive and far-reaching they are, compares in magnitude to the daunting fiscal challenges that lie ahead, even after the 2011 deficit reduction package is factored in.

Meeting the Federal Fiscal Challenge: Some Heretical Views

The famous baseball player and manager Yogi Berra, who had a special way with words, once suggested, "When you come to a fork in the road, take it." Which fork will the federal government take: the well-considered option that should be able to preempt a future deficit-triggered economic crisis, or the hasty, perhaps panic-driven one that follows a crisis? To be more precise, policymakers surely will confront several "forks" over the next century and beyond, because it is unrealistic to expect that any grand budget bargain, whenever it may take effect, before or after an economic crisis, will solve all fiscal problems forever. But whenever one or more decisions are made, we have some possibly heretical thoughts about their substance.

Given enormous projected future federal deficits, the once-conventional wisdom in Washington was that getting rid of them eventually would require roughly an even split of the two major policy options, program cuts and tax increases. With the top marginal federal income tax rate (taking into account the new taxes scheduled to go into effect under the Affordable Care Act) now exceeding 40 percent, and additional income taxes in most states on top of that, it is unlikely in our view that policymakers will ratchet up income tax rates even higher. Instead, any additional revenues are likely to come either from some loophole closing (as the Obama deficit commission, chaired by Alan Simpson and Erskine Bowles, recommended) or from some sort of consumption tax, such as a federal sales or value-added tax (VAT). The former approach may not be sufficient to solve the problem but could permit a lower marginal rate, which would make the economy more efficient by improving incentives for work and entrepreneurship. A consumption tax would encourage savings, thus facilitating long-term growth, rather than penalize personal efforts to earn more income. In short, either approach to raising more revenue would serve the interests of the economy well.

As for cuts in benefits, any measures with immediate impacts on current beneficiaries and those soon to be eligible would be political nonstarters. Senior citizens and those nearing that status are more likely to vote than younger citizens and they are likely to have especially strong feelings about any efforts to reduce entitlement benefits. This is surely the reason that President George W. Bush proposed his partial privatized plan for Social Security only for citizens under the age of fifty-five. Fairness is also important when considering future measures to restructure entitlements. The changes should affect those young enough to be able to change their behavior—in particular, to increase their savings—to make up for reductions in government-provided benefits in the future.

In *Good Capitalism, Bad Capitalism,* we shared the then conventional wisdom that deficit reduction should be split roughly fifty-fifty between more tax revenues and reduced future entitlement benefits. But the financial crisis, the recession, and the political reaction to the response by Congress and the administration have changed our minds about the likely outcome of the deficit reduction response, whenever that may come to pass. The crisis itself has significantly eroded public confidence in both government and large financial institutions; the former (federal regulators and policymakers) for not preventing and most likely contributing to the financial disaster, and the latter for both contributing to the crisis and, in the case of the large banks that took or were forced to accept government rescue funds, for paying large bonuses to their senior executives. Ironically, the agendas of the Tea Party that spontaneously formed in 2009 and the Occupy Wall Street movement, such as they are, seem to be aligned on these points.

Moreover, much of the public remains skeptical of the two-year stimulus plan enacted in 2009 even though the economy began to recover shortly after that plan was adopted, largely, we believe, because a healthy portion of the stimulus spending was perceived to be standard political pork. The gap between reality and political perception is even more evident in the case of the Troubled Asset Relief Program (TARP), which infused $700 billion into the banking system and eased the pain of the General Motors and Chrysler bankruptcies. Although economists from across the political spectrum now believe that TARP stabilized the banking system at a critical time, the program has been perhaps the most unpopular of the federal financial rescue efforts, likely because funds were channeled to the same banks that contributed to the financial crisis and the recession in the first place.

However effective the bailouts, large and small, may have been in averting a much deeper economic downturn—a debate that will surely continue for many years, if not decades—they seem to have contributed to strong feelings that too much government money was spent to reward the irresponsible, even though it looks like the lion's share of the bailout funds eventually will be repaid to the federal government.[5] For one thing, the media and the public tend to pay far more attention to the initial gross outlays than to the subsequent recoveries and repayments. Even if the public had known that *all* of the federal funds would later be repaid, the fact that only troubled large companies, but not smaller companies and banks, had access to what were essentially federal bridge loans probably would have resulted in a similar degree of distrust. Indeed, it is striking that in April 2010, even after the repayments and economic recovery, the Pew Research Center reported that nearly 80 percent of Americans did not trust the federal government to do the right thing, one of the highest levels of mistrust recorded in fifty years.[6]

Outrage over the bailouts and fears of "federal takeover" through health care reform played a major role in the congressional midterm elections in 2010, which had a huge impact on the deficit reduction package enacted during the summer of 2011. The first round of reduction was accomplished *entirely* through spending cuts, and it is likely that essentially the same outcome will result from the second stage of the package. The message we take away from these developments is that if and when additional deficit reduction measures are taken, they will consist overwhelmingly of additional cuts in entitlement benefits of future beneficiaries, and only modestly of increases in tax revenues. This message is not only consistent with the actions taken in the summer of 2011, but also with the budget plan put forward by the Obama deficit reduction commission's two co-chairmen in 2010. A majority of the commission members voted for a package that would keep federal spending as a share of GDP in the low twenties, implying that future deficit reduction would be split roughly as 75 percent entitlement cuts and just 25 percent in higher tax revenues (which again need not take the form of higher *tax rates*, but instead, as the commission suggested, can be generated by eliminating or capping various deductions and "tax expenditures").

Whole books and countless articles have been written on the new forms and mechanics the necessary benefit adjustments might take, and thus it makes no sense to tax our readers (pun partially intended) with detailed analysis of them all. Suffice it to say that when the changes come—either before or after a crisis—they are likely to include some combination of the following:

- later ages at which individuals can claim full benefits from Social Security and Medicare (all phased in over some reasonable period);
- indexation of Social Security benefits to the rate of price inflation rather than the historically higher rate of wage growth;
- the transformation of Medicare and possibly Medicaid benefits into vouchers (or the less politically toxic term "premium support") for the purchase of health insurance, indexed to some excess over general inflation but less than the roughly 2.5 percentage point "excess cost" growth that has historically been the case;
- if Medicare/Medicaid are not "voucherized," then deductibles paid by beneficiaries possibly will be enlarged over time, most likely on a progressive basis so that higher income retirees pay more out of pocket than do those with lesser incomes; and
- likewise, in the absence of Medicare/Medicaid vouchers, greater use of "comparative effectiveness analysis" in guiding reimbursements to health care providers, and possibly other more draconian means of rationing what treatments and procedures—especially costly end-of-life procedures—the federal government will fund.

This is only a small sampling of the possible range of ideas for reducing entitlement outlays. Clearly, many more details will need to be ironed out. For example, any voucher or premium support system most likely would have to take into account regional variations in health care costs due to wages and other costs, and the initial health of individuals when they become eligible for benefits, unless health insurance for seniors is tied only to age, sex, and location and not to their existing medical conditions. But make no mistake: a voucher system whose payments are tied to any measure of inflation that is less than the inflation of health costs themselves will lead, absent a significant bending of the health cost curve, to a gradual erosion of health care benefits that will likely affect most seniors (seniors with the lowest incomes should be most strongly shielded from benefit changes, but whether the political system will do so is not clear).

One idea not listed above, but which is already included in the 2011 deficit reduction package, is yet another round of across-the-board cuts in reimbursements to health care providers for services to Medicare-eligible patients if Congress does not develop an alternative plan that saves at least $1.2 trillion over a ten-year period (reimbursements to providers may be cut further in any case). This particular "reform" will simply aggravate an already growing problem: the shortage of physicians willing to see and treat Medicare patients. However, now that the federal government has become heavily involved in subsidizing and regulating health care insurance for nonretirees, it is possible that at some point, in the interest of cutting the deficit, it will force significant cuts in physician pay more broadly to rectify the gap between physician reimbursements for Medicare and non-Medicare patients. As it is now, U.S. doctors are much more highly paid than physicians in other developed countries.[7] This disparity in pay may not survive in the future era of required deficit reduction.

None of the foregoing options will be popular. But they are likely to be *less unpopular* with *future* retirees than the huge tax increases that would be required to keep entitlements from being cut in any way. When hard choices must be made—and certainly all the options for large cuts in the federal deficit will be politically unpalatable—then the least unpopular ones are likely to win out.

Of course, we could be wrong about the public's willingness to tolerate new and higher taxes to support the current Social Security and Medicare benefits structures even as more baby boomers continue to retire. The public today may not be ready to make this choice, but it is impossible to say how voters will feel in the decades to come. It is our judgment that public opposition toward a materially higher tax share of GDP will remain roughly as strong as it has been since the onset of the financial crisis and the recession that followed it. We could be wrong about this too: public anger at government could fade as the recovery continues, and voters and their elected representatives could be more willing to accept higher taxes in lieu of major entitlement benefit cuts. We just do not think so.

In any event, the continuing pressure to address the mounting federal deficit and rising health care costs, and the eventual response, will have a number of hugely important implications for our society. Other parts of the budget, how much individuals save, health care costs and innovation, how long Americans work, and Americans' attitudes toward immigrants will all be altered by these decisions. State and local governments that face even more pressing challenges will also be affected in various ways, but not all of them negative, in our view. We consider each of these to be a "silver lining" of an otherwise dark cloud in the remainder of this chapter.

Infrastructure Privatization

The late Senator Pat Moynihan and other Democrats have argued, with some merit, that a main purpose of the Reagan tax cut package of 1980—apart from the desire to stimulate more work and entrepreneurship through lower marginal tax rates—was to "starve the beast" of government spending. In fact, a number of studies since have demonstrated convincingly that whatever the surface appeal this argument may have had, its desirability notwithstanding, past deficits have not restrained federal spending.[8] But the future is likely to be very different, and a "starve the beast" effect may materialize in another form. Given the much larger projected deficits ahead than were present during the 1980s and 1990s, and regardless of any major new infrastructure spending approved as part of the Obama administration's jobs program during 2011 or 2012, elected officials in the future will have much stronger incentives than before to find other ways to cut federal spending beyond taking the highly unpopular route of cutting entitlement benefits of future seniors—even if those cuts merely have the effect of moving former federal expenditures "off-budget."

One such example, we predict, is the likely movement of future federal, state, and local spending for highway construction, federal buildings, and government facilities (including prisons) into private hands, perhaps through the sale of these capital items to private investors. Citizens today are not likely to remember, but the fact is that the predecessors to today's modern highways were privately owned, and paid for with tolls. In 1860, for example, over seven thousand private corporations operated bridges, canals, ferries, and roads. Only later in the nineteenth and twentieth centuries, when the public grew disenchanted with the poor condition of some roads, did state and local governments begin to take over the construction and ownership of this important part of the nation's infrastructure.[9] After World War II, President Eisenhower called on Congress to fund the construction of a massive interstate highway system in the interest of national security (so that roads could facilitate both civilian evacuations and transportation of troops in a national defense crisis). Congress has been handing out money to the states for road construction ever since.

The fact that public roads and other infrastructure may be classic "public goods," that is, goods that can be enjoyed by many without subtracting from the benefits they provide to each individual and that are also difficult to deny access to, does not necessarily mean that government must both *construct* and *own* such facilities. That view, coupled with the obvious need to upgrade and expand much of the rotting infrastructure in the United States, has led to calls for a new federally sponsored "infrastructure bank" to support massive new construction. But such an institution would be just another off-the-books entity, like the two government-sponsored housing enterprises, Fannie Mae and Freddie Mac, that eventually blew up and will probably cost taxpayers several hundred billions of dollars in the end. If this chapter has done nothing else, it should have made amply clear by now that the United States does not have that kind of money to spend, whether in after-the-fact subsidies of an entity that could eventually be destined for financial trouble, or by issuing off-the-books federal guarantees that really amount to adding to the federal debt itself—all at a time when one of the main challenges of government is to *reduce* long-term federal deficits. In short, the infrastructure bank idea is totally out of sync with fiscal reality.

But that does not mean the future of infrastructure is bleak. To the contrary, if the government cannot do something, then it ought to pave the way (pun intended) for the private sector to fill the gap. There are already some examples in the United States and elsewhere of privately owned toll roads. After all, the budget crises confronting states and municipalities across the nation already have driven governments in some areas to think creatively what they can sell off, lease back, or both.[10] In the new era of fiscal austerity, we would not be surprised if many states and localities turned to authorizing many more privately owned roads and buildings, so much so that private ownership eventually becomes the norm rather than the exception.[11] With current technologies like the E-ZPass electronic toll collection system or transponders in cars, tolls can be assessed without disrupting traffic with toll booths. One can imagine new technologies and contracting arrangements that would permit people to buy passes for fixed periods within certain geographic areas, for fixed distances, and so forth, with systems of transponders and computers allocating funds among different owners.

Of course, given the absence of alternative routes for drivers and flyers going to and from different destinations, any system of privatized roads and airports most likely would require both safety and possibly even some price regulation by the government. Road construction and maintenance also would have to meet minimum standards to ensure public safety. Public pressure will exist for government to regulate road or airport charges or tolls (much as local utility rates are now) where there are inadequate transportation alternatives to the privately owned roads. To be sure, price regulation itself, especially if based on cost-plus principles, can lead to inefficiencies such as gold-plating. Nonetheless, it is possible, if not likely, that private ownership of roads, airports, and other formerly public facilities would encourage more innovation and allow for more efficiency than would otherwise occur.

From a budget perspective, the privatization of new roads and other formerly public facilities would be a clear win. It would mean those expenditures would never find their way to the government's books, and thus not require taxpayer funding (whether paid in full at the outset, or through interest paid on debt issued to finance these projects). The sale of existing public infrastructure also could bring in substantial revenues, although to the extent local and state governments lease these facilities back, the sales would just shift the timing of the costs.

The sorry state of the nation's infrastructure—corroding bridges, highways, and public transportation in some places—requires fixing somehow if the economy is to grow at any reasonable pace, let alone at the preferred accelerated rate. By one account, the United States ranks twenty-third in the world in the quality of its overall infrastructure, an embarrassing standing for a country that has claimed, and wants to continue to claim, global economic leadership.[12] Highly congested roads in poor condition, for example, compel firms to look for potentially more costly work-arounds such as changes in work shifts, delivery schedules, and more telecommuting (which may save money in the short run, but harms esprit de corps and reduces spontaneous innovations that often grow out of face-to-face interactions). Time spent in traffic jams and airport delays could be put to better uses. Billions are wasted on vehicle repairs each year due to deteriorated road conditions. If public money is not available or cannot be borrowed, then private financing and ownership is the only way the nation will be able to tackle these problems.

Private ownership and financing of roads, airports, and perhaps other formerly public facilities has another important virtue: it should accelerate implementation of various forms of congestion pricing that would encourage more telecommuting and spread out road usage—through shifts in work hours and delivery schedules—more evenly over the course of each day. People expect government to treat the public fairly and equally without regard to the efficiency consequences and thus tend to resist attempts to adopt congestion pricing. In contrast, expectations are very different when private firms ration by price, for example, as airlines do in pricing seats. Because congestion pricing would considerably reduce (though not eliminate) the need for more construction, the privatization of infrastructure would help ensure that only completely necessary new infrastructure is brought to market.[13]

More Private Saving

For several decades after World War II, Americans were moderate savers, socking away roughly 8 percent of their income per year. But for various reasons still not fully explained by economists—most likely, rising housing prices and easier credit—the personal savings rate steadily dropped from the 1970s on, until it was close to zero before the Great Recession. Savings rates have edged up a bit since then and at the time of this writing were in the 5 percent range, but debate continues over how permanent this increase in the personal savings rate may be.

Although benefits of future retirees may not be cut in the near term, the mere threat that they eventually might or will be is likely to encourage Americans to save more than in the decades preceding the Great Recession. The new attitude toward thrift may not be evident for several years, but if government deficits continue to rise, more Americans will understandably fear that their retirement benefits could be at risk and will save accordingly.

In fact, one small but important step in this direction was taken when Congress enacted the Pension Reform Act of 2006, which allows employers' defined contribution retirement plans to default to the maximum permissible employee contribution. This "nudge" in pension policy is consistent with the finding of behavioral economists that people are heavily influenced by the default option; previously, employees had to opt in— otherwise they would contribute nothing to the fund. Under the new "opt out" regime, employee savings have already increased.[14] A larger impact on national saving would be realized if all employers offering defined contribution pension plans were *required* to adopt the opt-out approach now permitted under the 2006 act.[15]

Saving is important for both individuals and society as a whole. For individuals, these truly personal funds, assuming they are not put into ill-advised non-diversified investments, enable families to pay for big ticket items such as the purchase of a house, payment for college, and to supplement Social Security when they retire. For societies, higher savings rates generate a larger pool of funds to finance private- and public-sector investments. Although the globalization of finance has permitted countries to borrow more freely to finance domestic investment, borrowing from abroad still is not a perfect substitute for domestic saving. Accordingly, other things being equal, higher domestic savings translate into lower domestic interest rates, and higher rates of investment and thus economic growth. In addition, the greater the positive savings response to any change in entitlement benefits, the greater will be the demand for government bonds and domestic securities, and therefore, the lower will be the risk of a deficit-triggered recession.

Health Care Costs and the Worrisome Impacts on Future Innovation

We do not contend that increased personal saving alone will entirely offset the rising costs of government-financed health care in the future. Moreover, even a mandated opt-out system for defined contribution pension plans would not touch a substantial portion of the workforce whose employers do not offer such plans, or self-employed entrepreneurs who choose not to establish their own plans or whose businesses may not achieve sufficient success to cover those plans' costs. Both of these reasons, among others, may be why taxes must eventually be increased in some manner (ideally in the two ways suggested earlier in the chapter) to support even restructured benefits provided under Social Security and Medicare.

But since benefit restructuring eventually will require many Americans to bear more of their medical costs than they do now, a fundamental question arises. How will all but high-income and/or wealthy future retirees be able to afford the medical treatments and procedures that presumably will continue to become more expensive?

The best and most desirable answer to this question is for future health care innovations to be cost saving rather than cost enhancing. The basic cost control mechanism built into the 2010 health care reform bill—adjusting reimbursement rates (first for doctors, beginning in 2014, and later for hospitals, beginning in 2019)—may delay the inevitable explosion in health care costs, but is unlikely in our view to fundamentally "bend the cost curve" over the long run for at least two reasons. (For a summary of many of the key provisions and timelines in the health care reform legislation, assuming it goes into effect as originally enacted, see Box 8.1).

For one thing, we are skeptical about one of the fundamental cost control mechanisms of the bill, "comparative effectiveness analysis" (CEA), which has been promoted as an important way to rein in health care costs in high-cost regions of the country. Advocates of CEA as practiced by the government argue that if Medicare reimburses only the most proven cost-effective treatments, costs should drop to the level where the same or similar outcomes are achieved at much lower cost. However, these are still largely one-time events, even if they are realized over an extended period. Once all the inefficiencies are wrung out of the system—which we doubt is possible—health care costs will still remain on essentially the same, rapidly growing trajectory, but from a lower base. Eventually, unless that trajectory itself—the "health care cost curve"—is bent or slowed, rising costs will overwhelm the system.

Second, the history of medical innovation so far has been dominated by new *higher-cost* (and often less invasive) procedures, medicines, and

Box 8.1

Patient Protection and Affordable Care Act
Timeline and Summary of Key Provisions

2010
- Support Comparative Effectiveness research through new nonprofit institute
- Adults with preexisting conditions eligible to join a temporary high-risk pool (to be replaced by health care exchange in 2014)
- Insurers prohibited from discriminating on basis of preexisting conditions for anyone under age nineteen and from dropping policyholders when they get sick

2011
- Insurers required to spend 85 percent of large-group and 80 percent of small-group plan premiums, with certain adjustments, on health care, the improvement of health care quality, or as a rebate, returning the difference to policyholders

2014
- Insurers prohibited from discriminating or charging higher rates on the basis of preexisting conditions for all customers
- Medicaid eligibility expanded
- Tax credits to small businesses with fewer than twenty-five employees that offer health benefits
- $2,000 per-employee tax penalty imposed on employers with more than fifty employees who do not offer health insurance to their full-time workers. (The 2008 report by the Kaiser Family Foundation and Health Research & Educational Trust, "Employer Health Benefits: 2008 Summary of Findings," noted that more than 95 percent of employers with more than fifty employees offered health insurance.)
- Annual penalties imposed on individuals who do not buy health insurance
- Members of Congress and their staffs only can get health benefits through the health care exchange (instead of the current federal program designed only for them)
- Earned income of individuals above $200,000 annually or couples above $250,000 annually will be subject to a Medicare payroll tax of 3.8 percent
- New excise tax on pharmaceutical companies and medical device manufacturers

(Continued)

Box 8.1 *(Continued)*

2017
- States may apply to the secretary of health and human services for waivers of certain sections of the law, such as the individual mandate, provided the state has developed a detailed alternative that will provide coverage at least as comprehensive and affordable to a comparable number of individuals as the waived provisions

2018
- All existing health insurance plans must cover approved preventive care and checkups without co-payment
- New excise tax on high-cost insurance plans

treatments. MRIs and CAT scans are a good example, as they are routinely used by physicians as the diagnostic tool of first resort, rather than last resort as is the case in other countries. There is a fundamental reason that medical innovation continues to become increasingly expensive: it is paid for by third parties, namely insurance companies, or through government insurance programs. The 2010 health care reform legislation tries to change this dynamic largely through the use of CEA, which its advocates argue will encourage the development of new *cost-saving* medical innovations.

Yet as we noted in the introduction to this chapter, there are reasons to doubt this outcome, and in fact fear something worse. Even if CEA works— namely, rewards only the most cost-effective medical treatments—it cannot guarantee that those treatments will not also be far more expensive than the ones they replace. That may be an acceptable outcome for the patients who will be able to afford such treatments or for the public if the government continues to pay for treatment. But if because of their expense the government is not able to reimburse the costs of the best new technologies, then we are back to the conundrum we posed just a few paragraphs ago: how can we then assure that all senior retirees, regardless of financial status, have access to the best medical treatments?

Even more worrisome is the risk that government-operated CEA may end up stifling health care innovation, however much it may cost. Government authorities in charge of CEA must have sufficient databases on which to base their cost-effectiveness determinations. But these databases cannot be compiled without actually using the technologies or treatments and then being able to refine them on larger populations, as is standard practice in the health care industry. If bureaucrats are making cost-effectiveness decisions on the basis of only initial patient samples, when the full benefits of a treatment or drug may not be known and costs not yet reduced because providers have not had the chance to learn by doing, they run a great danger of killing off—through their reimbursement decisions—potentially lifesaving or life-extending treatments.

If the rate of health care innovation slows because of government's (unintentionally) heavy hand, then we will not have the access problem with which we began this section. But then we also will not have the innovations either.

The Eventual Appearance of Market-Guided Health Care

There is another course: introduce more market signals, namely prices, quality measures, and patient cost-bearing, into the marketplace so that the market rewards cost-saving innovation, which it can and will if given the chance. We recognize that the model of "consumer-driven" health care is controversial,[16] but its fundamental insight—that the current health system is essentially devoid of price signals—is right on target.

Critics of consumer-driven health care make several counterarguments, but we believe each is flawed. It has long been asserted, for example, that consumer health decisions are not well informed, since medicine is a classic example of a market with "asymmetric information." The doctor knows a lot more than the patient does about what courses of treatment are appropriate, and so patients are inclined to accept the doctor's recommendations even if they happen to be inappropriate in general or for that specific patient.

While this critique still has some validity, the Internet has revolutionized the availability of medical information. Today, as often as not, patients come to their doctor armed with a list of recommended treatments they see on websites such as WebMD, the National Institutes of Health, the Mayo Clinic, or any one of a number of other prestigious academic medical centers. And while these sites cannot diagnose, they help patients ask the right questions and be aware of their treatment choices.

What the Internet sites do *not* do, because of the opaque nature of the system, is enable patients to know what *net prices*—that is, the actual health insurance reimbursement rates—they or their insurance companies will be charged for the various treatments. Further, if they have met the deductibles in their health insurance policies, patients are unlikely to care. But if patients did have more out-of-pocket responsibility for their care, beyond the minimal office co-pays of $15 or $20 per visit, they would have far greater incentive to question their doctors about the comparative effectiveness of different treatments and to make their own decisions about how much "care" to purchase. Yes, we have just mentioned that phrase "comparative effectiveness" that we criticized earlier, but we believe patients are likely to be better served by having multiple third parties (insurers) compete to make those decisions rather than have those decisions effected through Medicare, which heavily influences reimbursements by private insurers.

Another criticism of consumer-driven health care is that patients often have no choice in what care to accept or what price to pay for it. This is obviously true for patients who require emergency care, but it is also alleged to be the case for patients with chronic illnesses, such as heart disease, lung problems, cancer, or diabetes. These ailments are estimated to account for roughly 75 percent of all health care costs, and treatment costs can and generally do exhaust a consumer's annual deductible relatively quickly. At that point, patients have essentially no economic incentive to shop for the best treatments.

These points are valid but do not negate the value of providing more price and quality information to patients and requiring them to have some of their own financial interest invested (the same requirement is now widely believed to be necessary for all parties in the mortgage origination and securitization business for that market to work properly). As health care costs continue to mount—both for employees covered by employer-provided plans and for individuals purchasing on the open market through the new health insurance exchanges—all consumers will have incentive to look for insurance plans that encourage the most cost-effective care. And even for patients who have chronic conditions, a more market-based system is likely to lead to more cost-effective care.

For example, there is no reason that providers of testing, monitoring, and treatment services for individuals with chronic diseases (such as infusion centers, dialysis treatment, and the like) cannot compete on price and quality. They would likely do so if individuals could purchase plans that rewarded them for shopping around, just as they do now for virtually every other product or service. Jason Furman, writing before he became the Deputy Director of the National Economic Council in the Obama administration, estimated that a system of health insurance plans with "progressive deductibles" (higher deductibles for higher-income consumers) could save the nation as much as 13–30 percent in annual health care costs.[17] However, the providers of health insurance plans will only offer innovative cost-saving features if they are permitted to compete with one another, something which "one-size-fits-all" federal health care plan regulation, or the government-run Medicare system, will not allow.

For the reasons just outlined, we are sympathetic to the view that markets can work a lot better than critics of consumer-driven health care give them credit for. More to the point, markets with accurate price and quality information give more power to *patients* to decide what services to purchase and from whom.[18]

Whether we are right or wrong about the virtues of a greater role for markets in health care ultimately may be beside the point. As health cost pressures mount and government pursues cost control by mandate, whether directly or indirectly in the form of CEA-guided reimbursements, a major political backlash by seniors and working Americans alike becomes increasingly likely. Complaints about government rationing of care and the growing unavailability of physicians willing to accept ever-stingier Medicare reimbursements are likely to become more common. If there were no effective cost constraints, policymakers would address these concerns by simply extending coverage, as Congress did in 2003 to Medicare prescription plans after complaints about the rising costs of drugs for seniors, or by canceling the cutbacks in physician reimbursements.

But in an environment where these options are not feasible, hard choices about what to cover and how much to pay providers must be made while considering budget targets. As these kinds of choices are thrust upon Congress year in and year out, the temptation will grow to take these choices out of the political arena and turn them over to markets. We recognize that this cannot be accomplished completely, since if the government pays for or subsidizes care, tough political decisions will still be required to control costs. Nonetheless, market-like mechanisms can at least remove political and regulatory decision makers from the immediate line of fire, thereby relieving them of the micro decisions concerning coverage and reimbursements.

Several such mechanisms come to mind. One approach, popularized in 2011 by Representative Paul Ryan and former OMB Director Alice Rivlin (each with different versions) but originally proposed many years ago by economists Henry Aaron and Robert Reischauer, would be to turn health care benefits into vouchers (which we have noted is euphemistically now called "premium support") that families and individuals can use to purchase insurance on the open market. As under the Affordable Care Act, insurers would be prohibited from discriminating on the basis of preexisting conditions, but free to offer varied combinations of benefits. There is a legitimate question whether, if the voucher or premium support idea is adopted and if health care costs continue their rapid escalation, elected officials will have the political will to adhere to any initial formula for determining the amount of such support. For this reason, some might prefer a revamping of Medicare that would offer various plans, with different levels of coverage and thus different prices.[19] The prices could also be adjusted in a way that makes the charges progressive. A related idea is to increase Medicare and Medicaid deductibles, ideally on a progressive basis, over time so that patients themselves pay more out of pocket.

Admittedly, for the federal government to turn to the market to address cost control after having downplayed it under the Affordable Care Act seems like a radical and unlikely about-face. However, if one takes a long-term view of how health care could evolve in the United States, one may be more optimistic. As the political climate changes, which it is likely to do as health care costs continue to climb, ideas that may now seem passé or unlikely may be revived. How elected officials, in particular, will behave in the future will be very much influenced by the constraints under which they are placed. Our educated guess is that if the cost and budget trends play out as we have suggested, and especially if the public becomes increasingly anxious, frustrated, and potentially angry about the federal government's micro decision making affecting their health care and what kinds of treatment they receive, political leaders will look far more closely at ways to extricate the government—and thus themselves—from the role of decision maker. That is why the market still has a chance to play a much larger role in health care in the future.

This will be good news for medical entrepreneurs, whose energy and innovation may yet bend the health care cost curve in ways that government rules and regulations never can. Indeed, only if consumers bear a greater portion of their out-of-pocket costs will they be motivated to search out the health insurance plans best suited to their needs. If the plans themselves are allowed to be innovative outside of a strict regulatory regime, consumers then will begin to demand the pricing and quality information that will permit more informed choices. Furthermore, as consumers have more information and incentives to shop around, health care providers—physicians, medical device manufacturers, health care networks, pharmaceutical companies—will have incentives that they only imperfectly have now to come up with new *lower-cost* innovations rather than more expensive treatments and procedures.

This future, we believe, offers our best hope of bending the health care cost curve so that when the budget crunch really comes, we will not end up rationing care significantly more than is already the case.

Working Longer

One of the possible, if not likely, policy changes to slow the growth in Social Security and Medicare costs is to gradually increase the age at which individuals are eligible for full benefits. Indeed, the Obama deficit reduction commission recommended a *very* gradual increase of the Social Security eligibility age over the next seventy-five years.

Whether or not this particular reform is adopted, one related way of reducing the need for painful benefit cuts is to encourage individuals to stay in the labor force for a longer period of time. The longer people work, the greater their total contribution to the collective level of production of goods and services, or GDP, and thus the larger the pool of resources available for paying a fixed set of government obligations, such as the entitlement promises. In mathematical terms, as more people work longer, the ratio of spending to GDP will become lower.

There are a number of forces, admittedly working in opposite direc-tions, which affect how long people voluntarily choose to work. On the positive side, as people live longer, they are more able and more willing to work longer, although this is true more for white-collar than blue-collar employees. The significant drop in equity and home values resulting from the financial crisis and the recession (even taking into account the market's partial rebound from its low in March 2009), coupled with the low inter-est rate environment since then, gives workers strong incentive to work longer in order to rebuild their retirement nest egg.[20] Moreover, technolo-gies like the Internet are making it possible for older Americans to con-tinue to work part time as consultants or entrepreneurs. Indeed, of any age group, individuals age 55–64 show the highest proclivity to start a business.[21] In addition, many workers with certain technical skills, such as engineers, are not being readily replaced by younger workers, who do not have either the requisite education or interest in filling these jobs. Employ-ers want these senior workers to stay on for longer periods.

Some factors offset these positive trends, however. In the short to me-dium run, older Americans laid off during or after the recession have found it more difficult than ever to find a job, a trend that may be neutral-ized only to a limited degree by the higher entrepreneurship rate among older Americans.. In addition, although age discrimination is technically against the law, in the real world there are many subtle ways that employ-ers can and still do discriminate against older workers.

On balance, it is our view that the average working age nonetheless will drift upward over time and thus somewhat mitigate budget pressure from the entitlement programs. Some additional policy nudges would further encourage older Americans to keep working. One obvious idea is to lift the earned income ceiling at which Social Security benefits are taxed. The income tax revenue from the additional work thereby stimulated should offset any loss in taxation of Social Security benefits.

More Tolerance for Immigration

In Chapter 5, we urged that the United States adopt a more entrepreneur-friendly approach to immigration by authorizing a new "job creator's" or "entrepreneur's" visa at a minimum, and if politically possible, staple a green card to the diploma for foreign students who receive STEM degrees awarded by American universities. Ideas such as these have yet to gain sufficient political traction given the much larger controversy over what to do about undocumented workers, who are largely low-skilled laborers.

The budget math we have outlined in this chapter ultimately could change the political dynamics of immigration policy. Faced with the need to generate more revenue to cover ever-increasing entitlement obligations, policymakers and voters may become more receptive to proposals to provide currently undocumented workers with gateways to green cards and citizenship. It is no secret that low-skilled immigrants are more than willing to take jobs that other Americans do not want, whether picking fruit or vegetables, washing dishes, cleaning up yards, or the like. Although the earnings from such endeavors may not be high enough to be subject to income taxes, these individuals would pay payroll taxes and thus help fund Social Security and Medicare payments to the rapidly growing number of retirees. If we are right that the individuals most threatened by cuts in those payments are younger individuals, then these voters one day may realize that it is in their self-interest to back more liberal immigration policies. Once again, the coming budget difficulties may help to break the deadlock on seemingly intractable political issues.

Addressing State and Local Budget Woes: Some Silver Linings

As many Americans surely know by now, the federal government is not alone in confronting enormous future deficits. Many, if not most, states and cities face similar challenges and for similar reasons. This was true even before the Great Recession, the economic pain of which was mitigated by the stimulus package enacted in 2009 but whose palliative effect wore off in 2011. Ever-increasing pension obligations are among the most important contributors to the dire fiscal position of many state and local governments as their workforces retire. Unlike most workers in the private sector, who if they have any pension savings at all have it in the form of a "defined contribution" plan with no guaranteed payments at retirement, most state and local government workers have pension plans that pay them "defined benefits." In the aggregate, these plans are under-funded. Reliable estimates indicate that the unfunded total may be as much as $3 trillion.[22]

Pension obligations, including retiree health benefits, are not the only factor contributing to the structural budget problems at the state and local government levels. The costs for Medicaid, law enforcement, prisons, infrastructure, and schools outstrip the growth in revenues for many jurisdictions. Without spending reforms, the Government Accountability Office projected in 2009 that state and local operating deficits—budgets that are supposed to be balanced—will approach 5 percent of GDP by 2050, in addition to projected federal deficits well into the double-digit percentages.[23]

Although the magnitude and urgency of the fiscal problems of certain states exploded into public consciousness in early 2011—with tense demonstrations by public employee unions primarily in midwestern states—not all states and municipalities are in such dire straits. Those with expanding populations, rising incomes, good governance, and reasonable public pension obligations and funding for them, are not in the same fiscal boat as states and municipalities without such policies—especially in California, Illinois, New Jersey, and New York—where deficit problems already are severe and, absent major policy changes, will only get worse. States with underlying fiscal challenges and constitutional protections for existing pension obligations will have an especially difficult time coping.

Until the program expired, many states papered over their fiscal problems by issuing Build America Bonds (BAB), which were authorized in the 2009 federal stimulus package but which Congress allowed to lapse at the end of 2010. The BAB program provided a federal subsidy of interest payments on taxable bonds issued by states and localities for specific projects. Although theoretically the BAB program could be resurrected, doing so effectively would amount to an unpopular federal bailout of states and localities with especially difficult fiscal problems, and in any event would not represent a long-run solution to these governments' deficits.

Nor do we believe that voters in the affected states will support tax increases to fully close the budget gap. The voter resistance to higher federal taxes that we have already posited is just as present at the state and local level. Moreover, the fact that businesses and people can and do easily move their legal residences from states with especially high tax burdens to states with lower burdens adds yet another powerful reason that higher taxes will not rescue states and localities with fiscal problems.

That leaves only a few other unpleasant options: significant cutbacks in state and local services, bankruptcy for municipalities where legally possible, or in the case of state governments that cannot legally go bankrupt, a repudiation of their debts. Indeed, at this writing, already a number of localities around the country have flirted with bankruptcy.

Many governments are not waiting for that prospect and are taking increasingly drastic steps to cut spending. A number of states have already cut back on educational expenditure, frequently in the form of teacher layoffs, leading to increased class sizes. Others are already doing what we suggest the federal government eventually will be forced to do: sell off infrastructure they own, primarily municipal sewer and water systems. Once transponder technology becomes more widely available, the privatization of local roads will not be far behind.

The cutbacks in state and local spending have slowed the recovery and will continue to offset the increase in private-sector demand. Over the longer run, however, there may be a few silver linings to the state and local budget crunch.

The privatization of infrastructure, for example, has positive elements to it. Free of the constraints of state and local wage requirements from any former union contracts and work rules, private-sector owners may be able to more efficiently build and operate sewer and water systems, roads, and perhaps other former governmental properties. Potentially more encouraging yet, even the bankruptcy of some municipalities may be just the sort of crisis needed to cut through teacher union opposition to work practices that have proved effective in the private sector: pay for performance, greater authority for principals to hire and fire teachers (and thus remove poorly performing teachers), and greater freedom to reconfigure school operations (hours, methods of teaching, and the like) that put the interests of students above all else.

If it takes governmental bankruptcies or the threat of them to help achieve all this, then future budget crises will have served at least one useful purpose. As we discussed in the last chapter, the political stability of capitalism depends on both the perception and the reality that everyone has the ability to benefit from the economic growth produced by capitalism, especially entrepreneurial capitalism. But ensuring these opportunities for the least advantaged citizens in the United States will require a fundamental overhaul of primary education, along with other aspects of our educational system. It would be unfortunate, but in the long run desirable, if the current and future budget crises at all levels of government proved necessary to accomplish this end.

Conclusion

Perhaps the greatest threat to uninterrupted rapid economic growth in the United States is the large and ultimately unsustainable deficits at all levels of government, but especially those at the federal level. Ideally, policymakers will take steps to address these problems before one or more financial and economic crises leave us all with no choice. The solutions to the deficits will involve very painful adjustments, but also have a few silver linings. Ideally, it would be nice to have the latter without the former, but it is unlikely that we will be so lucky.

9

ENTREPRENEURSHIP AND THE
OPPORTUNITY SOCIETY

Up to this point, we have discussed in some detail the virtues of
faster growth, outlined ways to achieve it, and highlighted the major threat
to its being realized. It is now time to address a question that we imagine
many readers have asked themselves at some point along the way: how do
we know that the benefits of added growth will be broadly distributed
across the population and not narrowly concentrated in just a few—
perhaps only the high-growth entrepreneurs we have been counting on to
move our economy ahead?

We do not know. That is because the answer to this question depends
to a significant degree on what our nation's policymakers do to assure that
as many Americans as possible, ideally all, have a reasonable shot at attain-
ing the American dream: a comfortable and rising standard of living
throughout their lives for themselves and their children. Note that we did
not say "equal" chance because that is unrealistic. Government cannot
eliminate the advantages of parents' wealth and education, growing up in
a two-parent family, one's genes, and luck, to name perhaps the most obvious factors aside from an individual's own hard work that determine
one's life course. Furthermore, we did not say it is the job of government
to ensure that everyone actually has the same standard of living. That
statement is totally at odds with the history of America and all free peoples where personal drive, coupled with inherited advantages, determines
economic outcomes. Instead, citizens rightfully look to their government
to simply help prepare them, mostly in their formative years but also

increasingly through the sometimes rocky turbulence of adulthood, to earn the greatest economic independence they can, given their willingness to work and the advantages (or disadvantages) with which they were born. In short, government should do its best to guarantee *opportunities,* not *results.*

Most Americans believe in the government's role in guaranteeing opportunities, even as median family income has stagnated, the financial bailouts have unfairly benefited the few, and more broadly, income inequality has widened. In the face of all this, most Americans still believe that people in this country are rewarded more for their own hard work and intelligence than for their family background. Yet despite this belief, which we suspect has eroded in the wake of the recession, upward mobility across generations in the United States is now actually lower for native-born Americans than for children in most other advanced countries.[1] Further, mobility in the United States appears to have declined relative to what it was in the 1960s and 1970s. The good news is that Americans born into the middle class (those in the middle 20 percent of the income distribution) still have plenty of opportunity to move up the economic ladder during adulthood (they have an equal chance of moving down as well).[2] We will expand on this fact later in this chapter, while expressing deep concern about the challenge and the difficulty of giving those born into deep poverty a better shot at realizing the American dream.

It is vital for the health of any economy and wider society for the vast majority of its citizens to continue believing in upward mobility. This belief is critical to maintaining popular support for the hugely important market-oriented policies that permit new businesses—the fountains of job growth and breakthrough innovations—to form and flourish. Policies such as trade protection ostensibly aimed at protecting specific jobs and the incomes that go with them only create higher hurdles for other firms to jump over and do little or nothing to advance the welfare of economies as a whole. Higher marginal income tax rates, designed to redistribute economic rewards from high earners and risk takers after the fact, up to a point can help reduce government deficits, but eventually can curtail the entrepreneurial risk taking that leads to more rapid growth and thus a larger economic pie.

Likewise, continued belief in the American dream—the colloquial label in the United States for upward mobility—also is essential for civility in politics, which is especially important in a political system such as that in the United States, which intentionally establishes checks and balances between the three main branches of government. A citizenry and its elected representatives that are deeply divided on major economic and social issues make it virtually impossible for government to help address many pressing national challenges, let alone put the finances of all levels of government back on a sustainable path.

Under normal circumstances, strong and sustained economic growth ensures widespread, although not equal, upward mobility, and thus validates the belief in its inevitability.[3] Growth also smoothes over the potential social frictions that can erupt into violence, or at the very least political stalemate, as Harvard University economist Ben Friedman has persuasively argued.[4] This benefit of growth is especially important for ethnically heterogeneous societies like the United States where ideas are the social glue that keeps things together. No idea, other than a commitment to democracy as a form of government, is as powerful and socially cohesive a force as the belief in the American dream.

But the continued and far-reaching belief in that dream will be tested if economic growth is tepid. The protest movements that have emerged from both ends of the political spectrum over the past few years indicate that such a test is already in progress. If the slow-growth pessimists turn out to be right, it will be especially important for policymakers to implement the right policies—about which we have more to say very shortly—to ensure that plentiful opportunities for upward mobility remain, even if actual rewards are not distributed any more evenly (or even less so) than they are now.

Ensuring opportunity also remains important in a high-growth environment, especially since, as we have argued throughout this book, higher growth is likely to be brought about through sustained innovation by successive waves of entrepreneurs. Like the enormous riches earned by the pathbreaking entrepreneurs of recent times, the future entrepreneurs of home run or even somewhat less successful companies are also likely to become very wealthy. Must, therefore, a future high-growth economy produce only a few "winners who take all"? And even if it does, can enough people have a shot at being among them, or riding along with them, that the *belief* in the American dream remains alive and well? What can be done to best ensure that this will be true—and specifically dispel fears of a shrinking middle class and the shrinking income growth of those who remain there? These are the central questions we address in the balance of this chapter.

Would Faster Growth Necessarily Lead to More Unequal Incomes?

The conventional answer to how well individuals are paid in any capitalist society is that it all depends on how productive they are. People who generate more income and wealth for society, either on their own as business founders and owners or as employees, earn more.

But how much money people earn and thus the living standards they can sustain (without putting themselves deeply into debt) in turn depends on multiple factors: primarily their skills, but also their social connections (which people inherit through their families and make on their own, increasingly with the aid of Internet social networking tools), and of course, luck. The best way to make your own luck, however, is through education—both formally through schooling and by working in the right environments that will teach you the right skills, so that you can use them in the right place and at the right time.

How would faster growth, made possible by accelerated waves of entrepreneurial innovation, affect this time-tested formula for personal economic success and satisfaction? The distribution of monetary benefits from these enterprises would depend primarily on the number of skilled jobs these new companies generate and how many people have the skills to fill them. But not to be overlooked is that the innovative products and services generated by innovative companies benefit the vast majority of individuals and their family members who do not actually work for the innovative firms, but who purchase the goods and services they produce, and who may work for other firms spawned by the initial innovators. Think, for example, of all the people who work for suppliers to the automobile or personal computer industry, or the entrepreneurs (and their employees) who build "apps" for the various hardware platforms that continue to be developed—for Microsoft, Apple, Google, and a spate of new companies that will surely follow in their wake.

At the end of the day, however, the distribution of the rewards from innovation will depend on its pace relative to the number of individuals who can adapt to and profit from it. As professors Lawrence Katz and Claudia Goldin of Harvard have put it in one of the most comprehensive studies of how people are paid, the distribution of income is determined primarily by what they term the "race" between technology and education.[5] The more rapidly technology changes, the faster do the skill requirements for workers. The more gradually the technology changes, the easier it is for all of us to adjust to the changes. Readers with white-collar jobs (and many with traditional blue-collar ones as well) will know how in their own lives they have gradually become accustomed to using word processing and spreadsheet programs, for example. Yet when the pace of change accelerates or when change comes too suddenly—the "Future Shock" scenario—it is difficult for a lot of people to quickly and constantly learn new skills. In such a world, the few who can keep up find employers bidding up their wages. Many software engineers, for example, have benefited greatly from the huge demand for their talents in the immediate post-recession years due to the boom in Web 2.0 companies.[6]

It would seem, therefore, that an economy with more rapid growth is more likely to generate increasing income disparity, because the technological advances behind faster growth are likely to be racing ahead more quickly than the supply of workers with sufficient skills to fill the jobs generated by the new advances. This will only be true, however, if the supply of individuals with the requisite skills remains constant. Fortunately, where people are free to learn new skills and move to new jobs or to create their own jobs through the firms they launch, in response to market signals, the supply of workers and entrepreneurs with the new skills will expand over time to meet the demand. In other words, skills and education will constantly be striving to catch up with technology, if always with a lag, which will keep income disparity from continuing to widen.

In fact, there is evidence from much of American post–World War II experience that rapid economic growth can lift the fortunes of all parts of the income distribution, from lowest to highest. The two periods of fastest productivity growth (and growth in per-capita income) were 1948–73 and 1993–2000. In both cases, the percentage gains in income in all five quintiles of the income distribution were about the same. In each of these cases, rapid growth turned out to be balanced, generating demand for workers with widely different levels of skills. The latter period, in particular, coincided with an entrepreneurial boom, making it clear that entrepreneurial growth does not necessarily lead to widening income inequality.

There is no guarantee that these patterns will repeat themselves in the future if growth escalates, as we argue here that it should and can. In part, if the patterns differ, it may be because education and skills are not the only factors determining income and its distribution across society. It helps to be in the right industry, and the right firm, at the right time—or, in other words, to be lucky. The early workers at Google, Microsoft, Apple, Intel, or at any of the other successful high-tech companies of recent years earned riches if they received stock or options. They took risks to work for fledgling companies at the time, but also surely count themselves lucky to have been there when economic lightning struck.

In recent years, those working for financial companies have been among the luckiest in our economy, riding along with the wave of their companies' successes. The overall numbers tell part of the story. As our colleagues Paul Kedrosky and Dane Stangler have documented, the financial sector accounted for a steadily growing share of GDP throughout the post–World War II period, hitting a high of 8.4 percent of the nation's GDP in 2009–10—surprisingly, in the two years *after* the financial crisis.[7] A rarefied few in finance, principally the founders of hedge and private equity funds, have earned enormous riches, some in the billions of dollars a year.[8] This almost surely explains the finding by economists Robert Gordon and Ian Dew-Becker that the incomes earned at the very, very top of the income distribution—those with the highest 10 percent of all incomes—increased more rapidly from 1977–2001 than the incomes in any other slice of the distribution.[9]

It is difficult to attribute the outsized gains of this very narrow class of financial entrepreneurs to their education alone. While a doctoral degree in a mathematics-oriented field is necessary today for some successful trading activities, it is certainly not the general rule for founders of hedge or private equity funds, who come from varied educational backgrounds, not all of them mathematical.[10] The skills—yes, there are skills to making it in the very cutthroat world of high finance—that have enabled most of these founders to rise to the top of the income distribution are a unique blend of market-relevant knowledge, sometimes networks, the willingness to run against the grain (which is difficult to do in a business like finance with such a strong herd mentality), and of course luck.

Yet even the distortions in the income distribution introduced by the outsized gains in finance earned by a few do not contradict the notion that it is *opportunity* rather than *results* that matters. The most important characteristic of the hedge and private equity fund kings, for purposes of this book, is that few of them came from wealthy families or were "born into the business." The rise to the top in this new high finance is about as meritocratic as can be. Investors care not a whit about your breeding, but about your investment philosophy and especially your returns. In this environment individuals born to families with modest means, or from foreign lands, have made it to the very top. Even in the slightly less-remunerative executive suites of the top banks, one finds today individuals from all kinds of backgrounds, not the aristocracy that once characterized most of this business. The acid test for any meritocracy is whether the children of those at the top will inherit the jobs of those who made it. The answer is clearly no, unless by chance a child has the drive and savvy that drove the father (or in the rare case, the mother) to the top of the investment world.

This is not to say that the wealthy cannot pass on huge advantages to their children, for certainly they do—not just money, but the finest schools, the best upbringing, and useful social networks. But what is true of high finance is also true for much of the rest of U.S. business, for both publicly held companies and entrepreneurial firms. Hard work in school and later on the job, combined with savvy and often luck at being in the right place at the right time, is still what counts. It may help to attend a prestigious private college but that, too, is no guarantee of success. According to a study by *U.S. News and World Report,* although Harvard was the most frequently attended college of CEOs of Fortune 500 companies in 2010, also ranking near the top were high-quality public universities such as Wisconsin–Madison, Michigan–Ann Arbor, Texas–Austin, and Ohio State.[11]

Where you went to school, or sometimes even how long you attended, matters even less if you found your own company. To be sure, it is important to gain certain skills from any school at any level you attend, and the evidence suggests you are more likely to try the entrepreneurial path if your parents were entrepreneurs or you worked while in high school or college in a family-owned business (not necessarily that of your parents).[12] But despite the popular myth that you need to get in and attend, at least for a time, an Ivy League or equivalent school to start a very successful company, it is just that—a myth. This is not to take anything away, of course, from the huge successes of individuals like Bill Gates or Mark Zuckerberg, both Harvard dropouts, but it is far from clear that either needed Harvard in any way to launch his company. More generally, the data show that they are clearly the exceptions and not the rule. Only 8 percent of successful high-tech startups, for example, were founded by individuals who received their terminal degree at an Ivy League school.[13] Even more to the point, most high-tech founders come from middle-class or upper lower-class family backgrounds. The common element among them is that they tend to be highly educated.[14] More broadly, among the wider population of all entrepreneurs, the evidence suggests that financial resources are not a determining factor as to whether someone launches a startup.[15]

In short, the rewards for success in America may be getting more unequally distributed—in part because U.S. firms increasingly compete in a global economy where the "winner-take-all (or most)" reward structure can generate huge payoffs for the successful, often because of the Internet, in astonishingly short periods of time—but it is still possible for the hardworking and the lucky to rise to the top. The land of opportunity, or the American dream, clearly remains alive and well if you work hard, get a good education, and (sometimes) get lucky (although those who work hard and become educated tend to *make* their own luck).

But What about Those Who Start Life Behind?

Sadly, however, the cards still are stacked against far too many Americans who are born to families or single parents with little or no income, and disproportionately to minorities locked in high-crime, low-income neighborhoods with poor schools and inadequate health care. For these individuals, making a successful life and realizing even aspects of the American dream can be and often is a difficult, if not impossible, struggle. A major reason for this, of course, is that too many children from these backgrounds, if they graduate, do not acquire the skills necessary for good jobs or careers in today's labor market. Too many simply drop out of school before they finish the twelfth grade. According to data from the Department of Education, since 2000, roughly 25–30 percent of high-school freshmen have failed to graduate high school on time. Graduation rates are far lower in many schools with large populations of students from low-income families (which are more likely to be found in cities), though not even schools with higher-income populations (more likely to be found in suburban areas) are untouched by the dropout problem.[16] And even among students who make it to college, only about half graduate on time (in four years).[17]

Some may be tempted to point to the success of first- or second-generation immigrants and ask: if they can do it, why can't native-born Americans who start from a similar, disadvantaged station in life? There certainly is no shortage of immigrant success stories. As we discussed in great detail in Chapter 5, immigrants account for a disproportionate share of successful high-tech startups. Many also have achieved remarkable educational success from families that have only been in America for a relatively short time. As one measure, consider the fact that over 30 percent of the undergraduate and graduate students at the University of California, Berkeley, one of the nation's leading public universities, now come from families with Asian backgrounds, a statistic that few would have believed a generation ago.[18] Asian and other immigrants account for high and growing numbers of students at other high-profile public and private universities. To be sure, as we have just argued, attendance at (and more importantly graduation from) an elite university does not automatically translate into huge wealth or top business positions later in life. Nonetheless, it is difficult to argue with the fact that the immigrant children who have achieved educational success are well on their way to realizing their own American dream.

But what is holding back native-born Americans, especially minorities, who are born into dire circumstances? Volumes have been written on this subject, and we do not have the space here (nor, we suspect, readers' attention) to give the subject the full attention it deserves. But clearly one key difference has to be that the children of immigrant families who find success later in life tend to be raised in a stable *family* environment, with two hardworking parents (either in the workplace or at home). Children born out of wedlock to single mothers, in contrast, start out life with huge disadvantages. As Brookings Institution senior fellows Ron Haskins and Isabel Sawhill have summarized it:

> Those who finish high school, work full time, and marry before having children are virtually guaranteed a place in the middle class. Only about 2 percent of this group ends up in poverty. Conversely, about three-fourths of those who have done none of these three things are poor in any given year.[19]

Emerging medical evidence suggests that some sort of abuse or trauma in childhood can also literally change the way the brain works, compounding the negative impacts of a poor economic environment and thus further impairing the financial and medical futures of children who grow up in low-income families and neighborhoods.[20]

There is only so much that governmental policies can do to break these vicious cycles of despair, aggravated by cultural norms that discourage some children with such backgrounds from achieving success by "acting white,"[21] and the vocabulary handicap that many poor children from single-parent households live with from their earliest years.[22] Welfare reform was supposed to help break these behavioral cycles that get passed from generation to generation by encouraging single mothers to work, and by doing so, discourage single parenthood in the first place. After fifteen years, the reform has had some success: welfare rolls are down,[23] and teen pregnancies that result in childbirth are at an all-time low.[24] However, welfare reform is clearly not a panacea, as teen births still persist at unacceptable levels, especially among low-income populations.[25]

We do not claim to have the answer to the hugely difficult problem of giving native-born children and their parent(s) a better chance to improve their station in life and, in their own way, realize the American dream. Indeed, we strongly doubt that there is any one answer or magic bullet. But two propositions, we believe, must be part of any solution.

First, since education vastly increases the earning power of individuals—the lifetime premium for completing college over finishing high school is still about $1 million—innovative ways must be found to give students the skills they need to keep learning throughout life and, at the very least, reduce the chances that they will drop out before they finish high school.[26]

We argue in the next section that teaching students how to launch a real business, along with the necessary skills, is likely to be an important part of both the in- and out-of-classroom school experience.

Second, public policy must find ways of harnessing the entrepreneurial energy of both private- and public-sector institutions and individuals to change the culture that condemns both children and adults to life at the bottom of the economic ladder. We have some sketchy answers below that address this challenge, but sketchy is better than none. Most important, the need to begin this particular conversation in order to stimulate more and better ideas could not be greater or more urgent.

The entrepreneurship we speak of in this chapter is different than the growth entrepreneurship we have emphasized in the book up to now. Here we refer to the need for as many people as possible to have an entrepreneurial *mind-set* and *set of skills*—that is, to be able and eager to engage in continuous innovative, out-of-the-box thinking, to be flexible and adaptable to changing circumstances, and perhaps most important, to be able *to implement ideas or seize opportunities by launching a real business, or to carry out the project within an existing organization*. These are real skills that must be taught and conveyed to all members of society and drawn on throughout their lives, especially for those who start out with huge disadvantages. It is both an economic and a moral imperative.

Entrepreneurship and Upward Mobility

Any reader of this book is likely to be highly familiar with the by-now standard list of remedies for improving the quality of K–12 education, especially in schools with high concentrations of minorities or students from low-income backgrounds. In brief, these solutions attempt to translate private-sector modes of operating and behavior into public schools by providing performance incentives for teachers, more freedom for principals to dismiss teachers who perform poorly, alternative methods of teacher certification outside of traditional education programs, and rigorous national standards for achievement to supersede states' looser standards, to name a few. The conventional reform list also includes more competition in the provision of schooling itself, whether through vouchers or charter schools, or both. One especially exciting source of competition is from unconventional entrants into education like Salman Khan, founder of the Khan Academy, whose growing number of YouTube videos on math and other subjects is subverting the use of standard, costly print textbooks and giving students and teachers alike powerful new ways of learning that hold great promise for improving the educational performance of students from any socioeconomic background.

Notably, the aforementioned list of remedies does not include more money per pupil, for several good reasons. First, there is no clear, documented link between per-pupil spending and educational outcome (this is clearly true with Khan Academy videos, which are free). Second, the money simply is not available. And third, even if more money were readily available, why pour more money into a broken system?

As a mental exercise, suppose that a magic wand were waved and all of the reform ideas mentioned above were implemented across the United States. We would be the last to dispute that such changes would represent major progress of the first order. But even repairing the overall K–12 educational system still does not necessarily ensure that it will equip students with all the skills they will need to succeed in twenty-first century labor markets.

The most important skills in the modern labor market include the desire to *continue learning well past formal schooling* and the ability to continuously adapt to, and ideally anticipate, the needs of employers and potential customers (for those thinking of launching a business or who already have one). Gone are the days when one could learn the basics, graduate and go work for a large corporation until retirement. Graduates from high school, college, or graduate school today can expect to be in many different jobs throughout their career, even if they do not start their own business. Indeed, technology and shifts in consumer wants give rise to new jobs and occupations. The positions of privacy officer or social networking supervisor, to name a couple, were unheard of several years ago but now are increasingly found in many companies.

To navigate this complicated terrain, people need to think of themselves as their own business, one that must continue to learn and to innovate by developing or adapting new skills that the marketplace requires. Most of these perpetual "students" will put their ever-evolving skills into the service of employers. But many will choose to work for themselves and hire others to follow them. Regardless, all of us, and especially our children, will need entrepreneurial skills our entire working lives.

Several key questions loom, however. What kind of formal school curriculum (primarily K–12, but also in college) will best equip individuals for the entrepreneurial challenges they will face as adults? Is entrepreneurial training best taught inside or outside the classroom, or a combination of both? Ideally, there would be clear and well-researched answers to both of these key questions. Unfortunately, that is not the case, at least so far. Instead, the best we can offer now are our own inclinations, which are rooted in nearly a decade of grant-making experience at a foundation committed to advancing both entrepreneurship and education.

Clearly, success in the workplace and in any entrepreneurial endeavor requires some mastery of certain basic skills—reading comprehension, mathematical reasoning (at least algebraic and ideally statistical), scientific understanding, and information technology proficiency. But these are hardly sufficient. Other less tangible skills are also crucial. Teamwork is important in any endeavor and can be learned through participation in sports or other group and school activities. Creative thinking, as expressed through art, design, music, or other mediums, is also important. Steve Jobs's and Apple's success provide clear proof. Jobs credited a calligraphy course he took in college (almost as an afterthought) as his inspiration to include multiple fonts in Apple's software.[27] Moreover, Apple would not be the successful company it is today without a strong commitment to elegant design accompanying its innovative engineering.

Unfortunately, we know of no K–12 school or set of schools that has successfully developed a curriculum centered on entrepreneurship—developing new ideas and implementing them by launching real enterprises—that can be easily duplicated by other schools. The Kauffman Foundation took some initial steps in this direction in September 2011 when it opened in Kansas City, Missouri, the first charter school in the United States operated and funded by a foundation. The school targets students from a low-income background starting in the fifth grade. Like many other charter schools, it had far more applicants than the hundred available spots in the first class, and so the first class was ultimately chosen by lottery. Although the new Ewing Marion Kauffman School will not teach "an entrepreneurial curriculum" in the sense in which we have just described it, the school will introduce entrepreneurial themes, both in and out of the classroom, in each of the grade levels until graduation.

What might an entrepreneurial curriculum actually look like? Answering that question well and implementing the answer is one of the great educational challenges of this century. We have only some preliminary thoughts on the matter, which we hope will stimulate others more qualified to flesh out other ideas or put real meat on the bare bones of the following.

First, teachers in all grades should have suitable materials and be able to use them to encourage students to be creative by solving actual problems. As just one example, consider as a model Stanford University's well-known, highly selective Bio-X program for doctors who want to be entrepreneurs. One of the first things that participants in this program are asked to do is to spend some time in the Stanford Hospital and come up with several hundred ideas for improving its performance. That simple but challenging exercise could easily be repeated in high schools (and perhaps earlier) by sending out students to the venues of their choice—retail stores, restaurants, airports, and the like—to identify myriad ways that these organizations could be improved and develop concrete plans for doing so, ideally as entirely new businesses to compete with the firms they observe, or by selling supplies and services to them.

Real-world entrepreneurial problem solving can also taught in the classroom by infusing math, science, and history at all levels with examples and stories that illustrate an entrepreneurial principle. For example, math classes can be centered on the real additions, subtractions, divisions, and multiplications (among other exercises) that real businesses confront every day. It is not too early, for example, to teach students math through spreadsheets as early as the fourth or fifth grade. Science courses should not only explain the basic principles of the material, but also demonstrate to students how the principles being taught are or have been incorporated in real products, and discuss the businesses that use them. Even many literature and history lessons can and should be taught with entrepreneurship and business themes in mind.

Second, students at some point—we believe before high school—should be taught how ideas can be translated into real businesses, and equipped with the skills to launch a business themselves. This includes testing markets (or as a substitute, doing market research, through surveys for example) to see whether customers will buy what they think they have to sell; figuring out ways to bootstrap their companies so they do not need much capital; and only as a last resort figuring out how much outside money may be really needed and in what form (debt or equity—yes, these terms can be taught to those in middle school, and perhaps even younger). In short, all high school graduates must be thoroughly financially literate and able to start a business if they want. Even if they never do launch a firm, having these skills and knowing that they are crucial to economic well-being in the twenty-first century will stand them in good stead throughout their lives.

Admittedly, an entrepreneurship-centered curriculum faces a classic chicken-and-egg problem. Textbook writers and software developers will not write or develop suitable materials unless they know there is an ample market for them. Conversely, teachers will find it difficult to teach math, science, literature, and history courses infused with entrepreneurial themes and examples unless the texts and supplementary materials are available. Foundations can help crack this problem by funding new materials and the schools that will use them. Ideally, the federal government would jump into the fray by awarding prizes for the best classroom materials making use of entrepreneurial themes and by funneling grant monies to low-income school districts that teach an entrepreneurial curriculum.

We believe—but admit we cannot yet prove—that an entrepreneurial secondary education is not only important pedagogically, but is also a potentially powerful way to address the dropout problem. One important reason driving high dropout rates surely is that too many kids are bored by school and see it as irrelevant to their lives, now or in the future (to the extent that kids, who are notoriously present-thinking, even think about the future—they should be taught this as well). How to earn money, however, is one thing that all kids understand. As a simple matter of common sense, instruction that equips them with the skills to legally earn a living and provides them with examples of how others whom they admire *and can identify with* have done so is central to keeping their interest.

Role models, of course, will vary from child to child and over time, but it should not be too difficult to figure out who they are, or for students themselves to point the way. Most teenagers, for example, would have a natural interest in how sports teams, various entertainers, television shows, and video game companies get started and generate earnings. Certain students may display interest in industries with narrower appeal, such as fashion, food, or retailing. Unlike participation in sports teams, which necessarily must be limited to a chosen few, the understanding of business and what it takes to start and grow one can be made available to all students. If taught correctly and constantly reinforced in different contexts throughout a student's K–12 education, launching a business can be placed within the grasp and dreams of everyone. The same cannot be said for a career in professional sports, or even music or the arts. As Scott Adams, creator of the famous *Dilbert* cartoon series, aptly puts it:

> I understand why the top students in America study physics, chemistry, calculus and classic literature. The kids in this brainy group are the future professors, scientists, thinkers and engineers who will propel civilization forward. But why do we make B students sit through the same classes? That's like trying to train your cat to do your taxes—a waste of time and money. Would it not make more sense to teach B students something useful like entrepreneurship?[28]

We agree wholeheartedly with this sentiment, but with one exception. Entrepreneurship is for A students too, for many of them also will change the world.

The key for educational funding organizations—government, foundations, or a combination of the two—is to support the development of a wide *menu* of materials from which teachers can pick and choose, depending on the interest of their students. As interest in entrepreneurial curricula grows, private entrepreneurs and even established textbook publishers and software developers will realize the market opportunities and greatly expand the "apps" that are available, much as PC and cellular device platforms have stimulated the development of hundreds of thousands of apps for their users.

One continued unresolved issue is whether schools can best institute this kind of entrepreneurial training in the classroom or out of it. For high school and possibly middle school students, we do not believe a choice has to be made. Both types of instruction should be pursued. The right in-school curricula can excite students about the possibilities created by entrepreneurial thinking, whereas extracurricular competitions, clubs, and programs can give them necessary hands-on experience. One does not learn basketball or football solely through the X's and O's on a blackboard, but rather through actually playing the game. Likewise, entrepreneurial interest is best stimulated through actual participation in a wide range of out-of-school activities. Equipping budding entrepreneurs with the right set of skills is no different than drilling gifted athletes, musicians, writers, and other professionals in extensive exercises. "Practice makes perfect" is much more than an aphorism—it is the key to success in any pursuit.[29]

Fortunately, there are some worthy out-of-classroom entrepreneurial activities to build on. The National Federation for Teaching Entrepreneurship (NFTE) organizes entrepreneurship competitions and encourages entrepreneurship in the classroom in twenty-one states and ten countries. Junior Achievement has a long record of encouraging entrepreneurship in an out-of-school environment. DECA (formerly known as the Distributive Economic Clubs of America) runs a highly popular national high school marketing competition. As successful as each of these programs is, none appears to us to have stimulated the kind of enthusiasm generated by First Robotics, a national engineering competition launched by inventor-entrepreneur Dean Kamen (and, in the interest of full disclosure, supported by the Kauffman Foundation for Kansas City–area schools). One challenge for a like-minded entrepreneur is to create one or more First Robotics equivalents for budding entrepreneurs in middle and high schools. For example, an ideal out-of-school entrepreneurial activity for older students could be the development of applications software promoting entrepreneurial learning. Such an activity could be accelerated by mentors with programming experience and by some sort of profit sharing among the students and the school, similar to universities and their faculty, but hopefully with liberal commercialization rules (see Chapter 4).

Are there enough qualified teachers to effectively incorporate and communicate any new entrepreneurial material to students? The easiest cohort of teachers to tap (with little persuasion needed) will be new teachers, especially those coming out of the Teach for America (TFA) program. But in the short run, even TFA is unlikely to be able to supply more than a fraction of the teachers needed in the cities where it is active. More help will be needed, and one of the best ways to provide it is for states to modify their teaching certification requirements to permit more individuals with real work experience, ideally entrepreneurial, to teach part or full time in the classroom. Although this idea has been slow to get off the ground, largely due to opposition from teachers' unions, state and local budget pressures should eventually change the dynamic. With more public school teachers retiring over the next decade, states and localities will not only have less opposition to alternative certification, but may find it easier and less expensive to recruit from an ample supply of workers who do not want to go back to the private sector or want to leave it altogether for a second (or third) career. Those teachers hailing from the business world would infuse new ideas and methods into teaching, and likely would be more amenable to experimenting with entrepreneurial teaching materials.

Of course, it will be necessary to find ways to reward teachers who successfully impart entrepreneurial skills to their students. This will require new methods of testing for which the government should provide development grants. In addition, teachers who supervise out-of-classroom entrepreneurial activities should be paid for their time and expertise. Mentors from the business world who want to volunteer their time, perhaps as part of a permanent Startup America campaign, should be recruited for these out-of-classroom activities. If special payments or bonuses are required to attract them to schools with a large number of low-income students, then these expenses would be well worth the cost. For example, why not enlist front office personnel from local sports teams to run summer camps for kids who want to learn about the *business of sports*—including the challenge of finding and recruiting talented athletes? In other words, turn the fascination with "fantasy" sports teams into something far more useful and productive, with life lessons added to boot. Keeping at-risk kids in school and interested in building their future surely will cut crime and the huge costs that go into preventing and punishing it. It's a lot cheaper to spend roughly $15,000 a year teaching a student something that interests them and keeps them in school than paying more than $40,000 to warehouse them in prison—not to mention the costs that go into putting them there.

Entrepreneurial training should not end with high school, of course. Students in college are likely to have more skills and be surrounded by more entrepreneurial opportunities. Many colleges have recognized this and increasingly are offering a range of programs to assist budding entrepreneurs in their midst. In Chapter 3, for example, we discussed The Launch Pad, which started at the University of Miami and is spreading to other campuses. There is no reason that *every* college should not have a similar program, centered in its career office and not put in a silo as they often are, most frequently in business schools. Other universities are beginning to establish entrepreneurs' dorms, and many schools have tech-oriented entrepreneurship mentoring programs that are either part of the regular curriculum or, more often, situated in an out-of-school setting.

Much experimentation and expansion in these post-secondary entrepreneurship efforts will be necessary. But these efforts also tend to be aimed at a limited, motivated, and self-selected audience: students that already have the entrepreneurial itch and are probably least likely to drop out of college—or if they do, it is to pursue an entrepreneurial dream that is strengthened while they are in school. These programs should *not* therefore be viewed as a panacea to the college dropout problem, although it is possible that some could attract and retain a limited number of students who might otherwise drop out.

We are fully aware of the ambitiousness of what we are suggesting. Turning schools into entrepreneurial engines is something that cannot be dictated from the top down by the federal government, especially in the highly decentralized school system that has long characterized the United States and is unlikely to change any time soon.[30] But this is not necessarily a bad thing. Decentralization allows ample opportunity for experimentation. Just as "good capitalism" is inherently messy, so must be the way schools impart entrepreneurial traits to their students. Governments can facilitate this process largely by removing roadblocks and providing incentives for enterprising school leaders who realize that they must impart the skills and mind-set to their students who will grow up to compete in an ever-more-rapidly changing economy than the one in which they must themselves compete. This truth only becomes more evident if growth accelerates, which we hope for and advocate throughout the rest of this book.

Entrepreneurship as One Ticket Out of the Underclass

As difficult as it is to transform and improve the U.S. K–12 educational system—especially for students from low-income families—an even more imposing challenge is how to provide opportunity for *adults* mired in poverty, not only for themselves, but for their children. If the parents' lives are not also improved then the children have a great chance of being trapped in the same depressing, vicious cycle of poverty.

Clearly, we are not the first to recognize or attempt to address this challenge. Lowering the poverty rate has been a pressing national goal for all of our adult lives, especially since President Lyndon Johnson's famous declaration of a "war" on poverty. Unfortunately, despite politicians' tendency to declare war on all kinds of domestic policy problems, such as cancer or drugs, these efforts have mixed results at best. Such is true of the war on poverty as well. Many approaches have been tried, ranging from just giving the poor more money in cash; in-kind vouchers or their equivalents, such as food stamps, health care, and housing allowances; and access to legal services and job training. Nothing seems to have made a significant impact. During times of economic expansion, small dents have been made in the poverty rate, although some measurements, such as consumption, indicate that the poverty rate has fallen on account of the cheaper prices of goods like food and appliances.[31]

Nonetheless, poverty, however it is defined, remains with us and is a disturbing reminder that a rising economic tide does not necessarily lift all boats. To some, what needs to accompany that tide is a cultural transformation that changes the mind-set of the poor.[32] To others, poverty is something that cannot be helped because those mired in it either do not have the intelligence to change their lives, or after growing up in dysfunctional schools and environments they are unable to change.[33]

We understand this pessimism, as well as the "poverty fatigue" that many citizens may have, given how impervious poverty seems to the many different public policy approaches that have been used in an attempt to remedy it. But we are not ready to give up. There are many anecdotal success stories of individuals who grew up in poverty and escaped to have hugely successful lives—Oprah Winfrey, Chris Gardner (the homeless salesman who became a stockbroker and is featured in the best-selling memoir and movie, *The Pursuit of Happyness*), and Robert Johnson, the founder of the BET network—to name a few. To write off the millions who are still caught in the underclass as being incapable of improving their fortune is shortsighted and wrongheaded.

Up to now, the generally accepted assumption about reducing poverty is that the poor must be trained to work for *someone else*. Few have dared to think that perhaps some of the poor, with the right training and policy reforms, might actually be able to *create a job for themselves* and perhaps *even for others as well*.

Policy reform must be the first step to make such a vision reality because, as with job training, there is no point to entrepreneurial training of any type unless there are entrepreneurial opportunities to pursue. At first blush, it would seem that there would not be sufficient possibilities in low-income neighborhoods that low-income individuals would have the financial wherewithal to follow. But that is in part because of unnecessary professional licenses or excessively burdensome municipal or state regulations that preclude low-income individuals from owning their own business.[34] Endeavors such as cutting hair, providing local transportation, child care, and other similar services and activities could turn into self-sustaining businesses that provide low-income individuals with jobs—not only for themselves but for others—if local governments eliminated or reduced the legal barriers to these activities. Existing requirements may be well intentioned and are ostensibly designed to protect consumers from shoddy or poor service, but they can also have the harmful side effect of preventing enterprising individuals from owning a business, while ignoring the power of the marketplace to weed out poor providers. Consumers, after all, have the power to simply say "no" and patronize others who deliver higher-quality service.

This is not to say that some occupational training might not improve the quality of these services. It may well be, but that is for the market and the providers and consumers themselves to determine. If they think that going to barber school, for example, will improve customer satisfaction and thereby lead to higher income, barbers will attend, but only after they have earned some cash to pay for the training.

Basic entrepreneurial training—bookkeeping with simple software, learning how to accept credit and debit cards, designing and maintaining a web page, marketing a service, and attracting and retaining customers—is likely to be even more important to budding and active entrepreneurs in low-income communities than occupational training. The Small Business Administration supports Small Business Development Centers around the country, but often these SBDCs are not focused on the kinds of business that low-income individuals are likely to start. Nor do we believe that entrepreneurship training classes offered at many community colleges, whether using their own curricula or the FastTrac course popularized by the Kauffman Foundation, are entirely able to fill this gap. Goldman Sachs launched a "10,000 Small Businesses" initiative in 2010 aimed at low-income areas and it is gradually being expanded to more cities, but this effort is targeted at already established businesses with at least $150,000 in revenue.

Accordingly, there is a vacuum to be filled. Would-be entrepreneurs in low-income neighborhoods need specialized assistance to get started. Current entrepreneurship training needs to be adapted to the skill levels of those attending, and even translated into different languages so that materials are accessible to individuals from diverse ethnic backgrounds. In addition, the people needed to conduct this kind of training require unique skill sets that are different from the skills required to serve as leaders and mentors for a primarily middle-class clientele.

With municipal and state budgets already stretched to breaking point, there is the obvious question of where the money for all this will come from. Local foundations are one obvious source, but so are local companies that stand to benefit from more prosperous and safer communities with stronger, more stable entrepreneurial roots. Ideally, this idea would have an entrepreneurial champion like Wendy Kopp, who started Teach for America. Hopefully, there are similar advocates out there, perhaps reading this book, who will launch a low-income entrepreneurship initiative equivalent to Teach For America, possibly to be staffed by recent college graduates and assisted by local entrepreneurs. Such a program would build an entrepreneurial path out of poverty for many enterprising, low-income individuals who have for too long been ignored by the policymaking community.

We do not want to oversell this agenda. Only a small minority of residents of low-income areas is likely to have the inclination to start a business and to be able to successfully run it. But even if that share is 10 percent—roughly the share of self-employment in the larger population—the jobs created for the entrepreneurs and the people they may be able to hire could make a sizeable impact on the poverty problem in various areas around the country. Moreover, as more low-income individuals become successful, they will become role models for their children and others in the community, giving them hope that they can move up the economic ladder, too. Revitalization of low-income neighborhoods will also attract mainstream businesses, retail stores, doctors, and other service providers, who also will create more jobs.

In short, an entrepreneurial growth agenda for low-income individuals and neighborhoods can become the impetus that begins to lift many out of poverty and toward a better life. Entrepreneurship may not be a silver bullet that cures poverty—there is no such thing—but it is one powerful weapon the potential of which is not yet even close to being fully deployed. If you are not convinced yet, then consider the entrepreneurial revolutions that are lifting huge numbers of people out of poverty in countries like China and India. Why not here?

Entrepreneurship and the Middle Class

The Great Recession clearly illustrated that the U.S. economy had inadequate financial regulation, which helped precipitate the financial crisis that preceded the economic downturn. But another weakness has been exposed as well: an absence of opportunities for the many millions who lost their jobs to return to meaningful and well-paying work. Further, the longer workers go without a job, the more difficult it is for them to find one.[35]

As we suggested at the outset of this chapter, many Americans are wondering what will happen to the middle class during the lengthy period required for a sustained recovery.[36] This is especially true in an increasingly global economy where skilled workers from around the world, willing to work for lower wages than are paid in this country (though they may not necessarily be as productive as our workers), are competing for a wider range of manufacturing and service jobs. A faster growing economy here—which we should want because it produces newer and cheaper goods and services at a more rapid pace—also may more rapidly change skill sets required of workers and thus intensify their anxieties.

The only way to assure a prosperous middle class freer from current worries about their future is to equip as many individuals as possible with the skills demanded by employers and the desire to continuously learn new things. Sound familiar by now? It should, because the same entrepreneurial mind-set and toolkit we need to give our current and future school graduates also must be shared by those already in the workforce.

Fortunately, for those willing to look for them, there are ample opportunities to gain basic entrepreneurial training in community colleges and even online, at minimal cost. Indeed, with the growing popularity of online universities and the marketplace's increasing acceptance of their degrees, individuals who put forth the effort to educate themselves have greater opportunities than ever before to learn and become certified for new jobs and careers. This trend will only continue as online education becomes mainstream. The federal government could help in this regard by urging accrediting organizations to *accredit individual online courses* for college credit, rather than restricting accreditation to entire online schools as is the case now. In the meantime, individuals who want face-to-face instruction can go to community colleges to learn new skills, including basic entrepreneurship.

Whether individuals work for themselves through the businesses they create or for others, they will be well equipped for the future if they constantly think like entrepreneurs. They must look for the *next* opportunity and plan for multiple outcomes. Indeed, individuals who only have a "Plan A" for their career, next job, or business will be at a disadvantage relative to those who have many different plans and are ready to implement those plans B, C, or D, either by seeking out the required training or starting new enterprises themselves. As the title of a book one of us (Schramm) has written puts it, we are all facing an "entrepreneurial imperative."[37]

Again, we are not claiming that entrepreneurial education, or even an entrepreneurial mind-set, will protect everyone in the middle class from the tumultuous changes in the marketplace's demand for skills, a circumstance that is likely to intensify with more rapid growth. We do argue, however, that a commitment to lifelong learning is the best insurance one can purchase against economic retrogression in this new environment. There are really no other alternatives.

Conclusion

As we have argued throughout this book, a faster-growing economy will not be possible without continuous entrepreneurial revolution. In turn, the entrepreneurs who lead these revolutions almost certainly will earn substantial rewards. Historically, Americans have not begrudged them these rewards so long as there are opportunities for everyone, regardless of their initial station in life, to realize their own American dream.

People throughout the world justifiably resent political and economic systems that do not reward merit. Resentment breeds backlash that can drive governments, whether autocratically ruled or democratically governed, to adopt policies that slow the pace of growth in the interest of slowing or preventing wider inequality gaps.

This is an outcome that must be zealously avoided, and can be as long as our society remains committed to keeping the doors of opportunity wide open. It is undeniable that they are more open to people with inherited abilities, especially those augmented by family status, just as the doors are more difficult to keep open to those who are born into families and neighborhoods of limited means. But even with these unequal starting positions, many Americans have found the way to level the playing field and climb to a higher socioeconomic status than the one to which they were born. Education has been, and must continue to be, central to that effort.

What is different about the twenty-first century, we posit, is that new kinds of education, throughout one's life, will be needed to keep the doors of opportunity open to as many people as possible. This is especially true for those who start out with huge disadvantages. An education that focuses on giving students and eventually adults a continuing thirst for learning and chances to satisfy that thirst is required. This, we suggest, is best accomplished by impressing upon all people, from the earliest possible age, that they are entrepreneurs who control their destinies. An entrepreneurial mind-set, augmented with the skills of recognizing and acting on opportunities, is the key to success in the future. It is also central to sharing the rewards of entrepreneurial growth, not by force, but because they have been earned. That has been America's history. It is also America's destiny.

10

CONCLUSION: THE POLITICAL ECONOMY OF GROWTH

Since the Great Recession, policymakers and voters in developed economies, including the United States, justifiably have been preoccupied with wanting a rapid recovery, even though we believe it is now also widely understood that this expansion will be slower and more gradual than after previous postwar downturns. This is because the recession of 2008–9 was the deepest of this era, but also—more importantly, at least in the case of the United States—American consumers and financial institutions were heavily leveraged going into the financial crisis that precipitated the large drop in output. Consumers therefore understandably have been cautious about returning to their former free-spending ways, too often facilitated by easy lending against what seemed for a long while like perpetually rising home values.

Yet as important as a healthy post-recession recovery is for the future economic, social, and political health of the United States and other developed countries, the main challenge that all of them confront is how to facilitate *rapid sustained* growth in output for decades to come, ideally with gains broadly shared by their populations. We have concentrated on helping to address this challenge for the United States in particular, but we believe that many of the ideas outlined here are equally or similarly applicable to other countries.

We write at a time of some considerable pessimism about the outlook for long-run growth in the United States, however. The consensus forecast for the growth of what economists call "potential GDP per capita" is in the neighborhood of 2 percent, about a percentage point lower than during the 1990s and the "golden" post–World War II quarter-century spanning 1948 to 1973. If instead the United States could somehow return to the annual growth rate of those former periods—in other words, go up to 3 percent per capita—our citizens, and those of the rest of the world who sell to us and routinely copy our ways, would all be considerably much better off.

Our main thesis is that the best way to achieve a sustained higher growth rate is through *continuous entrepreneurial revolutions*. This is not an outcome, however, that governments can simply mandate, even with the best of advice. By definition, entrepreneurial growth requires *entrepreneurs,* especially those who form and nurture the development of high-growth enterprises. Government cannot manufacture such individuals or the innovations they develop and commercialize. But suitable government policies can maximize the chance that economies will be led by such people and the enterprises they create. Our central purpose in writing this book has been to identify what those policies are and to encourage their adoption. Along the way, we have also suggested how private-sector organizations, universities in particular, can help.

At the same time, we recognize that growth never has been and almost certainly never will be smooth. There will be recessions and expansions along the way. Until the Great Recession, most were convinced that monetary policymakers in particular had permanently engineered a "Great Moderation," the term applied to the twenty-five-year period of relative quiescence and reasonable growth after the recessions of 1980–82. Whether we can get that stability back is beyond the scope of this book, but several aspects of that issue—whether the U.S. economy will be derailed by new and even deeper crises—are topics that we have not ignored.

For example, in Chapter 7, we suggested that the best way to avoid or at least minimize the impact of future OPEC-induced energy price shocks is to mandate fuel choice in new automobiles. In Chapter 8, we underscored the urgency of tackling our long-term federal budget deficits in a convincing way in order to avoid a future deep recession triggered by investors' loss of faith in policymakers' willingness to bring those deficits back to sustainable levels. And in Chapter 9, we applied the same entrepreneurial principles that run through the first part of the book to ensuring future opportunities for all Americans, especially those who start life furthest behind, to share in the faster growth that we hope continuous entrepreneurial revolutions will bring about.

Democracy has many virtues, but one of its difficulties is addressing long-term challenges, whether they threaten future crises or, if met, promise significantly better lives for people in the future. Voters and their elected representatives have difficulty taking steps to avoid future crises because even experts disagree as to their likelihood, and because actions required to prevent them typically require some sort of near-term sacrifice that people are not enthused about making, especially with regard to avoiding risks whose likelihood may be disputed and which in any event are highly uncertain. Likewise, it is hard to muster political support for measures that make a distant future look much better when people are struggling now to make ends meet and have difficulty thinking about that future—let alone whether they will be around to benefit from it.

What good, readers might wonder, does it then do (as we have done throughout this book) to develop ideas that are likely to enhance growth *in the future* or to avoid crises that could interrupt it, *also in the future?* Many years ago, John Maynard Keynes pondered this question and answered it with one of his most often-quoted phrases: "The ideas of economists and political philosophers, both when they are right and when they are wrong, are more powerful than is commonly understood. Indeed the world is ruled by little else. Practical men, who believe themselves to be quite exempt from any intellectual influence, are usually the slaves of some defunct economist."

Or, as Keynes put it even more simply: "Ideas shape the course of history." For living proof, look at the United States, a country powered only by ideas (the embrace of democracy and capitalism) and the unwelcome history of communism. We and all others who attempt to influence public opinion with research and writings about policymakers obviously find great comfort in Keynes's observations, which in any event are so sufficiently obvious that if he had not stated them, someone else of note would.

The critical question that political economists wrestle with is "How do ideas—from defunct (or not-yet defunct) economists, social scientists, religious leaders, or political leaders themselves—get implemented?" In a democratic system with three branches of government, such as that in the

United States, the answer depends on the particular branch. For changes in statutes, and to a lesser extent regulations (which "fill-in-the-blanks" statutes deliberately create), the almost tautological answer is policies change when elected officials perceive that a consensus exists for doing so among the electorate, or more frequently among the increasing number of interest groups that represent different electoral constituencies. Cynics may ascribe the same political motivations to judges, but in the vast majority of cases, judges at least claim to gain direction from other sources—the U.S. Constitution, past judicial decisions, and of course, existing statutes and regulations.

These answers, of course, beg the question of when consensus on a particular new course of action is reached. The framers of the Constitution deliberately created a complex system of checks and balances so that any one of the three governmental branches would have difficulty acting alone in any way, except through the president's commitment of military forces, and even those actions are typically subject to congressionally imposed time limits. Such a governmental system is thus deliberately constructed to be comfortable only with incremental change, especially through regulatory decisions by the executive branch or theoretically "independent" agencies and the judiciary, which exist to implement or better define what Congress supposedly once said in the laws that it passed.

Yet ironically, when it does come, statutory change (and to a much lesser extent, change in regulation) sometimes comes abruptly and disruptively, most often in response to a crisis, actual or perceived. Financial crises have been among the most reliable instigators of far-reaching policy change: the Federal Reserve was created in 1913 after the financial panic of 1907; a whole slew of laws and agencies was created in the wake of the Depression; the savings–and-loan and banking crises of the 1980s led to fundamental changes in banking regulation; the financial reporting scandals of the late 1990s and subsequent years led to the Sarbanes-Oxley Act in 2002; and most recently, the financial crisis of 2007–8 led directly to the comprehensive financial reform package embodied in the Dodd-Frank Act of 2010. A sense of political crisis, in contrast, helped spur passage of sweeping civil rights legislation and "Great Society" anti-poverty programs in the 1960s, environmental and social regulatory statutes in the 1960s and in the 1970s, and again, most recently, in comprehensive health care reform legislation enacted in 2010.

In short, big policy changes are possible and do happen, although debate often continues for long periods thereafter over the wisdom of those changes. Typically, when constructing new laws, elected officials and administrations take ideas off the proverbial "policy shelf" and write them into law. We have written this book with the hope that at least some of the ideas in it will now go on that shelf, for use either after future crises, or ideally before them.

At the end of the day, however, Americans do not rely on Washington, or either their state or local governments, to power the U.S. economy. If we have made anything clear in the preceding pages it is that entrepreneurs and the new firms they create and grow are the lifeblood of our economy and its future prospects. Government can help or hurt the growth process, but ultimately the culture of entrepreneurship is sufficiently infused in our society that it will continue under any circumstances to be the driving force for improvement in living standards, here and abroad.

As we have noted at several points throughout this book and are closing with now, the United States exists because of a shared commitment to a set of ideas about governance and the way our economy works. The Great Recession spoiled the faith of many in these ideas, and in the business and political leaders who espoused them. But the economic downturn has not shaken Americans' faith in the ability of entrepreneurs to lead us toward better times. We hope that readers of this book will be even more committed to this proposition now that they have read it, and supportive of policies and practices that will facilitate the entrepreneurial growth to permanently improve our lives and those of future generations.

NOTES

1. Toward Better Capitalism

1. Servan-Schreiber, *The American Challenge*.
2. Baumol has refined and extended this line of thinking in his sure-to-be classic, *The Microtheory of Innovative Entrepreneurship*.
3. Zakaria, "Yes, America Is in Decline."
4. See Reinhart and Reinhart, "After the Fall."
5. Baumol, Litan, and Schramm, *Good Capitalism, Bad Capitalism*, 16–25.
6. Stevenson and Wolfers, "Economic Growth and Subjective Well-Being."
7. Coy, "Why One Economist Predicts Slow Growth."
8. Cowen, *The Great Stagnation*.
9. Council of Economic Advisers, *Economic Report of the President, 2010*, 142.
10. Luft and Korin, *Turning Oil into Salt*.

2. Toward a New Understanding of the Economy

1. We arrive at this number by dividing the roughly 40 million new jobs added by the U.S. economy between 1980 and 2007 by total employment in that latter year.
2. Haltiwanger, Jarmin, and Miranda, "Jobs Created from Business Startups in the United States."
3. Stangler and Litan, "Where Will the Jobs Come From?"
4. Horrell and Litan, "After Inception."
5. Stangler, "High Growth Firms and the Future of the American Economy."
6. Stangler and Kedrosky, "Exploring Firm Formation."
7. Horrell and Litan, "After Inception."
8. Many economists have voiced this view. One of the better analyses supporting it is Reinhart and Reinhart, "After the Fall."

9. For more details on these and other related data, see Reedy and Litan, "Starting Smaller; Staying Smaller."

10. Baumol, *The Microtheory of Innovative Entrepreneurship.*

11. The discussion in the following several paragraphs draws on Schramm, "All Entrepreneurship Is Social."

12. For a great biography of this hugely important economist, see McCraw, *Prophet of Innovation.*

13. The discussion in this section through the rest of the chapter draws on Litan, "Inventive Billion Dollar Firms."

14. Technically, consistent with the qualification in the section immediately above, potential rather than actual GDP should be used as the base of the calculation. At the current writing, given the Great Recession and slow recovery since, actual GDP is probably about 10 percent below potential GDP, which implies a base level of GDP of more than $16 trillion. For illustrative purposes only, however, we use here the current level of GDP as the base from which to make the following calculations.

15. Nordhaus, "Schumpeterian Profits and the Alchemist Fallacy."

16. This 10 percent ratio may be a conservative estimate. Many of the most successful U.S. companies have returns well in excess of this ratio; see the most profitable companies of the Fortune 500 at http://money.cnn.com/magazines/fortune/fortune500/2010/performers/companies/profits/revenues.html.

17. See Stangler and Kedrosky, "Exploring Firm Formation."

18. Buchanan, "One Word," 78.

3. Toward a More Entrepreneurial Economy

1. See Lerner, *Boulevard of Broken Dreams,* and Maltby, "Where the Act Is."

2. See Maltby, "Where the Act Is."

3. The data in this paragraph are from the National Science Foundation, *New NSF Estimates Indicate that U.S. R&D Spending Continued to Grow in 2008.*

4. See Litan, "Fueling Local Economies."

5. The president of the Gates Foundation's Global Health Program, Dr. Tadataka Yamada, has written that "[p]eer review can kill truly novel ideas because they are, by definition, peerless." See Tadataka Yamada, "In Search of New Ideas for Global Health," *New England Journal of Medicine* 358 (2008), 1324–25.

6. Viard, "Tax Policy."

7. Data are from the National Science Foundation, *New NSF Estimates Indicate That U.S. R&D Spending Continued to Grow in 2008.*

8. Our colleague Ben Wildavsky has thoroughly documented this global race for university excellence. See Wildavsky, *The Great Brain Race.*

9. See Wessner, *An Assessment of the SBIR Program.*

10. In Chapter 8, we address the important issue of how and to what extent tax increases should be used to close the yawning and growing federal budget deficit. We put readers on alert here that we believe most of the necessary adjustment should and

will come on the spending side (specifically reform of the benefits structure of the major entitlement programs), but that to the extent additional revenues are required, and they are likely to be, they should come from taxes on consumption rather than additional taxes on income of any form.

11. For example, there is ample literature documenting the negative impact of corporate income taxes at the state level within the United States. For an excellent summary and new evidence of the effects of corporate, personal, and other taxes on locational decisions, see Rohlin, Rosenthal, and Ross, "State Tax Effects and Entrepreneurship." Likewise, Djankov et al. (2010) find a similar effect at the international level, across countries.

12. The most definitive study documenting a negative impact of higher marginal tax rates on entrepreneurship is Gentry and Hubbard, "Success Taxes, Entrepreneurial Entry, and Innovation." For studies showing the opposite result, namely that higher tax rates lead to more entrepreneurial activity, see Long, "Income Taxation and Self-Employment"; Blau, "A Time-Series Analysis of Self Employment in the United States"; Parker, "A Time Series Model of Self-Employment under Uncertainty"; and Robson and Wren, "Marginal and Average Tax Rates and the Incentive for Self-Employment."

13. Poterba, in "Venture Capital and Capital Gains Taxation," finds the capital gains–personal income tax differential influences whether workers at existing firms decide to become entrepreneurs.

14. For evidence about the age and other demographic characteristics of successful entrepreneurs, see Wadhwa, "Education and Tech Entrepreneurship."

15. Some better-known examples include Martek Biosciences of Columbia, Maryland; OraSure Technologies of Bethlehem, Pennsylvania; and Janssen Biotech Inc. of Horsham, Pennsylvania.

16. See Baumol, Litan, and Schramm, *Good Capitalism, Bad Capitalism*.

17. Zoller, "The Dealmaker Milieu."

18. Many universities also engage in some form of "economic development," especially in struggling communities, by providing technical help and training to both new and existing firms. See, e.g., Shaffer and Wright, "A New Paradigm for Economic Development."

19. That individual is Dr. William Green, and he is the only reason that the Kauffman Foundation can claim some indirect sponsorship of The Launch Pad. Shortly after Green opened the program at Miami, the Kauffman Foundation awarded a grant to the university to assist in replicating the Launch Pad at other schools. We are pleased that the Blackstone Foundation has since provided significant financial backing to make this expansion a reality.

20. See previous footnote.

21. Public data about these accelerators and incubators are hard to come by, but as of September 2011, here is what we were able to find. TechStars had funded seventy companies since 2007, of which half had been acquired (www.techstars.org /results). Y Combinator had funded over three hundred companies since 2006, and

collectively these companies were valued at $4.7 billion as of June 2011 (*TechCrunch,* June 1, 2011).

4. Unleashing America's Academic Entrepreneurs

1. Zucker and Darby, "Star Scientists, Innovation and Regional and National Immigration."

2. National Science Foundation website: www.nsf.gov.

3. The balance of this chapter draws heavily on the discussion of this topic in chapter 3 of Kauffman Task Force on Law, Innovation and Growth, ed., *Rules for Growth,* coauthored by Litan.

4. Jonathan Cole, *The Great American University: Its Rise to Preeminence, Its Indispensable National Role, Why It Must Be Protected* (New York: Public Affairs, 2009).

5. For a journalistic critique of university engagement in commercialization activities, see Greenberg, *Science for Sale.* Although this is a good account of the dangers of commercialization in some cases, we reject the core premise of this book and other critiques, which is that universities should not help commercialize innovations developed by their faculty.

6. National Science Foundation, *Nifty Fifty* (2000), available at www.nsf.gov/od /lpa/nsf50/nsffoutreach/htm/home.htm.

7. Fred Block and Matthew Keller, "Where Do Innovations Come From? Transformations in the U.S. National Innovation System, 1970–2006" (The Information Technology and Innovation Foundation, 2008).

8. Association of University Technology Managers, *AUTM U.S. Licensing Activity Survey,* available at http://www.autm.net/Surveys.htm. The AUTM data are not a complete census, but since they cover virtually all of the top research universities, the reported licensing figures are likely to come close to an actual total for all university licensing revenues.

9. The average annual rates of return are calculated by dividing total licensing income by total research expenditures for each university, and then dividing that figure by thirteen, or the number of years in the 1996–2008 period.

10. See Edward B. Roberts and Charles Eesley, "Entrepreneurial Impact: The Role of MIT" (Ewing Marion Kauffman Foundation, February 2009).

11. See Robert E. Litan and Lesa Mitchell, "A Faster Path from Lab to Market," *Harvard Business Review* (January–February 2010): 7.

12. U.S. Government Accountability Office, "New Drug Development: Science, Business, Regulatory, and Intellectual Property Issues Cited as Hampering Drug Development Efforts" (November 2006).

13. Thursby, Fuller, and Thursby, "U.S. Faculty Patenting."

14. None of this is to suggest that fixing the technology transfer model will necessarily improve the productivity of pharmacological research in particular, where the productivity statistics are especially disturbing. Many more far-reaching changes in the structure of that particular industry are probably necessary.

15. Nonetheless, there is limited evidence suggesting that faculty ownership of IP accelerates faculty entrepreneurship, which can only benefit their universities. See Kenney and Patton, "Does Inventor Ownership Encourage University Research-Derived Entrepreneurship?"

16. See, for example, a report on this subject issued by Pennsylvania State University, *Leveraging University Research for Industrial Competitiveness and Growth,* prepared by a distinguished panel of academic experts and sponsored by the National Science Foundation, that offered a series of recommendations for improving technology transfer at universities, but paid no attention to the legal hurdles universities have erected that inhibit their faculty members from more aggressively pursuing commercialization opportunities on their own.

17. Joseph M. DeSimone, William R. Kenan, Jr., and Lesa Mitchell, "Facilitating the Commercialization of University Innovation: The Carolina Express License Agreement" (The Ewing Marion Kauffman Foundation, April 2010), available at www.kauffman.org.

18. In the intra-university case however, which is frequent, the university administration does have many channels to address the problem without "taking it to the outside."

5. Importing Entrepreneurs

1. The financial threshold for the EB-5 visa is reduced to $500,000 if the investment is in a business located in an economically distressed area.

2. Partnership for a New American Economy, "The 'New American' Fortune 500" (June 2011).

3. According to the "Kauffman Index of Entrepreneurial Activity," compiled by Professor Robert Fairlie of the University of California at Santa Cruz using Current Population Survey data, over the 2008–9 period, 510 businesses were launched for every 100,000 immigrants per year, compared to the average of 300 businesses for all native-born Americans.

4. Wadhwa et al., "Skilled Immigration and Economic Growth," and Wadhwa et al., "Education, Entrepreneurship, and Immigration, Part II."

5. Wadhwa et al., "Skilled Immigration and Economic Growth," and Wadhwa et al., "America's New Immigrant Entrepreneurs, Part I."

6. Herman and Smith, *Immigrant Inc.*

7. NFPA, "H-1B Visas by the Numbers"; Herman and Smith, *Immigrant Inc.*; and Hunt and Gauthier-Loiselle, "How Much Does Immigration Boost Innovation?"

8. Wadhwa et al., "America's New Immigrant Entrepreneurs, Part I."

9. Hunt and Gauthier-Loiselle, "How Much Does Immigration Boost Innovation?"

10. West, *Brain Gain,* 26.

11. "The Chinese Must Go," *Illustrated Wasp,* May 11, 1878, in West, *Brain Gain,* 70.

12. E. J. Dionne, Jr., "Democracy in the Age of New Media: A Report on the Media and the Immigration Debate" (Washington, DC: Brookings Institution, 2008).

13. Jennifer Ludden, "1965 Immigration Law Changed Face of America" (*National Public Radio,* May 2006), http://www.npr.org/templates/story/story.php?storyId=5391395.

14. Hugh Davis Graham, *Collision Course: The Strange Convergence of Affirmative Action and Immigration Policy in America* (Oxford: Oxford University Press, 2002), 102–3.

15. Data from the State Department, http://travel.state.gov/visa/statistics/graphs/graphs_4399.html.

16. See, e.g., West, *Brain Gain,* 135–36.

17. Data are from the National Science Foundation.

18. For an excellent description of the EB-5 and its benefits, but also its limitations, see Lieber, "Want a Green Card?"

19. According to the Department of Homeland Security, there were roughly 930,000 temporary workers in the United States in 2008, but this figure is not broken out by specific visa type. One can safely assume, however, that the large portion of these workers had H-1B visas. See http://www.dhs.gov/xlibrary/assets/statistics/publications/ois_ni_pe_2008.pdf.

20. As most readers probably know, the estate tax reform eventually eliminated the tax in its entirety for just one year, 2010, after which the tax reverted to its pre-reform status. In late 2010, Congress enacted a maximum tax rate of 35 percent for all estates over $5 million (with certain exclusions).

21. Wadhwa et al., "Education, Entrepreneurship, and Immigration, Part II."

6. Improving Entrepreneurial Finance

1. Data from Figure 3.09, *2010 NVCA Yearbook,* available at http://www.nvca.org/index.php?option=com_content&view=article&id=257&Itemid=103\. This trend continued into 2010, which showed a decline in both new venture funds launched and money raised. See Tam and Ante, "Tech Wave Lifts Some Venture Firms."

2. One common way of defining angel investors is to refer to the definition of an "accredited investor" under the securities laws: an individual whose net worth (excluding primary residence) exceeds $1 million or has income exceeding $200,000 in each of the two most recent years or joint income with a spouse exceeding $300,000 for those years.

3. The most thorough study of angel investment, both in the United States and elsewhere, we have seen is Wilson, "Financing High-Growth Firms."

4. More information about the KFS can be obtained at www.kauffman.org/KFS. Researchers wanting to access the database for research use should review http://www.kauffman.org/kfs/Data-Files/NORC-Data-Enclave.aspx.

5. See generally Robb and Robinson, "The Capital Structure of New Firms," 10.

6. Banks are the largest source of credit provided to small businesses generally. See Congressional Oversight Panel, "The Small Business Credit Crunch and the Impact of TARP."

7. Gompers and Lerner, *The Money of Invention.*

8. See the NVCA report, *Venture Impact: The Economic Importance of Venture Backed Companies to the U.S. Economy,* available at http://www.nvca.org/index.php?option=com _content&view=article&id=255&Itemid=103.

9. See Kedrosky, "Right-Sizing the U.S. Venture Capital Industry."

10. Kaplan and Lerner, "It Ain't Broke."

11. Ibid.

12. The carry provisions in many hedge and private equity funds do not operate this way, and instead have "high water" benchmarks that do not reward fund managers unless their cumulative annual returns exceed some threshold.

13. Drawn from Vaughn, Barde, and Cherian, "Understanding the Early-Stage Eco-system of Entrepreneurship," unpublished paper made available to the authors.

14. For a more thorough guide to the dangers of government-backed venture funds, see Lerner, *Boulevard of Broken Dreams.*

15. Litan and Robb, "Market-Based Approach for Crossing the Valley of Death."

16. Provisions would have to be made to prevent old companies from reorganizing as new companies in order to take advantage of the more advantageous capital gains terms.

17. Wadhwa, "Education and Tech Entrepreneurship."

18. IPO Task Force. "Rebuilding the IPO On-Ramp: Putting Emerging Companies and the Job Market Back on the Road to Growth." Paper presented to the U.S. Department of the Treasury, October 2011, p. 2.

19. See, e.g., CRA International, *Sarbanes Oxley Section 404 Costs and Implementation Issues: Spring 2006 Survey Update,* available at www.complianceweek.com/s /documents/cra_survey.pdf.

20. Staff of the Office of the Chief Accountant, *Study and Recommendations on Section 404(b) of the Sarbanes-Oxley Act of 2002 for Issuers with Public Float Between $75 and $250 Million.* Our suggestion of giving companies with market capitalization under $1 billion different treatment under Sarbanes-Oxley is similar in spirit to the suggestion made by the IPO Task Force to the Treasury Department in October 2011 that all new public companies be given time to comply with various securities rules (namely, to have an "on ramp" before being subjected to full compliance with all securities rules).

21. See Bradley and Litan, "Choking the Recovery." We draw on only those arguments in this study relating to the impact of ETFs on IPOs. The study also raises disturbing questions about the systemic risks posed by the short selling of small cap ETFs and offers a number of remedies for this problem as well.

22. See Wallison and Litan, *Competitive Equity.*

23. See Bradley and Litan, "Testimony" (2011).

24. Bradley and Litan, "Choking the Recovery."

25. See also Bradley and Litan, "Testimony."

7. Toward Sustainable Growth

1. Meadows, *Limits to Growth*.

2. For an excellent rebuttal to the "peak oil" argument, see Smil, *Energy Myths and Realities*.

3. For a thorough history of the oil industry in both the United States and abroad, see Yergin, *The Prize*.

4. Ibid.

5. For an interesting account of Insull's activities, see Carr, *The Big Switch*, 33–41.

6. Luft and Korin, *Turning Oil into Salt*, 55.

7. Ibid.

8. Ibid., 56.

9. Based on a comparison of estimated five-year ownership costs of the most popular 2010 hybrid models versus their nonhybrid counterparts from *Kelley Blue Book*.

10. Luft and Korin, *Turning Oil into Salt*, 66.

11. Gray and Varcoe, "Octane, Clean Air, and Renewable Fuels."

12. Ibid., 53–54.

13. U.S. Energy Information Administration, Department of Energy, "Oil: Crude and Petroleum Products Explained," http://www.eia.doe.gov/energyexplained/index .cfm?page=oil_home#tab2.

14. Admittedly, there is one substantive drawback to any kind of variable fee price floor for energy or energy tax in general. Like other consumption taxes, the fee is likely to be regressive, since energy consumption is likely to account for a larger fraction of expenditures by low-income individuals than by those of middle or upper incomes. The standard way to address this problem is to use some of the proceeds of the fee to fund a tax rebate to low-income individuals, preferably through a credit on their income taxes. Because low-income individuals generally do not pay income tax, the credit should be refundable—that is, be written as a check to the individuals even though they pay no income taxes—just like the earned income tax credit. The amount of the credit would vary from year to year, depending on the amount of the fee.

15. Luft and Korin, *Turning Oil into Salt*, 59.

16. Wolak, "The Benefits of an Electron Superhighway."

17. The state calculus under such an approach would preempt or override any local rulings to the contrary.

18. U.S. Energy Information Administration, "Electric Power Monthly." See also Yergin, "Stepping on the Gas."

19. Fallows, "Dirty Coal, Clean Future," 68–74.

20. American Energy Innovation Council, "American Business Leaders Call for Revolution in Energy Technology Innovation."

21. President's Council of Advisors on Science and Technology, *Report to the President on Accelerating the Pace of Change in Energy Technologies through an Integrated Federal Energy Policy*.

8. Averting Future Economic Crises

1. Reinhardt and Rogoff, *This Time Is Different.*

2. Congressional Budget Office, *CBO's 2011 Long-Term Budget Outlook,* 22.

3. Simpson, "We Know What We Have to Do."

4. The Pew calculations are based on a rule of thumb developed by the Congressional Budget Office that a 0.1 percentage point increase in the GDP growth rate would shave the nominal ten-year cumulative deficit by $300 billion. See Pew Economic Policy Group, *No Silver Bullet.*

5. Through early April 2010, the estimated net cost of the Troubled Asset Repurchase Program (TARP) had fallen to less than $90 billion, from earlier estimates as high as $250 billion. In addition, AIG, which had borrowed $85 billion from the Federal Reserve at its peak, was on track to repay a substantial portion of those funds too.

6. Kohut, "Americans Are More Skeptical of Washington Than Ever."

7. Reid, *The Healing of America.*

8. See Niskanen, "Limiting Government," and Romer and Romer, "Do Tax Cuts Starve the Beast?"

9. Winston, *Last Exit.*

10. Lanthe, "Facing Budget Gaps, Cities Sell Parking, Airports, Zoos."

11. At this writing, for example, only a few roads around the country—the Dulles Greenway in Virginia, the South Bay Expressway in California, the Chicago Skyway in Illinois, and the Indiana toll road—are in private hands (and all are owned by a single investor, the Macquarie Group). The airport in Branson, Missouri, also is privately owned. In 2007, Citigroup attempted to take the Midway Airport in Chicago private but this effort failed (although some other entity may later succeed here and elsewhere in privatizing airports in this new age of fiscal austerity).

12. See World Economic Forum, *Global Competitiveness Report 2010–11.*

13. For two different but positive perspectives on infrastructure privatization, see Winston, *Last Exit,* and Geddes, *The Road to Renewal.*

14. Thaler and Sunstein, *Nudge.*

15. French et al., *The Squam Lake Report.*

16. See, e.g., Herzlinger, *Who Killed Health Care?* and Gratzer, *The Cure.*

17. Furman, "The Promise of Progressive Cost-Consciousness in Health-Care Reform."

18. For a more thorough discussion of ways to control the growth of health care spending while preserving, if not enhancing, the quality of care, see Kauffman Foundation, "Valuing Health Care."

19. This idea has been advanced by Tyler Cowen in one of his blog postings at www.marginalrevolution.com.

20. Munnell and Sass, *Working Longer.*

21. Fairlie, "Kauffman Index of Entrepreneurial Activity: National Report: 1996–2005."

22. Novy-Marx and Rauh, "The Liabilities and Risks of State-Sponsored Pension Plans"; Congressional Budget Office, *The Underfunding of State and Local Pension Plans.*

23. General Accounting Office, *State and Local Government Retiree Health Benefits,* and Milken Institute and the Kauffman Foundation, "Ensuring State and Municipal Solvency."

9. Entrepreneurship and the Opportunity Society

1. Corak, "Do Poor Children Become Poor Adults?"

2. Haskins and Sawhill, *Creating an Opportunity Society.* Those born into families at the extremes of the income distribution, the rich and the poor, appear to have little mobility—that is, little chance to move up (this is obviously of much greater concern for those at the bottom, who theoretically have much room to advance, than for those at the top, who cannot go much higher).

3. Okun, "Upward Mobility in a High-Pressure Economy."

4. See Friedman, *The Moral Consequences of Economic Growth.*

5. Goldin and Katz, *The Race between Education and Technology.*

6. The *Future Shock* reference comes from a famous book from the 1970s of that title by Alvin Toffler.

7. Kedrosky and Stangler, "Financialization and Its Entrepreneurial Consequences."

8. Mallaby, *More Money Than God.*

9. Dew-Becker and Gordon, "Where Did the Productivity Growth Go?"

10. See Mallaby, *More Money Than God.*

11. Burnsed, "Where the Fortune 500 CEOs Went to College."

12. Fairlie and Robb, *Race and Entrepreneurial Success,* 49–96.

13. Wadhwa, Freeman, and Rissing, "Education and Tech Entrepreneurship."

14. Wadhwa et al., "The Anatomy of an Entrepreneur."

15. Keister, *Getting Rich.*

16. Aud et al., "The Condition of Education 2010."

17. Bowen et al., *Crossing the Finish Line.*

18. "UC Berkeley Enrollment Data," http://opa.berkeley.edu/institutionaldata/campusenroll.htm.

19. Haskins and Sawhill, *Creating an Opportunity Society,* 9.

20. See the evidence cited in Tough, "The Poverty Clinic."

21. See Lindsey, "Culture of Success."

22. James Heckman, "Schools, Skills, and Synapses" (IZA Discussion Paper Series, May 2008).

23. U.S. Department of Health and Human Services, *Temporary Assistance for Needy Families Program, Eighth Annual Report to Congress.*

24. Ventura and Hamilton, *U.S. Teenage Birth Rate Resumes Decline,* report that teen birth rates fell by more than one-third from 1991 to 2005, and after a two-year increase are again on the decline, reaching the lowest level on record in 2009.

25. Finer and Henshaw, "Disparities in Rates of Unintended Pregnancy in the United States, 1994 and 2001," find that individuals from low-income families are more likely to have unintended pregnancies.

26. Carnevale, Smith, and Stroh, "Help Wanted."

27. Jobs, commencement address, Stanford University, 2005.

28. Adams, "How to Get a Real Education."

29. Gladwell, *Outliers*.

30. On the need for innovation in higher education more broadly, see Wildavsky, Kelly, and Carey, *Reinventing Higher Education*.

31. There is evidence that the government-reported measures of consumer price inflation, which are used to deflate nominal GDP to arrive at real incomes and output, are overstated for two reasons: they take insufficient account of innovative new products and services, and the ability of consumers to substitute for other less expensive products. When account is taken of both factors, real wages of the poor may have increased, and thus the poverty rate would have substantially declined over the past forty years, or at least until right before the Great Recession. See Broda and Weinstein, *Prices, Poverty, and Inequality*. See also Eberstadt, *The Poverty of "The Poverty Rate,"* 4.

32. See Lindsey, "Culture of Success."

33. See Murray and Hernstein, *The Bell Curve*.

34. For a more thorough discussion of the impediments to entrepreneurship by low-income individuals, see Kleiner, *Licensing Occupations* and Koppl, *Enterprise Programs*.

35. See Greenstone and Looney, "The Great Recession's Toll on Long-Term Unemployment."

36. For one excellent survey of the challenge and issues, although we do not agree with all of his recommendation, see Peck, "Can the Middle Class Be Saved?"

37. Schramm, *The Entrepreneurial Imperative*.

BIBLIOGRAPHY

Adams, Scott. "How to Get a Real Education." *The Wall Street Journal,* April 9–10, 2011, C1–C2.

American Energy Innovation Council. "American Business Leaders Call for Revolution in Energy Technology Innovation." News release, June 10, 2010.

Aud, Susan, et al. *The Condition of Education 2010 (NCES 2010–028).* National Center for Education Statistics, Institute of Education Sciences, U.S. Department of Education. Washington, DC, 2010.

Baumol, William J. *The Microtheory of Innovative Entrepreneurship.* Princeton, NJ: Princeton University Press, 2010.

Baumol, William J., Robert E. Litan, and Carl Schramm. *Good Capitalism, Bad Capitalism, and the Economics of Growth and Prosperity.* New Haven, CT: Yale University Press, 2007.

Blau, David M. "A Time-Series Analysis of Self Employment in the United States." *Journal of Political Economy* 95 (1987): 445–67.

Block, Fred, and Matthew Keller. "Where Do Innovations Come From? Transformations in the U.S. National Innovation System, 1970–2006." The Information Technology Foundation, 2008.

Bowen, William G., M. Chingos, and M. McPherson. *Crossing the Finish Line: Completing College at America's Public Universities.* Princeton, NJ: Princeton University Press, 2009.

Bradley, Harold, and Robert E. Litan. "Choking the Recovery: Why New Growth Companies Aren't Going Public and Unrecognized Risks of Future Market Disruptions." Kansas City, MO: Ewing Marion Kauffman Foundation, November 2010. http://www.kauffman.org/uploadedFiles/etf_study_11–8-10.pdf.

———. "ETFs and the Present Danger to Capital Formation: Prepared Testimony." Kansas City, MO: Ewing Marion Kauffman Foundation, October, 2011. http://www.kauffman.org/uploadedFiles/ETFs-and-the-Present-Danger-to-Capital-Formation.pdf.

Broda, Christian, and David E. Weinstein. *Prices, Poverty, and Inequality: Why Americans Are Better Off Than You Think.* Washington, DC: AEI Press, 2008.

Buchanan, Leigh. "One Word: Jobs." *Inc.* September 2011, 66–78.

Burnsed, Brian. "Where the Fortune 500 CEOs Went to College." *U.S. News and World Report,* January 3, 2011. www.usnews.com/education/articles/2011/01/03/where-the-fortune-500-ceos-went-to-college.

Carnevale, Anthony P., Nicole Smith, and Jeff Strohl. "Help Wanted: Projecting Jobs and Education Requirements through 2018." Georgetown University Center on Education and the Workforce, 2010. http://cew.georgetown.edu/.

Carr, Nicholas. *The Big Switch: Rewiring the World, from Edison to Google.* New York: W. W. Norton and Company, 2008.

Cole, Jonathan. *The Great American University: Its Rise to Preeminence, Its Indispensable National Role, Why It Must Be Protected.* New York: Public Affairs, 2009.

Congressional Budget Office. *CBO's 2011 Long-Term Budget Outlook.* Washington, DC, June 2011.

———. *The Long-Term Budget Outlook.* Washington, DC, November 2010.

———. *The Underfunding of State and Local Pension Plans.* Washington, DC, May 2011.

Congressional Oversight Panel. *The Small Business Credit Crunch and the Impact of TARP.* 111th Cong., 2nd sess., May 13, 2010.

Corak, Miles. "Do Poor Children Become Poor Adults? Lessons for Public Policy from a Cross-Country Comparison of Generational Earnings Mobility." *Research on Economic Inequality* 13 (2006): 143–88.

Council of Economic Advisers. *Economic Report of the President, 2010.* Washington, DC: U.S. Government Printing Office, 2010.

Cowen, Tyler. *The Great Stagnation.* Kindle Edition e-book: Dutton, 2011.

Coy, Peter. "Why One Economist Predicts Slow Growth." *Bloomberg Businessweek,* October 4–10, 2010.

CRA International. *Sarbanes-Oxley Section 404 Costs and Implementation Issues: Spring 2006 Survey Update.* Boston: Charles River Associates, April 2006. www.compliance week.com/s/documents/cra_survey.pdf.

Dew-Becker, Ian, and Robert J. Gordon. "Where Did the Productivity Growth Go? Inflation Dynamics and the Distribution of Income." *Brookings Papers on Economic Activity* 36, no. 2 (2005): 67–127.

Dionne, E. J., Jr. *Democracy in the Age of New Media: A Report on the Media and the Immigration Debate.* Washington, DC: Brookings Institution, 2008.

Djankov, Simeon, et al. "The Effect of Corporate Taxes on Investment and Entrepreneurship." *American Economics Journal: Macroeconomics* 2, no. 3 (2010): 31–64.

Eberstadt, Nicholas. *The Poverty of "The Poverty Rate": Measure and Mismeasure of Want in Modern America.* Washington, DC: AEI Press, 2008.

Fairlie, Robert W. "Kauffman Index of Entrepreneurial Activity: 1996–2009." Kansas City, MO: Ewing Marion Kauffman Foundation, May 2010. http://www.kauffman .org/uploadedfiles/kiea_2010_report.pdf.

——. "Kauffman Index of Entrepreneurial Activity National Report: 1996–2005." Kansas City, MO: Ewing Marion Kauffman Foundation, 2006.

Fairlie, Robert W., and Alicia M. Robb. *Race and Entrepreneurial Success.* Cambridge, MA: MIT Press, 2008.

Fallows, James. "Dirty Coal, Clean Future." *The Atlantic,* December 2010, 64–78.

Finer, Lawrence B., and Stanley K. Henshaw. "Disparities in Rates of Unintended Pregnancy in the United States, 1994 and 2001." *Perspectives on Sexual and Reproductive Health* 38, no. 2 (2006): 90–96.

Fishback, Bo, et al. "Finding Business 'Idols': A New Model to Accelerate Start-Ups." Kansas City, MO: Ewing Marion Kauffman Foundation, 2007. http://www.kauffman.org.

French, Kenneth R., et al. *The Squam Lake Report: Fixing the Financial System.* Princeton, NJ: Princeton University Press, 2010.

Friedman, Benjamin M. *The Moral Consequences of Economic Growth.* New York: Alfred A. Knopf, 2005.

Furman, Jason. "The Promise of Progressive Cost-Consciousness in Health-Care Reform." Discussion Paper 2007–05, Hamilton Project, Brookings Institution, April 2007.

Geddes, R. Richard. *The Road to Renewal: Private Investment in U.S. Transportation Infrastructure.* Washington, DC: AEI Press, 2011.

General Accounting Office. *State and Local Government Retiree Health Benefits.* Report to the Chairman, Senate Special Committee on Aging, 111th Cong., 1st sess., 2009.

Gentry, William M., and R. Glenn Hubbard. "Success Taxes, Entrepreneurial Entry, and Innovation." National Bureau of Economic Research, Inc. *Innovation Policy and the Economy* 5 (2005): 87–108.

Gladwell, Malcolm. *Outliers: The Story of Success.* New York: Little, Brown and Company, 2008.

Goldin, Claudia, and Lawrence Katz. *The Race between Education and Technology.* Cambridge, MA: Harvard University Press, 2008.

Gompers, Paul A., and Josh Lerner. *The Money of Invention: How Venture Capital Creates New Wealth.* Boston: Harvard Business School Publishing, 2001.

——. "What Drives Venture Capital Fund-Raising?" *Brookings Papers on Economic Activity: Microeconomics* (1988): 149–92.

Graham, Hugh Davis. *Collision Course: The Strange Convergence of Affirmative Action and Immigration Policy in America.* Oxford: Oxford University Press, 2002.

Gratzer, David. *The Cure: How Capitalism Can Save American Health Care.* New York: Encounter Books, 2008.

Gray, Boyden, and Andrew R. Varcoe. "Octane, Clean Air, and Renewable Fuels: A Modest Step toward Energy Independence." *Texas Review of Law and Politics* 10 (2006).

Greenberg, Daniel S. *Science for Sale.* Chicago: University of Chicago Press, 2007.

Greenstone, Michael, and Adam Looney. "The Great Recession's Toll on Long-Term Unemployment." Brookings Institution *Up Front* blog, November 5, 2010.

Haltiwanger, John, Ron Jarmin, and Javier Miranda. "Jobs Created from Business Startups in the United States." Kansas City, MO: Ewing Marion Kauffman Foundation, January 2009. http://www.kauffman.org/uploadedFiles/BDS_Jobs_Created_011209b.pdf.

Haskins, Ron, and Isabel Sawhill. *Creating an Opportunity Society.* Washington, DC: Brookings Institution Press, 2009.

Herman, Richard T., and Robert L. Smith. *Immigrant Inc.: Why Immigrant Entrepreneurs Are Driving the New Economy.* Hoboken, NJ: John Wiley & Sons, 2010.

Herzlinger, Regina E. *Who Killed Health Care? America's $2 Trillion Medical Problem—and the Consumer-Driven Cure.* New York: McGraw-Hill, 2007.

Horrell, Michael, and Robert E. Litan. "After Inception: How Enduring Is Job Creation by Startups?" Kansas City, MO: Ewing Marion Kauffman Foundation, July 2010. http://www.kauffman.org/uploadedFiles/firm-formation-inception-8–2-10.pdf.

Hubbard, Glenn and Peter Navarro. *Seeds of Destruction.* Upper Saddle River, NJ: FT Press, 2011.

Hunt, Jennifer, and Marjolaine Gauthier-Loiselle. "How Much Does Immigration Boost Innovation?" Bonn, Germany: Institute for the Study of Labor, January 2009.

IPO Task Force. "Rebuilding the IPO On-Ramp: Putting Emerging Companies and the Job Market Back on the Road to Growth." Paper presented to the U.S. Department of the Treasury, October 2011.

Jobs, Steven. Commencement address, Stanford University, Palo Alto, CA, June 14, 2005. http://news.stanford.edu/news/2005/june15/jobs-061505.html.

Kaiser Family Foundation and Health Research & Educational Trust. *Employer Health Benefits: 2008 Summary of Findings.* 2008.

Kane, Tim. "The Importance of Startups in Job Creation and Job Destruction." Kansas City, MO: Ewing Marion Kauffman Foundation, July 2010. http://www.kauffman.org/uploadedFiles/firm_formation_importance_of_startups.pdf.

Kaplan, Steven N., and Josh Lerner. "It Ain't Broke: The Past, Present, and Future of Venture Capital." *Journal of Applied Corporate Finance* 22, no. 2 (2010): 36–47.

Kauffman Foundation. "Valuing Health Care." Kansas City, MO: Ewing Marion Kauffman Foundation, 2012. http://www.kauffman.org.

Kauffman Task Force on Law, Innovation and Growth, ed. *Rules for Growth: Promoting Innovation and Growth through Legal Reform.* Kansas City, MO: Ewing Marion Kauffman Foundation, 2011.

Kedrosky, Paul. "Right-Sizing the U.S. Venture Capital Industry." Kansas City, MO: Ewing Marion Kauffman Foundation, June 2009. http://www.kauffman.org/uploadedFiles/USVentCap061009r1.pdf.

Kedrosky, Paul, and Dane Stangler. "Financialization and Its Entrepreneurial Consequences." Kansas City, MO: Ewing Marion Kauffman Foundation, 2011. http://www.kauffman.org.

Keister, Lisa A. *Getting Rich: America's New Rich and How They Got That Way.* Cambridge: Cambridge University Press, 2005.

Kenney, Martin, and Donald Patton. "Does Inventor Ownership Encourage University Research-Derived Entrepreneurship? A Six University Comparison." University of California, Davis, May 2011. http://www.ssrn.com/abstract=1847184.

Kleiner, Morris M. *Licensing Occupations: Ensuring Quality or Restricting Competition.* Kalamazoo, MI: Upjohn Institute for Employment Research, 2006.

Kohut, Andrew. "Americans Are More Skeptical of Washington Than Ever." *The Wall Street Journal,* April 19, 2010, A19.

Koplow, Doug. *Subsidies in the U.S. Energy Sector: Magnitude, Causes, and Options for Reform.* Cambridge: Earth Track, 2006.

Koppl, Roger, ed. *Enterprise Programs: Freeing Entrepreneurs to Provide Essential Services to the Poor.* Dallas, TX: National Center for Policy Analysis, 2011.

Lanthe, Jeanne Dugan. "Facing Budget Gaps, Cities Sell Parking, Airports, Zoos." *The Wall Street Journal,* August 23, 2010, A1.

Lerner, Josh. *Boulevard of Broken Dreams.* Princeton, NJ: Princeton University Press, 2009.

Lieber, Nick. "Want a Green Card? Fund an American Business." *Bloomberg Businessweek,* August 14, 2011, 49–50.

Lindsey, Brink. "Culture of Success." *The New Republic,* March 12, 2008.

Litan, Robert E. "Fueling Local Economies: Research, Innovation and Jobs." Testimony before the U.S. Congress Joint Economic Committee, 111th Cong., 2nd sess., June 29, 2010.

———. "Inventive Billion Dollar Firms: A Faster Way to Grow." Kansas City, MO: Ewing Marion Kauffman Foundation, December 2010. http://www.kauffman.org/uploaded/Files/inventive billion dollar firms.pdf.

Litan, Robert E., and Alicia Robb, "A Market-Based Approach for Crossing the Valley of Death: The Benefits of a Capital Gains Exemption for Investments in Startups." Kansas City, MO: Ewing Marion Kauffman Foundation, January 2012. http://www.kauffman.org/uploadedFiles/crossing-valley-of-death-report.pdf.

Long, James E. "Income Taxation and Self-Employment." *National Tax Journal* 36 (1982): 491–501.

Ludden, Jennifer. "1965 Immigration Law Changed Face of America." National Public Radio, May 2006, http://www.npr.org/templates/story/story.php?storyId=5391395.

Luft, Gal, and Anne Korin. *Turning Oil into Salt: Energy Independence through Fuel Choice.* Charleston, SC: BookSurge Publishing, 2009.

Mallaby, Sebastian. *More Money Than God.* New York: Council on Foreign Relations, 2010.

Maltby, Emily. "Where the Act Is." *The Wall Street Journal,* August 22, 2011, R1.

McCraw, Thomas K. *Prophet of Innovation: Joseph Schumpeter and Creative Destruction.* Cambridge, MA: Harvard University Press, 2007.

Meadows, Donella H., et al. *Limits to Growth.* Boston: MIT Press, 1972.

Milken Institute and the Kauffman Foundation. "Ensuring State and Municipal Solvency." *Financial Innovations Lab Report,* October 2010.

Munnell, Alicia H., and Steven Sass. *Working Longer: The Solution to the Retirement Income Challenge.* Washington, DC: Brookings Institution Press, 2008.

Murray, Charles, and Richard Hernstein. *The Bell Curve.* New York: Free Press, 1994.

National Foundation for American Policy. "H-1B Visas by the Numbers: 2010 and Beyond." NFAP Policy Brief, March 2010.

National Science Foundation. *New NSF Estimates Indicate That U.S. R&D Spending Continued to Grow in 2008.* Washington, DC: NSF, January 2010. http://www.nsf.gov.

Niskanen, William A. "Limiting Government: The Failure of 'Starve the Beast.'" *Cato Journal* 26, no. 3 (Fall 2006).

Nordhaus, William D. 2005. "Schumpeterian Profits and the Alchemist Fallacy." Discussion Paper Number 6, Yale Working Papers on Economic Applications and Policy, Yale University. http://www.econ.yale.edu/ddp/ddp00/ddp00006.pdf.

Novy-Marx, Robert, and Joshua D. Rauh. "The Liabilities and Risks of State-Sponsored Pension Plans." *Journal of Economic Perspectives* 23, no. 4 (Fall 2009): 191–210.

NVCA report. *Venture Impact: The Economic Importance of Venture Backed Companies to the U.S. Economy.* http://www.nvca.org/index.php?option=com_content&view=article&id=255&Itemid=103.

Okun, Arthur M. *Equality and Efficiency: The Big Tradeoff.* Washington, DC: The Brookings Institution, 1976.

———. "Upward Mobility in a High-Pressure Economy." *Brookings Papers on Economic Activity,* 1973, 4.

Olson, Mancur. *The Rise and Fall of Nations.* New Haven, CT: Yale University Press, 1982.

Parker, S.C. "A Time Series Model of Self-Employment under Uncertainty." *Economica* 63 (1996): 459–75.

Peck, Don. "Can the Middle Class Be Saved?" *The Atlantic,* September 2011, 60–79.

———. "How a Jobless Era Will Transform America." *The Atlantic,* March 2010. http://www.theatlantic.com/magazine/archive/2010/03/how-a-new-jobless-era-will-transform-america/7919/.

Pennsylvania State University. *Leveraging University Research for Industrial Competitiveness and Growth: Report of Findings and Recommendations.* NSF Project Number 0650124, National Science Foundation, September 2010.

Pew Economic Policy Group. *No Silver Bullet: Paths for Reducing the Federal Debt.* Washington, DC: Pew Charitable Trusts, September 2010.

Poterba, James M. "Venture Capital and Capital Gains Taxation." In *Tax Policy and the Economy,* vol. 3, edited by Lawrence H. Summers, 47–67. Cambridge, MA: MIT Press, 1989.

President's Council of Advisors on Science and Technology. *Report to the President on Accelerating the Pace of Change in Energy Technologies through an Integrated Federal Energy Policy.* Washington, DC: Executive Office of the President, November 2010.

Rauch, Jonathan. *Government's End*. New York: Public Affairs, 1999. Updated from *Demosclerosis*. New York: Times Books, 1994.

Reedy, E. J., and Robert E. Litan. "Starting Smaller; Staying Smaller: America's Slow Leak in Job Creation." Kansas City, MO: Ewing Marion Kauffman Foundation, July 2011. http://www.kauffman.org/uploadedFiles/job_leaks_starting_smaller _study.pdf.

Reid, T. R. *The Healing of America: A Global Quest for Better, Cheaper, and Fairer Health Care*. New York: Penguin Books, 2009.

Reinhart, Carmen M., and Vincent R. Reinhart. "After the Fall." Paper presented at the Federal Reserve Bank of Kansas City Economic Symposium, Jackson Hole, WY, August 26–28, 2010. http://www.kansascityfed.org/publicat/sympos/2010/2010 -08-17-reinhart.pdf.

Reinhart, Carmen M., and Kenneth Rogoff. *This Time Is Different: Eight Centuries of Financial Folly*. Princeton, NJ: Princeton University Press, 2009.

Robb, Alicia M., and David T. Robinson. "The Capital Structure of New Firms." Working Paper 16272, National Bureau of Economic Research, August 2010.

Robsen, M. T., and C. Wren. "Marginal and Average Tax Rates and the Incentive for Self-Employment." *Small Business Economics* 10 (1998): 199–212.

Rohlin, Shawn, Stuart S. Rosenthal, and Amanda Ross. "State Tax Effects and Entrepreneurship: Estimates from a Border Model with Agglomeration Economies." Department of Economics, Syracuse University, 2010.

Romer, Christine, and David Romer. "Do Tax Cuts Starve the Beast? The Effect of Tax Changes on Government Spending." In *Brookings Papers on Economic Activity*, edited by David H. Romer and Justin Wolfers. Washington, DC: Brookings Institution Press, 2009.

Roush, Wade. "There Is an Incubator Bubble—and It Will Pop." *Xconomy*, August 12, 2011. http://www.exconomy.com/national/2011/08/12.

Rushe, Dominic. "AIG Ready to Cut Link with U.S. Government." *Guardian*, January 13, 2011.

Schramm, Carl. "All Entrepreneurship Is Social." *Stanford Social Innovation Review*, Spring 2010, 21–22.

———. *The Entrepreneurial Imperative*. New York: HarperCollins, 2006.

Senor, Dan, and Saul Singer. *Start-up Nation*. New York: Hachette Book Group, 2009.

Servan-Schreiber, Jean Jacques. *The American Challenge*. Translated by Ronald Steel. New York: Atheneum, 1968.

Shaffer, David F., and David J. Wright. "A New Paradigm for Economic Development: How Higher Education Institutions Are Working to Revitalize Their Regional and State Economies." The Nelson A. Rockefeller Institute of Government, University of Albany, State University of New York, March 2010.

Simpson, Alan. "We Know What We Have to Do." *Bloomberg Businessweek*, August 14, 2011, G3, 28.

Smil, Vaclav. *Energy Myths and Realities: Bringing Science to the Energy Policy Debate*. Washington, DC: The AEI Press, 2010.

Staff of the Office of the Chief Accountant. *Study and Recommendations on Section 404(b) of the Sarbanes-Oxley Act of 2002 for Issuers with Public Float between $75 and $250 Million.* Washington, DC: U.S. Securities and Exchange Commission, 2011.

Stangler, Dane. "High-Growth Firms and the Future of the American Economy." Kansas City, MO: Ewing Marion Kauffman Foundation, March 2010. http://www.kauffman.org/uploadedfiles/high-growth-firms-study.pdf.

Stangler, Dane, and Paul Kedrosky. "Exploring Firm Formation: Why Is the Number of New Firms Constant?" Kansas City, MO: Ewing Marion Kauffman Foundation, January 2010. http://www.kauffman.org/uploadedFiles/exploring_firm_formation_1-13-10.pdf.

Stangler, Dane, and Robert E. Litan. "Where Will the Jobs Come From?" Kansas City, MO: Ewing Marion Kauffman Foundation, November 2009. http://www.kauffman.org/uploadedFiles/where_will_the_jobs_come_from.pdf.

Stephan, Paula. "Job Market Effects on Scientific Productivity." Georgia State University, 2011.

Stevenson, Betsey, and Justin Wolfers. "Economic Growth and Subjective Well-Being: Reassessing the Easterlin Paradox." *Brookings Papers on Economic Activity,* Spring 2008.

Tam, Pui-Wing, and Spencer E. Ante. "Tech Wave Lifts Some Venture Firms." *The Wall Street Journal,* February 18, 2011, C1.

Thaler, Richard H., and Cass R. Sunstein. *Nudge: Improving Decisions about Health, Wealth and Happiness.* New York: Penguin Group, 2008.

Thursby, Jerry, Anne Fuller, and Marie Thursby. "U.S. Faculty Patenting: Inside and Outside the University." *Research Policy* 38 (2009): 14–25.

Toffler, Alvin. *Future Shock.* New York: Random House, 1970.

Tough, Paul. "The Poverty Clinic." *The New Yorker,* March 21, 2011, 25–32.

U.S. Department of Health and Human Services. Administration for Children and Families. Office of Family Assistance. *Temporary Assistance for Needy Families Program, Eighth Annual Report to Congress.* Washington, DC, 2009.

U.S. Energy Information Administration. "Electric Power Monthly," January 2011. http://www.eia.doe.gov/cneaf/electricity/epm/epm_sum.html.

———. "Oil: Crude and Petroleum Products Explained." http://www.eia.doe.gov/energyexplained/index.cfm?page=oil_home#tab2.

Vaughn, Denzil, Karsten Barde, and Sanjeeth Cherian. "Understanding the Early-Stage Ecosystem for Entrepreneurship: Challenges, Emerging Innovations, and Potential for Future Innovations." Tuck School of Business, Dartmouth University, 2011.

Ventura, Stephanie J., and Brady E. Hamilton. *U.S. Teenage Birth Rate Resumes Decline.* National Center for Health Statistics Data Brief No. 58, 2011. http://www.cdc.gov/nchs/data/databriefs/db58.pdf.

Viard, Alan. "Tax Policy." In *Rules for Growth,* edited by the Kauffman Task Force on Law, Innovation and Growth. Kansas City, MO: Ewing Marion Kauffman Foundation, 2011.

Wadhwa, Vivek, Raj Aggarwal, Krisztina Holly, and Alex Salkever. "The Anatomy of an Entrepreneur: Family Background and Motivation." Kansas City, MO: Ewing Marion Kauffman Foundation, 2009. http://www.kauffman.org.

Wadhwa, Vivek, Richard Freeman, and Ben Rissing. "Education and Tech Entrepreneurship." Kansas City, MO: Ewing Marion Kauffman Foundation, 2008. http://www.kauffman.org.

Wadhwa, Vivek, AnnaLee Saxenian, Ben Rissing, and Gary Gereffi. "America's New Immigrant Entrepreneurs, Part I." Science, Technology & Innovation Paper No. 23, Duke University, 2007a. http://www.ssrn.com/abstract=990152.

——. "Education, Entrepreneurship, and Immigration: America's New Immigrant Entrepreneurs, Part II." Kansas City, MO: Ewing Marion Kauffman Foundation, 2007b. http://www.kauffman.org/uploadedfiles/entrep_immigrants_2 61207.pdf.

——. "Skilled Immigration and Economic Growth." Applied Research in Economic Development 5, no. 1 (2008): 5–14.

Wallison, Peter J., and Robert E. Litan. Competitive Equity: A Better Way to Organize Mutual Funds. Washington, DC: AEI Press, 2007.

Wessner, Charles W. An Assessment of the SBIR Program. Washington, DC: National Academies Press, 2008.

West, Darrell M. Brain Gain. Washington, DC: Brookings Institution Press, 2010.

Wildavsky, Ben. The Great Brain Race. Princeton, NJ: Princeton University Press, 2010.

Wildavsky, Ben, Andrew P. Kelly, and Kevin Carcy, eds. Reinventing Higher Education: The Promise of Innovation. Cambridge, MA: Harvard University Press, 2011.

Wilson, Karen. "Financing High-Growth Firms: The Role of Business ANGELS—Project Update." Prepared for the CHE Meeting, March 31–April 1, 2011, OECD.

Winston, Clifford M. Last Exit: Privatization and Deregulation of the U.S. Transportation System. Washington, DC: Brookings Institution Press, 2010.

Wolak, Frank A. "The Benefits of an Electron Superhighway." Stanford Institute for Economic Policy Research, 2003. http://www.stanford.edu/group/fwolak/cgi-bin/sites/default/files/files/The%20Benefits%20of%20an%20Electron%20Superhighway_Nov%202003_Wolak.pdf.

World Economic Forum. Global Competitiveness Report, 2010–11. New York: World Economic Forum, 2011.

Yamada, Tadataka. "In Search of New Ideas for Global Health." New England Journal of Medicine 358 (2008): 1324–25.

Yergin, Daniel. The Prize: The Epic Quest for Oil, Money and Power. New York: Simon and Schuster, 1991.

——. "Stepping on the Gas." The Wall Street Journal, April 2–3, 2011, C1.

Zakaria, Fareed. "Yes, America Is in Decline." Time, March 14, 2011.

Zoller, Ted Douglas. "The Dealmaker Milieu: The Anatomy of Social Capital in Entrepreneurial Economics." PhD diss. University of North Carolina, 2010.

Zucker, Lynne, and Michael Darby. "Star Scientists, Innovation and Regional and National Immigration." NBER Working Paper, 2007.

INDEX

Page numbers in italics refer to figures.